MW00709871

New Approaches to Religion and Power

Series Editor
Joerg Rieger
Vanderbilt University
Nashville, TN, USA

While the relationship of religion and power is a perennial topic, it only continues to grow in importance and scope in our increasingly globalized and diverse world. Religion, on a global scale, has openly joined power struggles, often in support of the powers that be. But at the same time, religion has made major contributions to resistance movements. In this context, current methods in the study of religion and theology have created a deeper awareness of the issue of power: Critical theory, cultural studies, postcolonial theory, subaltern studies, feminist theory, critical race theory, and working class studies are contributing to a new quality of study in the field. This series is a place for both studies of particular problems in the relation of religion and power as well as for more general interpretations of this relation. It undergirds the growing recognition that religion can no longer be studied without the study of power.

More information about this series at
http://www.palgrave.com/gp/series/14754

Becca Whitla

Liberation, (De)Coloniality, and Liturgical Practices

Flipping the Song Bird

Becca Whitla
Saint Andrew's College
Saskatoon, SK, Canada

ISSN 2634-6079   ISSN 2634-6087   (electronic)
New Approaches to Religion and Power
ISBN 978-3-030-52635-1   ISBN 978-3-030-52636-8   (eBook)
https://doi.org/10.1007/978-3-030-52636-8

© The Editor(s) (if applicable) and The Author(s), under exclusive licence to Springer Nature Switzerland AG 2020
This work is subject to copyright. All rights are solely and exclusively licensed by the Publisher, whether the whole or part of the material is concerned, specifically the rights of translation, reprinting, reuse of illustrations, recitation, broadcasting, reproduction on microfilms or in any other physical way, and transmission or information storage and retrieval, electronic adaptation, computer software, or by similar or dissimilar methodology now known or hereafter developed.
The use of general descriptive names, registered names, trademarks, service marks, etc. in this publication does not imply, even in the absence of a specific statement, that such names are exempt from the relevant protective laws and regulations and therefore free for general use.
The publisher, the authors and the editors are safe to assume that the advice and information in this book are believed to be true and accurate at the date of publication. Neither the publisher nor the authors or the editors give a warranty, expressed or implied, with respect to the material contained herein or for any errors or omissions that may have been made. The publisher remains neutral with regard to jurisdictional claims in published maps and institutional affiliations.

Cover illustration: lfreytag / Getty Images

This Palgrave Macmillan imprint is published by the registered company Springer Nature Switzerland AG.
The registered company address is: Gewerbestrasse 11, 6330 Cham, Switzerland

ACKNOWLEDGEMENTS

The work in these pages is undergirded by the many communities in which I have sung and taught over many years. I am particularly grateful to the Church of the Holy Trinity in downtown Toronto, the Echo Women's Choir, the H.E.R.E. Local 75 Choir, and the Toronto School of Theology Choir. The book itself is also the result of a rich engagement with many people who have accompanied me in my scholarly journey. To each and every one of you, too numerous to name, thank you!

My doctoral research was supported generously by the Social Sciences and Humanities Research Council of Canada through a Joseph-Armand Bombardier Canada Graduate Doctoral Scholarship and by an Ontario Graduate Scholarship. This support, along with funding from Emmanuel College, made possible my scholarly research and analysis. Thanks also to the students, staff, and faculty at Emmanuel for journeying with me, especially Emmanuel Principal Mark Toulouse and Acting Principal Phyllis Airhart for travel funds to present earlier versions of my research at the following: the Conference of the International Academy of Practical Theology in Pretoria, South Africa (2015); the Christian Congregational Music Conference in Rippon, UK (2015); and the "Reforming Imagination" Conference of the United Reformed Church, in Birmingham, UK (2017), which was also supported by a grant from the Oxford Fund of The United Church of Canada. I am also grateful to the Seminario Evangelico de Teología de Matanzas for supporting two study retreats in 2017 and 2018 during which I wrote outlines for two chapters and my conclusion.

Many thanks to the members of my doctoral committee, Pamela Couture, Lim Swee Hong, and William Kervin. They warmly accompanied me from the beginning, critically engaging with my work, gently and firmly pushing me where I needed to be pushed. In my work as his research fellow, Lim Swee Hong cheerfully encouraged me by offering me opportunities to teach, to travel, to present my ideas in academic and community settings, and by having countless conversations over coffee. As my doctoral supervisor—and as my friend—William Kervin went above and beyond, guiding me every step along the way and emboldening me with his careful and clear advice which I usually followed. It was an honour to reflect on some of the principles of this work with him as we together midwifed the worship life of the Emmanuel College community.

As I prepared the manuscript for publishing, I was nurtured by my community of colleagues and students at St. Andrew's College in Saskatoon. I am grateful to William Whitla and Carol Zollinger for editorial assistance in the final stages of preparing the manuscript, along with series editor Joerg Rieger and the team at Palgrave Macmillan, including the anonymous reviewers who carefully engaged my work. Thanks also to Keith Nunn, Ian Sowton, Mark MacDonald, and Susan Beaver for reading sections of the manuscript.

The scholarship in this book was deeply enriched through my involvement with the Canadian Decolonial Theology Project: my heartfelt thanks go to these colleague-friends—Néstor Medina, Michel Andraos, and Lee Cormie. Our work together deeply challenged me and sharpened my use of post and decolonial theory. In particular, I would like to pay tribute to Néstor Medina who introduced me to Latin American decolonial thinking as my professor before I began my doctoral studies. His scholarship, ongoing mentoring, and critical engagement with my work have provided a rich source for reflection throughout these pages.

Finally, I would like to thank my family for their patience, love, and support. To my brother and his boys, Mike, Jake, and Kyle Whitla, I love you. I carry the memory of your beloved wife and mother, Lisa Haberman, in my heart. To adopted family members Karen Haberman, Marty Crowder, and Dick Moore; to friends Natalie Celuch and Loreto Freire; to my children's godfather, Peter Turner; to my parents, Nancy and Bill Whitla, thank you for meals, walks, laughter, and encouraging words. To cousin Richard Norman, thanks for being a fellow traveller. Deepest thanks go to my children Emma Whitla and David Gasser and their father, Alan Gasser. Thank you for believing in me and in my work. Thank you for loving me. Thank you for being part of my syncopated liberating praxis of life!

Praise for *Liberation, (De)Coloniality, and Liturgical Practices*

"'Singing in a decolonial key' is the project here, with invigorating and demanding insights about how to achieve it. The cheeky sub-title—'Flipping the Song Bird'—indicates the defiant energy at play as autobiographical narrative (in its work of 'reconfiguring [the] self') and liberation and contextual theologies (especially from Canadian perspectives) agitate against 'musicoloniality.' Sound/music, words, and performances all come in for scrutiny, as both questions arise of post-colonial theological strategies and proposals emerge towards a more liberating liturgical theology. The result is a very vivid picture of singing as 'a living out of God's image in us.' Highly recommended!"
> —Stephen Burns, Professor of Liturgical & Practical Theology,
> *Pilgrim Theological College, University of Divinity, Australia*

"Becca Whitla carefully and critically undertakes multiple discourses while grounding them in this project of liberating congregational singing. The arguments are well thought-out, finely crafted, deeply researched, and carefully nuanced. This book presents various examples to analyze, interrogate, and critique liberationist, decolonial, and postcolonial perspectives. It also presents a specific and practical place for these interrogations to occur, so the work of this thesis does not remain for the elite or the ivory tower of academia. I highly recommend this manuscript for anyone looking at religion and culture, liturgical studies, as well as liberationist, decolonial, and postcolonial thought-in-action."
> —Neomi De Anda, Associate Professor,
> *Department of Religious Studies, University of Dayton, Ohio, USA*
> and President, *Academy of Catholic Hispanic Theologians of the United States*

"In creative defiance of Cartesian assumptions, Becca Whitla flips the equation and declares *We sing, therefore we are!* Singing embodies community empowerment, not an individual cognitive state of being. Singing has a long history of subversion and, by implication, the potential for liberation. Whitla is not a casual observer of the liberating potential of singing, but an instigator of communal singing as a way of empowering those on the margins of privilege. Her passionate rhetoric—"Flipping the Song Bird"—is matched by a creative, provocative methodology exposing deep-seated colonial privilege as a façade for patriarchal power manifest in human oppression."

—C. Michael Hawn, University Distinguished Professor Emeritus of Church Music, *Southern Methodist University, USA*

"Here is the most rigorously sustained engagement in liberationist, postcolonial, and decolonial theory and theology yet in practical and liturgical theology. A host of hermeneutical tools that have previously tended to remain theoretical and abstract (e.g., border thinking, intermixture, hybridity, mimicry) come alive in Becca Whitla's hands and are elegantly employed to original and empowering results. What starts out about congregational singing becomes nothing short of a hope-filled and Spirt-inspired call to conversion beyond Eurocentrism in music and liturgy, theology and faith."

—William S. Kervin, Associate Professor of Public Worship, *Emmanuel College of Victoria University at the University of Toronto, Canada*

"Drawing on a variety of social science methodologies, Becca Whitla examines the practice of congregational song music-making in a variety of contexts, particularly through a decolonial approach. This is an emerging area of study and the approach is ground-breaking. I foresee this work as generating vigorous discussions that will help further research work in the field for years to come."

—Lim Swee Hong (林瑞峰), Deer Park Associate Professor of Sacred Music and Director, Master of Sacred Music program at *Emmanuel College of Victoria University at the University of Toronto, Canada*

"Whitla's book moves us into a profound reflection on the ways in which incarnational song guides us into a path that makes the invisible visible. She has obviously spent time in careful exploration and deep meditation on the symbiotic relationship between traditional liturgical music structures and the so-called anti-structure of other particular styles and genres. Whitla's book will be of tremendous value to academia, the ministerial community, as well as the larger community of faith alike."

—Cynthia A. Wilson, Executive Director of Worship Resources for Discipleship Ministries and Director of Liturgical Resources, *United Methodist ChurchGeneral Agency, USA*

CONTENTS

LIST OF FIGURES

CHAPTER 1

Introduction: Flipping the Song Bird

Singing in Christian contexts has always involved the embodied action of particular peoples. From the earliest days, Christians have sung their faith to express their religious zeal and distinguish themselves from their cultural surroundings by singing "psalms and hymns and spiritual songs" (Ephesians 5:19). Music (and singing) was understood to be a gift from God which could enflame human religious passions and enable praise of God. Augustine of Hippo, for instance, writes in an oft-quoted passage from his fourth-century *Confessions*, "How copiously I wept at your hymns and canticles, how intensely was I moved by the lovely harmonies of your singing Church! Those voices flooded my ears and the truth was distilled into my heart until it overflowed in loving devotion; my tears ran down, and I was the better for them."[1] The medieval mystic, theologian, and composer, Hildegard of Bingen, was inspired to write down her visionary insights, including music, through an all-consuming process: "heaven was opened and a fiery light of exceeding brilliance came and permeated my whole brain and inflamed my whole heart and my whole breast."[2] In a similar vein, sixteenth-century reformer, Martin Luther, believed in the power and goodness of music so much so that he felt incapable of

---

[1] Augustine, "Book 9, Chapter (6) 14" in *The Confessions*, trans. Maria Boulding. (New York: New City Press, 1997), 220.

[2] Hildegard of Bingen, *Scivias* trans. Columba Hart and Jane Bishop (New York: Paulist Press, 1990), 59.

© The Author(s) 2020

B. Whitla, *Liberation, (De)Coloniality, and Liturgical Practices*,
New Approaches to Religion and Power,
https://doi.org/10.1007/978-3-030-52636-8_1

comprehending its magnitude. "I would certainly like to praise music with all my heart as the excellent gift of God which it is and to commend it to everyone," he wrote, "but I am so overwhelmed by the diversity and magnitude of its virtue and benefits that I can find neither beginning nor end or method for my discourse. ... For who can comprehend it all?"[3]

At the same time, singing has also often been viewed as threatening or even dangerous, especially in Christian contexts. Powerful historical voices have articulated suspicion and distrust of singing (and music) precisely because of its embodied power. For instance, though he clearly recognized and appreciated the power of music, Augustine also expressed discomfort with the passionate stirrings it elicited and the ways music was used in pursuit of more sensual Dionysian—and morally suspect—purposes. Liturgical theologian Don Saliers notes that this discord manifested itself in Augustine's attitudes to music and continued to resonate throughout history. He summarizes this development as follows:

> In his *Confessions* we overhear his attraction to the sound that made him weep, yet that he knows also may distract him from the Word itself. This suspicion of music has also been part of Christian liturgical tradition, again surfacing in the Protestant Reformation with the so-called 'left wing' traditions represented most austerely by Quaker silence. The sensual character of music and its emotional power over human beings was noticed especially in the neo-Platonic strands of Christian sensibility and theology.[4]

This tug between what could be broadly characterized as the body and the mind resurfaces throughout European Christian history. Early Christian discourses that were suspicious of music's emotional impact—and everything associated with it, including nature, women, and the body—were reinforced by the Cartesian privileging of the mind over the body in the seventeenth century and the entrenchment of the individualistic, rationalist, patriarchal ideals of the Enlightenment in the eighteenth century. As a result, hymns which were judged to be expressions of the rational/intellectual/mind were understood to be superior to hymns

---

[3] Martin Luther, "Preface to Gerog Rhau's Symphoniae Iucundae," in *Luther's Works, American Edition: Volume 53—Liturgy and Hymns*, Ulrich S. Leupold (Philadelphia: Fortress Press, 1965), 321–22.

[4] Don Saliers, "Liturgical Musical Formation," in *Liturgy and Music: Lifetime Learning*, ed. Robin A. Leaver and Joyce Ann Zimmerman (Collegeville, MN: Liturgical Press, 1998), 385.

which were perceived to be more embodied and emotional, or passionate expressions of the heart.[5]

This suspicion of singing in its more embodied forms was exported with European ideas and cultural paradigms in the colonial/imperial projects of Europe post-1492. At the same time, and partly because of its recognized power, hymns were used as a tool of the modernist/civilizing-cultural/colonial project to impose Christianity throughout the world. The canons of Western European and Anglo North Atlantic hymnody were understood to be the most appropriate modes of congregational singing. As a result, and also because of the suspicion against more embodied modes of singing, songs and musical traditions from outside these canons were often stigmatized. They were associated with the body, the sensual/erotic, the "primitive," and the passionate. As European cultural expressions, Christian hymns were understood to represent the pinnacle of human achievement.

In fact, in the Canadian Protestant churches of my inquiry—the United and Anglican Churches of Canada—the pervasive authority given to the inherited canons of Western European and Anglo North Atlantic hymnody in congregational singing still thwarts embodied congregational participation. It impedes the full expression of diverse and complex cultural identities which are, in my view, part of our *imago dei*. As a result, this impediment actually undermines God's gift to us; we are prevented from fully expressing and experiencing God's image in us.

Instead, congregational singing can embody a liberating praxis that serves to unmask these Western European and Anglo North Atlantic colonial forces—empire at the heart of song. A liberating praxis of congregational singing both challenges the suspicion against singing as an embodied action and aims to reclaim it from the domination of pervasive Western

---

[5] A culmination of this distrust is exhibited in the rigid belief that music must always be subordinated to the Word and was exemplified by sixteenth-century Swiss reformer Huldreich Zwingli who completely banned music from public worship. Ibid., 386. Zwingli's austere approach did not generally take hold, but the impulse to control and constrain music remained a strong thread in ecclesial practices. For example, French reformer John Calvin distrusted music's power due to its potential to "greatly turn or bend in any direction the morals of men." John Calvin, "Epistle to the Reader" from *Cinquante Pseaumes en Français par Clem. Marot* (1543), in David Music, ed. and comp., *Hymnology: A Collection of Source Readings* (Lanham, MD: Scarecrow Press, Inc., 1996), 66. A denominational imprint may also be discerned in the degree of distrust; contrast the Calvinistic focus on psalm singing, for instance, with a more Wesleyan allowance for an engagement with the affections.

European Anglo North Atlantic cultures in liturgy. It advocates a participatory embodied spirit-infused practice of congregational singing. Liberating singing, animated by the Holy Spirit, thus creates new spaces for the inclusion of the wide array of cultural traditions that are either ignored presently, relegated to the exotic, or segregated away from the mainstream—in other words, for the diverse polycultural, multilingual, multiethnic expressions of God's image in us.[6]

These diverse and often marginalized expressions help us reclaim singing as a profoundly embodied act which can usher in an experience of the Divine and contribute to a deeply spiritual experience as the corporate body of Christ reverberates.[7] This passionate, powerful, sensual, unequivocally physical, and body-centered ritual activity is thus both profoundly incarnational *and* communal. It is this experience of community—of singing in relation with each other—that allows us to experience the Divine within and among us when we sing as part of the body of Christ. Initiated by drawing or "inspiring" breath—*ruach* in Hebrew or *pneuma* in Greek—into ourselves, we activate our vocal cords by pushing the air back out through our mouths into the world. From this space, the liberating action of the Holy Spirit invites us to be open to the transforming and creative power of our collective action as we re-enact and participate in God's original and ongoing action of creation. Together the human and the Divine become eschatological co-workers, building and embodying God's kin-dom through the deepest kind of concrete engagement, simultaneously listening and "speaking" in our sung expressions, feeling, and breathing together, mutually attentive in the song and its singing.[8] Our

[6] Polycultural refers positively to the multiple cultures present in many contexts. In contexts outside Canada, the term multicultural is often used to describe this dynamic. In the Canadian context, however, multiculturalism was adopted as an official government policy by the federal government under Pierre Elliot Trudeau in 1971. We return to a critical analysis of this notion of multiculturalism in the Canadian context in Chap. 3.

[7] Divine is capitalized throughout when I am referring to Christian experience of the ultimate. It is not capitalized when it is an adjective or in a direct quotation.

[8] I use Kin-dom, after Ada Maria Isasi-Diaz. Ada María Isaisi-Díaz, "Kin-Dom of God: A Mujerista Proposal," in *In Our Own Voices: Latino/a Renditions of Theology*, ed. Beahamín Valentín (Maryknoll, NY: Orbis, 2010), 171–89. Isasi-Díaz insists that the *mujerista* "*proyecto histórico*" includes an "unfolding of what is called 'the kingdom of God'" which rejects "present oppressive systems and institutions" and encourages the flourishing of liberation. Liberation along *mujerista* lines is: deeply praxical, rooted in a "'doing,' a way of claiming our right to think, to know critically"; communal and accountable; "embedded in a 'grassroots ecumenism' that skirts traditional doctrinal purity and embraces diversity"; and

personal vocalizations are transformed into a collective action that is one of the primary modes of embodied ritual expression, integrating our whole selves—our bodies, minds, and spirits.

A liberating approach begins with a recognition that we sing with our bodies and in community. It insists that all are welcome to sing; all voices regardless of training or timbre are enjoined to praise God. It confronts the reality that our bodies are not abstract entities; they/we are situated in particular historical, geographical, and cultural locations, times, and ecclesial spaces. We are formed by the concrete circumstances in which we find ourselves. Our singing reveals something about who we are, and it also invites us to express our responses to our settings, articulating who we can become and how we understand the divine intent for us.

I would locate such liberating singing praxes within the long line of liberationist theologians who choose and affirm the embodied participatory nature of the work of the people. These theologians are opposed to "hierarchical structures of power [which] have in many cases alienated the people's participation in liturgy and worship, and have walled them off into a state of being no more than receivers of the holy things."[9] Spirit driven, such a liberating praxis witnesses to people's concrete lived experience just as it illuminates God's work in the midst of that reality. It also forms and enfolds the participants into a vocal community prepared (or "conscientized") for the work of liberation.[10] As such, it affirms the collective experience of the people as a place for doing theology, as a *locus theologicus*, drawing on the embodied knowledge acquired in the struggles and joys of daily living. When people sing thus engaged in a social praxis of liberation their very act of singing is a living out of God's image in us. We then more fully express and form our identities, enabling the

personal and political at the same time, 178–79. For her, "the deep *nosotras/nosotros* made possible by the ties of *familia*, the mutuality and reciprocity it entails, is at the heart of the new world order that is intrinsic in the Gospel proclamation, which is precisely why we believe kin-dom of God—*famila de Dios*—can function as a metaphor for what Jesus referred to as the "kingdom of God," 182. I am aware that notions of family can be problematic, especially for those who have experienced violence within the family. But her insistence on mutuality and reciprocity, as well as praxis, invites a reconfiguring of notions of family—or kingdom—to be truly inclusive and free from violence.

[9] Cláudio Carvalhaes, "Liturgy and Postcolonialism: An Introduction," in *Liturgy in Postcolonial Perspectives: Only One is Holy*, ed. Cláudio Carvalhaes (New York: Palgrave Macmillan, 2015), 4.

[10] Paulo Freire, *Pedagogy of the Oppressed*, trans. Myra Bergman Ramos (New York: Herder and Herder, 1971).

transformative purposes of liberation to emerge and be actualized, all animated by the liberating action of the Holy Spirit.

METHODOLOGY AND OUTLINE

In order to examine the multiple ways in which congregational singing can become liberating, I work with liberationist, decolonial, and postcolonial frameworks to analyze the implications of the colonizing legacy of Western European and Anglo North Atlantic hymnody in liturgy. Each of these intellectual traditions represents vast and deep histories and trajectories. I draw on them with appreciation for their rich inheritances.

A clarification is in order at this point. I understand *liberating praxis* along the lines of Paulo Freire and others as "reflection and action directed at the structures to be transformed."[11] For Freire, liberation entails a conscientization which provokes people to act to change their social context in order to dismantle structures of poverty and oppression. This Freirian bedrock undergirds my interpretation of liberation. But my understanding of liberation is also enriched by communities of liberation theologians. They have insisted on unmasking, interrogating, and unsettling the social forces of oppression which are predicated on theological understandings that privilege the rich and neutralize the poor, preventing them from gaining agency to struggle against those same oppressive social structures. Their aim has been to create the conditions so that the poor, the marginalized, and the excluded can gain their historical sense of agency (praxis) so that they can contribute to the establishment of a society that more closely resembles the divine promise of the realm of God.

Liberation theologians in their multiple expressions drew on the Marxist notion of praxis but reconfigured it to include the reflective act *for* liberation inspired by the gospel, understood to be the transformation of history by working to build the kin-dom of God.[12] In their context, it first took on a specifically classist approach which was eventually expanded to include concerns about racialization and gender. More recent liberationist approaches have included questions of ethno-cultural background, sexual orientation, and (dis)ability. I am indebted to all these understandings of

---

[11] Ibid., 120.
[12] Gustavo Gutiérrez, *A Theology of Liberation*, trans. Caridad Inda and John Eagleson (Maryknoll, NY: Orbis, 1973); Juan Luis Segundo, *Liberation of Theology*, trans. John Drury (Maryknoll, NY: Orbis, 1976).

praxis. My own understanding also includes a decolonial impetus toward a disentangling of coloniality within present social structures and dynamics both inside and outside the church. Colonizing strategies are thus unmasked—as operative in the manner in which people interrelate and as embedded in the interconnected social markers of class, race, gender, and so on.[13]

For Christians committed to struggles of liberation from oppression, a liberating singing praxis includes a commitment to struggle against all forces that dehumanize in singing. Through critical analysis of songs and their singing, liberating singing can contribute to building God's kin-dom of justice and radical love. Such a praxis draws on the inheritance of liberation theologies in emphasizing, among other things: the particular contexts and concrete historical reality of the oppressed or marginalized; the importance of self-critical awareness, consciousness-raising, and narrative in liberating processes; the power of the community and the church as liberating forces; the experience of the people as an epistemological source for theology, a *locus theologicus*; and the rooting of a liberating praxis in "life as a whole as a new way of being and doing" in history.[14]

After more than twenty-five years of animating and studying congregational and community singing in Canada, Cuba, the USA, and elsewhere, I have come to learn that the realities of life for the people who gather to sing are extremely diverse, representing many cultures, languages, social and economic classes, abilities, genders, sexual orientations, and so on. These messy, intercultural, often conflictual, and socially contested realities are always present when we sing. They also shape and condition the way people sing and why they sing. Inspired by liberationist thinkers, I have sought to lift up these experiences—the experience of people's daily lives—along with the cultural traditions of the people, as a place for doing

---

[13] Briefly put, coloniality can be described along the lines of decolonial scholars as the ubiquitous residue and ongoing manifestations of the modern-colonial capitalist world-system, the superstructure which encompasses the co-constitutive and global forces of colonialism, modernity and capitalism. The notion of coloniality as applied to congregational singing will be developed in subsequent chapters, especially Chaps. 3 and 4.

[14] Rebecca S. Chopp, "Toward Praxis: A Method for Liberation Theology," in *The Praxis of Suffering: An Interpretation of Liberation and Political Theologies* (Maryknoll, NY: Orbis, 1986), 139, 143. These points will be elaborated upon throughout the book. For foundational treatment of these theme, see Gutiérrez, *A Theology of Liberation*; Segundo, *Liberation of Theology*. I would argue that liberating praxis also includes liberation from forces of capitalism, individualism, and consumerism, which threaten not only the very fabric of our communities but also the delicate fabric of the interconnected web of God's creation.

theology. Over time, these theologies and my relationships in a variety of communities have helped to shape how I have come to understand my vocation as a song enlivener or song leader.[15] The overarching methodology of my thesis reflects these multiple influences and relationships. It is what I call a *syncopated liberating approach.*

Another word of clarity is in order here; while I would locate my work in the realm of practical theology, I do not see it as ethnographic. Recent scholarship has productively turned toward ethnographic approaches, especially in the realm of practical theology, including in analyses of church music.[16] These approaches often take a participant-observer stance, with clearly defined fieldwork and interview procedures outlined from the outset. In my work, I did not set out as a participant-observer, or even as a researcher, to "go to the places where people live, work, or pray in order to take in firsthand the experience of group life and social interactions."[17] Rather my methodological approach draws from my own lived experience recalled from memory. I reflect on this experience, in conversation with multiple people, scholars, and communities, with a view to work toward transformation, in this case, liberating congregation singing. It is, to repeat, a liberation-oriented praxis-based approach. Like some ethnographic (and auto-ethnographic) approaches, my work does draw on narrative, as I recall the events upon which I reflect. In addition, conversations with friends and colleagues animate my work, as sites for shared reflection. But these narratives and conversations are part of the living out of praxis rather than structured observations or interviews based on fieldwork, in the ethnographic sense. In every case, when I cite a conversation, I have

[15] I appreciate Michael Hawn's term "song enlivener." I use "song leader" along these lines. Hawn, "Chapter Eight: The Church Musician as Enlivener" in *Gather Into One: Praying and Singing Globally*, (Grand Rapids: Eerdmans Publishing, 2003).

[16] Early examples of an ethnographic approach in church music are C. Michael Hawn's *One Bread, One Body: Exploring Cultural Diversity in Worship*, (Wisconsin: Alban Institute, 2003), in which he used a participant-observer approach; and *Gather Into One: Praying and Singing Globally*, (Grand Rapids: Eerdmans Publishing, 2003) which features several interviews with global song leaders from around the world. More recently, scholars with an ethnographic approach in Christian congregational music have been gathering for a bi-annual conference at Ripon College, Cuddesdon, Oxford, UK. Scholars in this field include: Monique Ingalls, Carolyn Landau, Tom Wagner, Mark Porter, Anna Nekola, and Jonathan Dueck, among others (see bibliography). See: Christian Congregational Music, accessed, March 8, 2020, https://congregationalmusic.org/

[17] Mary Clark Moschella, *Ethnography as a Pastoral Practice: An Introduction* (Cleveland: Pilgrim Press, 2008), 25.

shared the manuscript with my conversation partners for their feedback and approval.

As such, this syncopated mode therefore reflects the rhythm of the liberating praxis I try to live out as I move between spaces, between my privilege and the "other" spaces of those who are marginalized, as well as in relationship, both personally and professionally.[18] It also resonates with my interdisciplinary scholarly approach which draws on multiple currents to identify and illuminate the interconnectedness of the issues I am raising. A syncopated rhythm interrupts the "normative" *beat* of the status quo while simultaneously responding to the heartbeat of life, with its provocative offbeat interjections that transform the overarching rhythmic structures.

Methodologically speaking, this praxis is not constrained by one approach or current, but emerges from the weaving together of multiple beats to form a rhythmic structure in which rhythms play off each other, often in tension, but also as a coherent frame/methodology. It allows distinct discourses to cooperate in articulating new unaddressed sets of issues which continue to unfold, not as finished products or neatly packaged theories but as unfolding multiple processes. Much like the human experience of life, it entails an ongoing praxical commitment toward liberating action and reflection that does not foreclose itself or pretend to arrive at a definitive endpoint. A syncopated liberating approach is multi-factorial, contestatory, and strategic. It entails a stance that depends on ongoing processes of self-interrogation in relation to power, struggles against systems that oppress, and accompanies those who are on the margins.

The foundational beat that lies underneath this book is a syncopation between human and divine impulses. As such, a syncopated liberating praxis taps into the energy and movement of the Holy Spirit. It follows that when leadership does not create the conditions for the people to sing or when it turns their singing against God's intention for humanity, it is stifling the Spirit's liberating breath. By liberating congregational singing, the people collaborate and conspire with God's created intent for life, while working against forces that dehumanize. Undergirding my vocation

---

[18] The idea of a syncopated liberating approach was suggested by Néstor Medina. Néstor Medina, Email correspondence with the author (25 October 2016). In Chap. 3, issues of identity and how they impact song leadership, among other things, will be explored in far more detail. However, since I am raising the question of privilege and "other" spaces here, I note, for now, that I am a university-educated, Anglo-Euro-Canadian settler, middle-class, cisgender, able-bodied, adult woman, and a mother.

as a song leader—and this scholarly reflection on that work—is a deep commitment to make space in which the people feel empowered to sing.

This work is rooted in my life; I draw from my particular experience with particular communities in the city of Toronto. However, it is my hope that practitioners and church music scholars from many contexts will find something here to help them dismantle coloniality and liberate congregational singing and worship where they are. Similarly, both the methodology and proposed techniques could be expanded for use in interrogating coloniality in broader church structures and activities. Such rigorous ongoing critical engagements with scholars from a variety of disciplines, including especially ethno/musicology and post- and decolonial studies, have the potential to transform the ways we think and act.

There is also a fundamental tension in my project between affirming and drawing from grassroots approaches and knowledges and engaging in critical discourse with "big theory." To address this tension, the book has a spiral structure in which my own experience continually draws us back to concrete community contexts, rooting the analysis in practice. With each circling back the theoretical analysis is also opened up and rendered more complex. My goal is that the questions raised in one chapter will be answered, or at least wrestled with, in the next. For me, this spiral of engagement is ongoing. This work continues as I teach, lead worship and singing, and research and reflect on these issues.

With all of this in mind, Chap. 2 begins with praxis by reflecting on and analyzing three seminary chapel services in order to propose some preliminary rubrics for liberating congregational song leading. Here I also situate my project within the field of church music scholarship and begin my own self-reflective and praxical journey.

Chapter 3 suggests ways to unmask our identities by examining some of the processes of identification and contextualization that hinder the creation of a robust, embodied, and accountable liberating approach to congregational singing. Insisting that we must always begin with ourselves, I examine questions of power and deconstruct the "coloniality of being" in ourselves, our relationships, our communities, and our institutions.[19] Several techniques are considered, drawn from a range of post and decolonial thinkers, as well as critical race theorists: decolonizing

---

[19] Nelson Maldonado-Torres, "On the Coloniality of Being," *Cultural Studies* 21, no. 2–3 (March/May 2007): accessed July 25, 2018, http://www.decolonialtranslation.com/english/maldonado-on-the-coloniality-of-being.pdf

autobiographies, unsuturing, unbleaching, engaging intermixture, and unforgetting. In order to begin to liberate our singing we must understand the superstructures of these contexts, which means we need to confront the coloniality of our denominations and broader contexts.

Chapters 4 and 5 include textual and some musical analyses of hymns which are generally considered part of the hymnic canons in the Anglican and United Churches of Canada. The expression of the complex cultural identities explored in Chap. 3 is impeded by the dominance of the inherited canons of Western European Anglo North Atlantic hymnody. Chapter 4 sets out to unmask the ways in which hymns from the Victorian era preserve, reproduce, and reinscribe ideologies and theologies of empire, in order to expose coloniality in music. To help in this analysis, I draw on current debates in the field of ethnomusicology in which scholars are beginning to dismantle eurocentrism in the study of music.

Chapter 5 problematizes the forthright unmasking of empire at the heart of hymnody from Chap. 4 by drawing on post- and decolonial scholarship. Exploring Homi Bhabha's concepts of mimicry, hybridity, and Third Space in this and the following chapter, I show that these hermeneutical moves help to deconstruct coloniality and point toward liberating potential, especially by unmasking and interrogating the pervasive cultural influence of European colonialism and imperialism. Yet, they are also circumscribed by the colonial gaze, Eurocentric epistemological frames, and overly abstract deconstructive thinking. Meanwhile, decolonial scholars are more interested in affirming the agencies of those from the Global South and (re)claiming other ways of knowing that are "de-linked" from Europe.[20] Both currents, the first deconstructive, the second more constructive, offer rich perspectives for the task of complexifying the methodology of the previous chapter.

Along these lines, Chap. 5 opens up the themes of Chap. 4 by examining how marginalized peoples sing the hymns of empire as well as their own songs. By drawing on the decolonial categories of "epistemic disobedience" and "other ways of knowing," this chapter analyzes the dynamics of congregational singing, along with the texts and performance practices of two "colonial" hymns: "From Greenland's Icy Mountains" and "How Great Thou Art." What becomes evident is that hymns clothed in the

---

[20] Walter D. Mignolo, "Epistemic Disobedience, Independent Thought and Decolonial Freedom," *Theory, Culture & Society* 26, no. 7–8 (2009): 178, accessed July 25, 2018, http://waltermignolo.com/wp-content/uploads/2013/03/epistemicdisobedience-2.pdf

garments of European hymnody can be inverted (flipped) by the people who sing them, subverting theologies of empire and colonialism and becoming instruments of resistance and sources of forbearance, strength, and hope. To conclude, a song from the Global South/Majority World, "El Espíritu de Dios," offers an opportunity to explore how fragile spaces have already been opened up by those from the underside.

In Chap. 6, the theoretical framings of both post- and decolonial scholars are further developed, often in tension with each other, by examining two Christmas events at the Church of the Holy Trinity in downtown Toronto. By comparing and contrasting the church's pageant, "The Christmas Story," with intercultural practices from the community's Christmas Eve service—the Mexican and Central American celebration of *Las Posadas* and the singing of a new Christmas Carol, "The Midwife's Carol," I examine how decolonial thinking goes beyond postcolonial frames. Voices that challenge the dominance of Eurocentric worldviews through other ways of knowing and being in song can be fruitfully read along decolonial lines as Walter Mignolo's border thinking and my reconceptualization of it as border singing.

Chapter 7 extends border thinking/singing beyond Mignolo's paradigm to encompass the multiplicity and complexity of our identities and our intermixing in congregational singing. The singing of the H.E.R.E. Local 75 Union Choir as a locus for doing theology through song elicits germinative principles for a liberating liturgical theology, animated by the Holy Spirit. Despite the dangerous daily lived reality of choir members, the choir embodies a sacramental praxis and shows how the work and grace of the Holy Spirit can guide us through the risks of dismantling coloniality toward liberating our singing. Such a praxis can lead to a change of heart and life for those involved and calls the churches to be open to their own conversion.

It is important to emphasize again that all this work is rooted in my life; working toward liberating congregational singing is a critical self-reflective process. I wanted to find words to articulate what I have been experiencing over the years in my singing, song leading, and church communities. My own faith journey, a journey riddled with doubt, has been sustained and renewed in encounters along the way with people who help me to see the hundreds of tiny epiphanies—fleeting glimpses of the Divine—that interweave into the fabric of my conversion to this syncopated liberating vision. I have come to understand my vocation as but a part of the work of the whole community of God which plunges "itself into [the] love that builds up humanity in history."[21] I believe that in this work—and through our singing—the church can become a concrete communitarian sign of liberation, enacting the radical love that is at the heart of Christianity.

POSTSCRIPT: FLIPPING THE (SONG) BIRD

Finally, and as the title of this book suggests—with, admittedly, both playful and subversive intent—I contend that congregational singing needs to be "flipped" to be liberating. Of course, I am well aware that the idiomatic expression "to flip the bird" is an obscene gesture in Anglo North American contexts, designed to affront. When Jesus felt a need to challenge the *status quo* in temple behaviour, he prophetically and unapologetically flipped over the money lenders tables (Matthew 21:12; John 2:15). My intention is to startle and deeply provoke the reader into considering what's at stake—how much our hymnody and our practices really need to change in order to be liberating. The songbird at the centre of this potent and provocative metaphor underscores the extent of the necessary commitment. Known for passion and dedication, songbirds, like the nightingale, were reputed to be so passionate and committed to singing that they used all their being, including their very last breath, in song.[22]

Consider the obscenity and travesty of the personal and cultural damage done by the colonization of congregational singing. Simply changing a few hymns here and there and adding an exotic instrument is insufficient. What is needed is a deep engagement that takes the embodied and enacted theology of singing very seriously. What are we saying with our texts? Or even, what multiple meanings can we discern? How does the way we sing change the meaning? How do song enliveners sustain prophetic witness in increasingly diverse and resource-challenged contexts? What are the real implications of moving from what Michael Hawn calls "center to spectrum?"[23] Are those with power really prepared to give it up? How much of our theological inheritance are we prepared to put on the table in our engagements? How can the gospel guide us toward commitment as Christians to make space for the diversity of the *imago dei* embodied in the

---

[21] Juan Luis Segundo, *The Sacraments Today, Volume Four of a Theology for Artisans of a New Humanity*, trans. John Drury (New York: Orbis, 1974), 7.

[22] David Badke, "Nightingale," in *The Medieval Bestiary: Animals in the Middle Ages*, accessed July 25, 2018, http://bestiary.ca/beasts/beast546.htm

[23] Hawn, *Gather Into One.*

songs of fellow human beings? How do we lift up and honour our own tradition and still make room for others? Will we recognize our hymnody, our faith, and our church if we let it be transformed by the presence of an-other?

These are challenging questions which outline a complex map of profound reconfigurations and reorientations of our understanding of singing, both in its powerful destructive force and its potentially pneumatic transformative promise. Being polite is not enough. Perhaps we/I need to be astonished into action. In my own experience, articulated in part in these pages, these kinds of questions require us to wrestle with deep dislocation and discomfort. They invite a profound epistemological and theological re-orientation for singers and song leaders who are committed to liberating congregational singing. They invite us to take the risk and think about what it might mean to actually flip the (song) bird.

BIBLIOGRAPHY

Augustine. 1997. Book 9, Chapter (6) 14. In *The Confessions*, trans. Maria Boulding. New York: New City Press.

Badke, David. Nightingale. In *The Medieval Bestiary: Animals in the Middle Ages*. http://bestiary.ca/beasts/beast546.htm. Accessed 25 July 2018.

Calvin, John. 1996. Epistle to the Reader. In *Cinquante Pseaumes en Français par Clem. Marot* (1543). Reprinted in Music, David, editor and compiler. *Hymnology: A Collection of Source Readings*. Lanham: Scarecrow Press.

Carvalhaes, Cláudio. 2015. Liturgy and Postcolonialism: An Introduction. In *Liturgy in Postcolonial Perspectives: Only One is Holy*, ed. Cláudio Carvalhaes. New York: Palgrave Macmillan.

Chopp, Rebecca S. 1986. Toward Praxis: A Method for Liberation Theology. In *The Praxis of Suffering: An Interpretation of Liberation and Political Theologies*. Maryknoll: Orbis.

Christian Congregational Music. https://congregationalmusic.org/. Accessed 8 Mar 2020.

Freire, Paulo. 1971. *Pedagogy of the Oppressed*. Trans. Myra Bergman Ramos. New York: Herder and Herder.

Gutiérrez, Gustavo. 1973. *A Theology of Liberation*. Trans. Caridad Inda and John Eagleson. Maryknoll: Orbis.

Hawn, C.Michael. 2003a. *Gather into One: Praying and Singing Globally*. Grand Rapids: Eerdmans Publishing.

Hawn, C. Michael. 2003b. *One Bread, One Body: Exploring Cultural Diversity in Worship*. Wisconsin: Alban Institute.

Hildegard of Bingen. 1990. *Scivias*. Trans. Columba Hart and Jane Bishop. New York: Paulist Press.

Ingalls, Monique, Carolyn Landau, and Tom Wagner. 2013. *Christian Congregational Music: Performance, Identity, and Experience*. Farnham: Ashgate Publishing.

Isaisi-Díaz, Ada María. 2010. Kin-Dom of God: A Mujerista Proposal. In *In Our Own Voices: Latino/a Renditions of Theology*, ed. Beahamín Valentín. Maryknoll: Orbis.

Luther, Martin. 1965. Preface to Gerog Rhau's Symphoniae Iucundae. In *Luther's Works, American Edition: Volume 53—Liturgy and Hymns*, trans. Ulrich S. Leupold. Philadelphia: Fortress Press.

Maldonado-Torres, Nelson. 2007. On the Coloniality of Being. *Cultural Studies* 21 (2–3), March/May. http://www.decolonialtranslation.com/english/maldonado-on-the-coloniality-of-being.pdf. Accessed 25 July 2018.

Medina, Néstor. 2016. Email Correspondence with the Author, October 25.

Mignolo, Walter D. 2009. Epistemic Disobedience, Independent Thought and Decolonial Freedom. *Theory, Culture & Society* 26 (7–8). http://waltermignolo.com/wp-content/uploads/2013/03/epistemicdisobedience-2.pdf. Accessed 25 July 2018.

Moschella, Mary Clark. 2008. *Ethnography as a Pastoral Practice: An Introduction*. Cleveland: Pilgrim Press.

Nekola, Anna, and Tom Wagner, eds. 2015. *Congregational Music Making and Community in a Mediated Age*. Farnham: Ashgate.

Porter, Mark. 2017. *Contemporary Worship Music and Everyday Musical Lives*. Abingdon/New York: Routledge.

Saliers, Don. 1998. Liturgical Musical Formation. In *Liturgy and Music: Lifetime Learning*, ed. Robin A. Leaver and Joyce Ann Zimmerman. Collegeville: Liturgical Press.

Segundo, Juan Luis. 1974. *The Sacraments Today, Volume Four of a Theology for Artisans of a New Humanity*. Trans. John Drury. New York: Orbis.

———. 1976. *Liberation of Theology*. Trans. John Drury. Maryknoll: Orbis.

CHAPTER 2

(Trans)forming Praxis: Initial Rubrics for Liberating Song Leading

INTRODUCTION

This chapter roots the project of liberating congregational singing in praxis, that is to say, I reflect on the action of song leading for the purpose of transformation.[1] A brief historical sketch of recent trends toward the renewal of congregational singing concentrates particularly on opening up hymnic canons to include songs from the Global South/Majority World.[2] An analysis of three examples of congregational song leading using global hymnody follows and yields some preliminary rubrics for liberating congregational singing that are contextual, accountable, and liberating.[3] The

---

[1] As outlined in the introduction, praxis includes the notion of transformation, along the lines of Freire and others. See chapter 4 of Paulo Freire, *Pedagogy of the Oppressed* (New York: Herder and Herder, 1971), 119–86. A "liberating" praxis of song leading therefore entails a reflection on the practice of song leading for the purpose of transformation—the transformation of liturgy and church structures which can in turn contribute to broader liberation struggles, against forces of dehumanization and toward movements that build up humanity as part of God's wider creation.

[2] Global South/Majority World refers to the geographical Global South as well as communities in the Global North which are marginalized, especially along ethno-cultural or racialized lines.

[3] Emerging out of ethnomusicology and popular music discourses, the terms global music and world music refer to music of a non-Western origin. The terminology remains contested and fluid, striking at the heart of the tension in ethno/musicology which sets every "other" music against European art music, what Stuart Hall calls the "West and the Rest." Similarly, in church music circles, global song and global hymnody refer to music that comes from the

---

© The Author(s) 2020   17
B. Whitla, *Liberation, (De)Coloniality, and Liturgical Practices*,
New Approaches to Religion and Power,
https://doi.org/10.1007/978-3-030-52636-8_2

rest of the book will extend, expand, and problematize the issues raised here in an ongoing praxiological process that roots theoretical proposals and mechanisms in concrete experiences of song leading and congregational singing. As a critical reflection on the vocation of song leading, the book draws from my experience, deepens it, and provides an opportunity to share a range of observations and techniques with others. It is intended to embody what Freire refers to when he says "critical reflection is also action."[4]

HISTORICAL CONTEXT: THE BLOSSOMING OF CONGREGATIONAL SINGING

In Euro-North Atlantic contexts, the recent blossoming of congregational singing practices as a sub-field in church music scholarship has been strongly influenced by ecclesial trends over the last seventy years—toward fuller congregational participation, local/indigenous Christian expressions, and an awareness of global Christianity through worship. Massive shifts in geo-political realities in the twentieth century, especially toward political and cultural independence from European nations, had an enormous influence in church contexts and resulted in regional church gatherings throughout the world. For example, the Christian Conference of Asia first met in 1964; the All Africa Conference of Churches, in 1969; and the Latin American Council of Churches, in 1982. These bodies, along with national ecumenical church councils and regional church coalitions, contributed to important intercultural and interdenominational conversations about liturgy and frequently dedicated time and staff resources to the development of worship resources.[5] Churches and church organizations in

---

Global South, along with marginalized contexts in the Global North. For further discussion, see: Stuart Hall, "The West and the Rest: Discourse and Power," in *Formations of Modernity*, ed. Stuart Hall and Gieben, Bram (Cambridge, U.K.: Polity Press in association with the Open University, 1992), 185–227; Martin Stokes, "Globalization and the Politics of World Music," in *The Cultural Study of Music: A Critical Introduction,"* eds. Martin Clayton, Trevor Herbert, and Richard Middleton, 107–116, (New York: Routledge, 2012); Timothy D. Taylor, *Beyond Exoticism: Western Music and the World* (Durham: Duke University Press, 2007).

[4] Freire, *Pedagogy of the Oppressed*, 123.

[5] World Council of Churches 24, "Member Churches," in *World Council of Churches*, accessed February 11, 2018, https://www.oikoumene.org/en/member-churches/wcc-regions

the Global North responded to these social, political, and cultural shifts. As churches in the Global South instituted radical changes, used innovative approaches, pushed back, and sometimes outrightly rejected Eurocentric ways of doing things, churches and church bodies in the Global North were called to account.

Four key historical moments signify these trends: the revolutionary liturgical Catholic edict for "fully conscious and active participation" from *Sacrosanctum Concilium* of the Second Vatican Council in 1963[6]; the prominence of global music at the World Council of Churches meeting in Vancouver in 1983[7]; the Lutheran affirmation that worship must be transcultural, contextual, counter-cultural, and cross-cultural in the 1996 Nairobi Statement on Worship and Culture[8]; and the United Methodist Global Praise program which began in the 1990s in the USA.[9] The resulting new approaches to worship and congregational singing were put into practice in ecumenical settings that focused on congregational singing, as in the Taizé Community in France and the Iona Community in Scotland. They have also been emboldened by and articulated in recent academic currents that take Christian congregational "musicking"[10] seriously in ethno/musicology.[11]

---

[6] Pope Paul VI, "Constitution on the Sacred Liturgy Sacrosanctum Concilium," II: 14, accessed October 27, 2017, http://www.vatican.va/archive/hist_councils/ii_vatican_council/documents/vat-ii_const_19631204_sacrosanctum-concilium_en.html

[7] See chapters by Per Harling and Pablo Sosa which examine these influences on ecumenical congregational singing practices in S. T. Kimbrough, ed., *Music and Mission: Toward a Theology and Practice of Global Song* (New York: GBGMusik, 2007).

[8] "Nairobi Statement on Worship and Culture," Calvin Institute of Christian Worship, accessed April 16, 2018, https://worship.calvin.edu/resources/resource-library/nairobi-statement-on-worship-and-culture-full-text

[9] "Global Praise," Global Ministries, accessed July 25, 2018, https://www.umcmission.org/Find-Resources/Global-Praise

[10] Christopher Small's book *Musicking* transformed discourses about music, particularly in the field of musicology. Insisting that music ought to be the verb to music, he writes that *"to music is to take part, in any capacity, in a musical performance, whether by performing, by listening, by rehearsing or practicing, by providing material for performance (what is called composing), or by dancing* (italics his)." Christopher Small, *Musicking: The Meanings of Performing and Listening* (Hanover, NH: Wesleyan University Press, 1998), 9.

[11] The scholarship in this new sub-field is driven by emerging scholars, many of whom are themselves Christian practitioners. It is characterized by a commitment to take the theo-religious meaning-making in Christian congregational musicking seriously. See, for example, Monique Ingalls, Carolyn Landau, and Tom Wagner, *Christian Congregational Music: Performance, Identity, and Experience* (Farnham, U.K.: Ashgate Publishing, 2013); Mark

The very rise of the study of congregational singing in and of itself as a particular focus in church music studies also signals these shifts. Congregational singing advocates are encouraging people to take hymns and songs seriously—both text and music—from a theological point of view. They insist that congregational singing, the singing of the people, is fundamental for meaningful worship, for meaning-making in worship, for theological formation, and even for ecclesial transformation. These ecclesial and academic currents have also fostered an emphasis on the recovery of the singing voice, which in turn has encouraged greater congregational participation and a greater diversity of repertoire. The political implications of empowering the voice are especially evident when the voices of those who were excluded or silenced are welcomed and the canon of hymnody is opened to include "other" musics, especially from the Global South/Majority World.

This inclusion of songs from the Global South and other marginalized communities has been understood by key practitioners in the Global North as a means to open up theological perspectives, enliven worship practices, and build solidarity through prayer and song.[12] To this end, John Bell decries the "patronising colonial mentality with regard to the universal mission," S. T. Kimbrough resoundingly enjoins us not to "colonize the music," and Michael Hawn argues for an "abundant, sung faith,"

Porter, *Contemporary Worship Music and Everyday Musical Lives* (Abingdon and New York: Routledge, 2017; Anna Nekola and Tom Wagner, eds. *Congregational Music Making and Community in a Mediated Age* (Farnham, Surrey, U.K.: Ashgate, 2015).

[12] It is worth mentioning a few of the key players in the field of global congregational song leading. These include John Bell, S. T. Kimbrough, Michael Hawn, and Lim Swee Hong, among others. The work of both Kimbrough and Hawn is particularly notable for their commitment to partner with practitioners and scholars from the Global South/Majority World. Lim Swee Hong distinguishes himself not only by providing a rare foray into a scholarly analysis of Christian congregational song beyond Western European Anglo North Atlantic contexts, but also by engaging postcolonial and ideological concerns in his study. See John L. Bell, *The Singing Thing: A Case for Congregational Song* (Chicago: GIA Publications, Inc., 2000); John L. Bell, *The Singing Thing Too: Enabling Congregations to Sing* (Chicago: GIA Publications Inc., 2007); Kimbrough, *Music and Mission*; C. Michael Hawn, *Gather Into One: Praying and Singing Globally*. Grand Rapids, MI: Eerdmans Publishing, 2003); C. Michael Hawn, comp. and ed., *New Songs of Celebration Render: Congregational Song in the Twenty-First Century* (Chicago: GIA Publications, 2013); Swee Hong Lim, *Giving Voice to Asian Christians: An Appraisal of the Pioneering Work of I-To Loh in the Area of Congregational Song* (North Charleston, SC: VDM Verlag, 2008).

which broadens theological perspectives and is undergirded by ethical approaches in song leading.[13]

Yet there remains a tendency to justify an expansion of hymnic canons to include global hymnody by somewhat romantically arguing that praying with particular "others" through their songs is sufficient reason to do it or that by simply singing global music, the imperial theologies of Anglo North Atlantic mainline churches can be transformed. In some cases, the move to incorporate global hymnody continues to be tied to outdated notions of mission which risk reinforcing and entrenching patronizing imperial/colonial theologies. In these contexts, the colonial paradigm of the mission-driven "centre" still holds, the shift from "centre to spectrum" is not made, and a tokenistic use of music from the Global South/Majority World prevails.[14]

Toward Rubrics for Liberating Song Leading

At their best, seminary chapel services model Christian worship leadership for today's web of complex ecclesial settings. In theory, they provide an environment in which liberating practices can be tried on and affirmed, as well as a setting in which coloniality in worship practices can be interrogated. In the analysis that follows, three services that took place at an Anglo North American seminary will be examined as case studies to help articulate some of the pitfalls and possibilities of global song leading in order to glean some initial best practices for liberating congregational song leading.[15] In the first example, a service drawing from the rich and moving wells of global music lacked something important in leadership. In the second, shared leadership addressed important concerns, but still didn't go far enough. In a comparative example, I proved guilty of not following my own best practices. And in the third and final example, we will see how some liberating approaches could become more clearly embodied in congregational song and song leadership. Each service

---

[13] Bell, *The Singing Thing Too*, 138; Kimbrough, *Music and Mission*, 105–6; Hawn, *New Songs*, XLV.

[14] Hawn argues for an opening up from "center to spectrum" that involves "polyrhythmic worship [which] embodies both the depth and heritage of liturgical tradition and the breadth of diverse ways of praying with the world church and fresh movements of the spirit." Hawn, *Gather Into One*, 273.

[15] Names, locations and some identifying details have been omitted to allow the focus to be on the liturgical/musical questions at stake.

provokes questions that have led me to establish some preliminary best practices for song leading.

Context and Accountability

The first service we consider was presented as a recognition, appreciation, and celebration of diverse expressions of Christianity, drawing on global song. The service followed a conventional structure with prayers, songs, three readings from scripture, and a sermon. Songs were from Korea, Syria, Cameroon, South Africa, the Philippines, and Canada.

On the surface, there was nothing intrinsically wrong with the service, per se. Yet, there are two significant ways in which the song leader's choices impeded both community participation and leadership accountability. To begin with, the leadership was not shared. The diverse and capable student body at the seminary included people who come from the same ethno-cultural groups as some of the songs chosen, yet their leadership was not included. In addition, the choir had rehearsed with the leader the night before, yet they were not invited to support the song leadership in any meaningful or visible way, beyond providing a body of people in the congregation who were familiar with the songs. The result of these leadership choices was that the whole service came across as univocal and largely led by one person. As a consequence, when students read prayers in their own languages, the gesture came across as tokenistic rather than genuine. The effect was exacerbated when a Euro-Canadian read in Spanish, not their mother tongue. The context of the community was not considered; the identities of the people in the room were not taken into account; and their agencies were therefore not affirmed.

Second, no context was given for any of the songs. The songs were thus misrepresented and misappropriated by the leader. It must be noted that the notion of cultural appropriation or misappropriation means different things in different contexts. In some places, it may be considered a sign of appreciation to sing an-other people's music, but in my own diverse Canadian context, best practices do *not* include using a song from some-one else's tradition or culture without acknowledging and honoring where it came from. Even then, and especially for songs from Indigenous contexts in Canada, it may still be unacceptable to use a song from another culture without permission. In this setting then, and though the song leader likely intended the opposite, they instead risked (re)colonizing the songs. By not contextualizing the songs, the style of leadership came across presumptive, off-hand, and even disrespectful. In addition, the congregation struggled to participate because of a number of other factors: the bulletin was hard to read, a pre-service run through of the songs was poorly led, and it was assumed that everyone could read music and read in multiple languages.

Néstor Medina calls this leadership style "cultural poaching," because it keeps power differentials intact and inflicts cultural and epistemic violence.[16] In this case, the leader seemed to be relying on their credentials as a "global" song leader to assume or build trust even though there was little accountability to the people in the room or the peoples of the songs. As a white Anglo leader, they also appeared to be very far removed from the experience of the marginalized peoples whose songs they represented. By not taking the contexts into account—both the original contexts of the songs as well as the contexts of the peoples in the room—the distance between the "West and the rest" was accentuated; the opportunity to invite differences into an intercultural engagement was lost.[17] There may well have been many other factors that influenced this song leader's capacity for best practices on this particular occasion. However, their leadership illustrated how an entrenchment in cultural privilege can preclude the possibilities of creating a more enriching intercultural space. By monopolizing the power of leadership and failing to consider song contexts, this leader did not practice accountability. What can we glean from this example to develop better practices?

Consider the question: who is in the room? Song leaders who are entrusted with the responsibility of animating congregational singing move us from one state to another, from the singular state of isolated personhood to a collective state of belonging, forming the very vocal community to which we belong through the act of our singing. They are also the point of connection, performing a kind of "sacramental" function which opens the door for the energy of the Spirit to connect all those present, an instrumental node that connects the congregation to the Divine. At the same time, the resulting "we" of our singing, as we form the body of Christ and community of believers, is heterogeneous, and reflects the

---

[16] Néstor Medina, Email correspondence with the author (19 September 2013). Medina was drawing on Gayatri Chakravorty Spivak's notion of epistemic violence. Gayatri Chakravorty Spivak, "Can the Subaltern Speak?" in *Marxism and the Interpretation of Cultures*, ed. Cary Nelson and Lawrence Grossberg (Illinois: University of Illinois Press, 1988), 283.

[17] Hall, "The West and the Rest."

increasingly complex realities of our social locations based on race, class, gender, language, sexual orientation, ability, and other factors. Even within us, our identities are often multiple and contradictory.[18]

These factors influence the power we have (or don't have) to act as agents in the shaping of our communities, as well as in singing, speaking, and acting on behalf of our communities. Being aware of the context of the singing means attending to the diversities of race, ethnicity, gender, class, sexual orientation, and ability in the people who gather. An explicit welcoming of the people in the room affirms identities and draws out people's agencies, both personal and collective, and contributes to a potentially rich intermixture. Moreover, as the people are enabled to sing "with" each other and from their lived experience, the singing becomes a concrete expression of theology, a *locus theologicus*.[19] Such singing—and worship practices, generally—which are concrete and rise out of the people's daily lived reality, is a fundamental criterion for liberating practices, a point to which we will repeatedly turn throughout this volume. Song leaders can draw on and affirm this diversity and experience when they are sensitive to the multiple contexts that are represented by the people present. Even better, they can encourage leadership from among the community gathered.

Being accountable also elicits considerations of the original contexts of the songs. To avoid poaching, a song leader needs to highlight—as much as possible—these original contexts, including information about a song's creators and the community from which it arose. This task is especially important when a song comes from the oral tradition and/or from a marginalized community where the origin may be more easily forgotten, obscured, sanitized, or even erased. Otherwise, the spectre of cultural

---

[18] Catherine Keller, Michael Nausner, and Mayra Rivera note that "our colors and cultures, our sexualities and nationalities, crisscross each of our identities, forming complex mazes of power. Whatever our bloodlines or our religious backgrounds, we find ourselves within these mazes. We find these mazes within us." Catherine Keller, Michael Nausner, and Mayra Rivera, eds., *Post-Colonial Theologies: Divinity and Empire* (Danvers, MA: Chalice Press, 2004), 3. Questions of identity will be examined in much more detail in the next chapter.

[19] Gloria Kehilwe Plaatjie calls such a process "reading with and reading from" in her own South African context in which she aims to establish a Post-Apartheid Black Feminist reading of the bible by lifting up the agency of non-academic black women, affirming their identities, and seeking to transform systems of oppression. Gloria Kehilwe Plaatjie, "Toward a Post-Apartheid Black Feminist Reading of the Bible: A Case of Luke 2.36–38," in *Voices from the Margin: Interpreting the Bible in the Third World*, ed. R.S. Sugirtharajah (Maryknoll, NY: Orbis Books, 2006), 467.

misappropriation looms when a well-intentioned leader inadvertently engages in cultural poaching of the songs of an-other people. Communities may thus be inadvertently recolonized by having their songs stolen, whether by intention or not, in a process of cultural violence that disregards their cultural claim to ownership and their cultural sovereignty.[20]

Ideally, a model of sharing power would be sought by giving over song leadership to people from the community of the song or by sharing power through co-leadership. While partnership in song leading *is* optimal and could have been considered at least to some degree in this instance, it is often not possible. Given that reality, we need rubrics for accountability. Pablo Sosa's threefold process for musical appropriation, as articulated by Michael Hawn, offers one possibility. It involves what Sosa calls contextualization, de-contextualization, and recontextualization. In the first phase, attention is paid to the original singer, the original hearers to whom the song was addressed, and how the song relates to its culture of origin—in short, its original context. Sosa's de-contextualization involves an attempt to interpret the essential meaning of the song as an artifact, on its own, apart from its context of origin. Finally, in the recontextualization stage the *"significado* (meaning) is given a new 'code' or takes on a new *significante* (significance) because of the current situation."[21] In other words, the song takes on a new meaning in its new context. Through recontextualization we can seek to understand how new contexts change the original meaning of the song as well as what the original meaning has to offer its new contexts. Sosa's analysis of musical appropriation brings to bear a contextual awareness of what Hawn calls both the "sending" culture and the "receiving" culture, or, said another way, the context of the original singers/community and the context of those who have appropriated the song.[22]

Such an awareness helps song leaders to be accountable to the creators/communities of the song, especially when song leading partners from those communities are not available. Establishing a kind of "right

---

[20] The question of who owns a song is complex and culturally conditioned, a point which will be developed especially in Chap. 5 in the analysis of *"El Espíritu de Dios."* Whether authorship is claimed or not, songs do originate from specific contexts and often become meaningful for other peoples and other cultures far from their source, "belonging" to their new contexts. There are also legal copyright implications which are explored briefly in this chapter (see footnote 24) and in Chap. 5.

[21] Hawn, *Gather Into One*, 60–61.

[22] Ibid., 19.

relations" in this way begins with contextualizing out loud when leading songs, but it can also be sought in more tangible ways.[23] Models for singing an-other's songs can be expanded to include the sharing of material benefits that accrue to organizations or artists who reproduce or record them.[24] Such tangible actions deepen practices of accountability. By the same token, a lack of attention to power dynamics and accountability can inadvertently (or intentionally) silence particular voices, especially of those who are marginalized, and especially by assuming to sing or speak on their behalf.

Interrogating Power in Song Leading: Epistemic Humility and Kenosis

The second service under consideration took place one month later in the same space and was also led by a white Anglo global song leading expert. In stark contrast, this service modelled practices of global song leading that celebrated diversity and affirmed identity and agency. How was this service different from the previous one? First, this worship leader was attentive to the people in the community. Over the course of their two-day visit they

---

[23] I use the phrase here expansively. In Canada "right relations" refers to an ongoing commitment to restore broken relationships between settler Canadians and Indigenous peoples. Indigenous peoples in Canada understand all newcomers as settlers even while acknowledging the complexity of settler identities depending on the ethnocultural backgrounds of people and their stories of immigration to Canada.

[24] James Poling suggested some helpful questions to guide practices of accountability in a reflection on his work as a white academic man working with marginalized peoples. His questions about his teaching work include the following: To whom, to what and how is a teacher or scholar accountable? Whose work and traditions has one appropriated? Who has the power to challenge a teacher or scholar and to hold them accountable? Who has benefited from one's work and how? And was the benefit emotional, intellectual, or material? These questions are applicable to song leaders who "borrow" from cultural traditions that are not their own. James Poling, "Postcolonial Theologies," Roundtable Response, International Academy of Practical Theology (Victoria University, University of Toronto, 13 April 2013). I also note that Pete Seeger along with Guy Carawan and Frank Hamilton copyrighted the well-known civil rights anthem "We Shall Overcome" in a deliberate move to control the potential income from the song as it became more popular. They then established a fund called the "We Shall Overcome Fund" which is chaired by African-American activist and singer Dr. Bernice Johnson Reagon. According to Seeger, "all royalties from any recording of the song go to this non-profit fund, which distributes the funds 'for black music in the South.'" Pete Seeger, *Where Have All the Flowers Gone? A Singalong Memoir* (Pennsylvania: Sing Out Corporation, 2009), 33.

made it a priority to work with students and invite student leadership throughout the service; in other words, by sharing power, they affirmed the identities and agencies of the gathered assembly. They modelled collaborative leadership.

Second, their approach to the material was contextual. The song leader shared information about the people and contexts of the songs we were singing. The Japanese hymn "Here, O God, Your Servants Gather," for instance, was introduced by sharing the fragile ecumenical postwar origin of the song. Similarly, the Masai "African Affirmation of Faith," which was followed by a sung response from South Africa "Amen, Siyakudumisa" by S. C. Molefe, was introduced with explanations of the cultural context of the song. By contextualizing the songs and through the song leader's posture of respect, they modelled a commitment to honour where the songs came from.

Attention to context certainly helps to mitigate against the great risk of the misappropriation of an-other's culture, a phenomenon that can recolonize whenever music is taken and sung that belongs to another people. But, can we go further and if so, what would that look like? By scrutinizing issues of power that are inherent in song leadership, especially when songs are from marginalized communities, leaders can actively work against reinscribing empire and make space for marginalized expressions and people that have been excluded. This work requires deep respect and self-critical awareness in order to appropriately engage with songs and discourses outside of their original contexts, especially for leaders from the dominant culture.

Such an approach evinces what Otto Maduro proposes as a stance of epistemic humility. In song leading, practicing epistemic humility lifts up other kinds of music and other ways of leading, beyond the privileged realms of written-down hymnody in European styles led by highly trained musicians. Maduro's proposal consists of practical and praxical rubrics for self-critical US LatinaXo "counter knowledges" that oppose Western "arrogant" epistemologies which are "hierarchical, binary, authoritarian, patriarchal, racist, (and) elitist."[25] His intervention is applicable beyond

---

[25] Otto Maduro, "An(Other) Invitation to Epistemological Humility: Notes Towards a Self-Critical Approach to Counter-Knowledges," in *Decolonizing Epistemologies: Latina/o Theology and Philosophy*, ed. Ada María Isasi-Díaz and Eduardo Mendieta (New York: Fordham University Press, 2012), 87, 88. Throughout the book, I use the term LatinaXo, following Neomi DeAnda who writes that "the inclusive 'a' and 'o' expresses the feminist critique of the male dominant in the Spanish language" and also, "the 'X' between the 'a'

his own US LatinaXo context in that it suggests a kind of epistemic dis-obedience—a notion to which we return in Chap. 5 along the lines of Latin American decolonial thinking—by advocating for "a witness of another way of not just knowing, but of knowing justly: knowing in a way that contributes to enhancing life on earth for all."[26] It unmasks what he calls "the dangerous ideal of a universal, eternal, and singular true knowl-edge—a delusion that is habitually part of imperial designs of forced uni-fication, subjection, and homogenization of a variety of ways of being human."[27] When it comes to singing, epistemic humility affirms oral musics, community cultural ownership, and a wide range of leadership styles, among other things.

Epistemic humility resonates theologically with the Pauline notion of *kenosis*, or self-emptying. Opening out through self-emptying invites song leaders to understand that decolonizing can mean getting out of the way by relinquishing one's privilege, especially when one is from the dominant culture. For our purposes, Medina helpfully re-casts *kenosis* culturally and pneumatologically with a proposal in which "the cultural dimension of life, the complex and messy process of cultural formation, is understood as the unique place of the Spirit's involvement."[28] For Medina, "it is through their human cultural reality that people not only interpret their world but also act, seek justice and equality, and oppose all that distorts the original divine intent of fellowship with an-other, nature and the divine."[29]

Pneumatological cultural *kenosis* as part of an intercultural song leading praxis would thus entail a commitment to: deep respect for an-other, self-critical awareness, and epistemic humility. It offers a theological paradigm for interrogating song leading practices that is animated by the Spirit and draws on the kinds of self-reflective and self-critical mechanisms which we

and the 'o' points to the need to omit an often created gender binary and allows for more fluidity." DeAnda, Neomi, "Jesus the Christ" in *The Wiley Blackwell Companion to Latino/a Theology*, edited by Orlando O. Espín, 155–171. New Jersey: John Wiley & Sons, Ltd., 2015, 169, footnote 1.

[26] Ibid., 103.

[27] Ibid., 102–3.

[28] Néstor Medina, "Jürgen Moltmann and Pentecostalism(s): Toward a Cultural Theology of the Spirit," in *Love and Freedom: Systematic and Liberation Theology in the Canadian Context*, ed. David John C. Zub and Robert C. Fennell (Toronto: Toronto School of Theology, 2008), 109. See also Néstor Medina, *Christianity, Empire and the Spirit: (Re) Configuring Faith and the Cultural* (Leiden: Brill, 2018), especially chapter seven: "Understanding the Cultural Pneumatologically," 311–360.

[29] Medina, "Cultural Theology of the Spirit," 109.

will consider in more detail in the next chapter.[30] The resulting rigorous self-critique can lead to discomfort and dislocation. Sometimes a song leader who adopts a kenotic approach will consider not singing by choosing silence instead when there is no leader available from the culture of the song.[31]

Messing Up

At an event that was concurrent with the second service, I was asked to lead the song *"El Espíritu de Dios."*[32] It was for the closing of a conference on music, theology, and justice. Flattered by the invitation to lead a song and energized by the possibility of sending us off with a flourish, I dove in. The people danced and used their bodies to emphasize the text—praying, praising, dancing, jumping, and laughing—echoing the actions of David, the psalmist, and joining together to shout out our praise to the Holy Spirit. One participant, a well-known liturgical theologian, got so excited that he broke the glass he was using as an improvised clave. It was a wonderful finish to a rigorous and engaging conference. But my elation with the success of my song leading, affirmed by the community's enthusiastic response, gave way to a feeling of guilt when I realized I had not given witness to the people whose song it was, especially Guillermo, the Salvadorian refugee who had taught it to me. By neglecting to tell the story of the song, I had momentarily erased the voice of the people whose song I was borrowing.

In subsequent conversation with me about the complex issues of "global" song leadership, the leader of the second service reassured me about my own leadership of this song which I had learned from Guillermo of the Toronto LatinaXo Anglican community, San Esteban. According to the leader, I had given voice to the voiceless. But I am not so sure. In a rush to reassure me and perhaps to justify their own leadership, might the leader of the second service have too quickly stepped past uncomfortable questions about whether or not I could really claim to justly represent that

---

[30] These include autobiographical narratives, unsuturing, unbleaching, engaging intermixture, and unforgetting.

[31] Such a moment would be rare, but could involve a public prayer lamenting the absence of a singer from the culture of the song and praying for the community from which the song came, with silence following. Praying for the community of any given song is an appropriate way to contextualize it.

[32] *"El Espíritu de Dios"* will also be considered in greater detail in Chap. 5.

community? Were my own song practices, and theirs, really making space for voices that had been excluded? Had I really opened up the possibility for a more diverse and inclusive repertoire? Or had I—or perhaps, how had I—re-exoticized an "other" culture by singing an appealing and lively song with a nice rhythm, making myself look good? A commitment to self-interrogation requires me to sit with the painful possibility that I had actually misappropriated Guillermo's voice in a move that was potentially (re)colonizing. That is the real risk and the danger of leading songs that belong to an-other people. The stakes are high. A kenotic and epistemologically humble stance invites an acknowledgment of the risk and danger of singing an-other's song. It also calls us to open out to the liberating potential of doing so. Let us turn to what such practices of liberating song leading might look like.

Toward Liberating Accompaniment

The third service was created and curated by a third global song leader. The theme of the service and the sharing of their leadership suggest two liberating possibilities. First, by wrestling with complex theological and political issues in the service instead of simply celebrating the exoticism of global hymnody, the leader allowed the reading and songs to speak in their own right, offering critical engagement and passionate expression for the participants. The theme was not global hymnody, but global justice—in the form of a concrete theme on stewardship of the land, particularly in relation to land reform and justice in Asia. By building the service on a concrete justice-focused theme, the service drew from the people's experience, especially those impacted by the misuse of the land.[33]

Second, student leadership, including in the use of the choir, was incorporated extensively throughout the service. Every song and reading had been carefully chosen not only for its relationship to the global justice theme but also by considering who among the student body could be invited to lead. In the end, the leader who had created and curated the service took an accompanying role by supporting the singing on the piano

---

[33] Even the category "Asian" was subverted by the inclusion of hymns that challenged stereotypical notions of "Asian" geography. By including a Palestinian song, "The Olive Tree," and a US-Singaporean collaboration, "Make Us One" by Ruth Duck and Lim Swee Hong, the essentialized identity of the oriental "other" was thus unfixed.

on only a few of the songs.[34] In what I am naming as a "kenotic" move, the leader gave up leadership to others—and it must be noted that this leader was not from the dominant white Anglo culture. This open and inviting approach was so keenly felt by one Indian student that he invited one of his own mentors to lead the congregation in a musical offering sung in Tamil at the beginning of the service. By partnering in leadership, the service was rooted in and rose up from the seminary community. Moreover, marginalized and racialized voices were given priority.

Michael Hawn writes that when we sing global music "we are not just learning to sing new songs from other places. We are learning to pray in new ways, and in solidarity with others who embody these sung prayers."[35] He recognizes that worship with space for a diversity of repertoire, what he calls polyrhythmic worship, can challenge "the community with the prophetic witness of the 'other' beyond our cultural expectations."[36] Solidarity and prophetic witness through singing are important steps in liberating congregational singing—and liturgy more generally. But in diverse North American urban settings, music from the Global South/ Majority World also often represents the actual people who are present in the room and certainly those who live in the community. When leadership from marginalized peoples is encouraged as it was in this example, when songs are chosen to emphasize the liturgical and theological themes of the service (and not as an exotic flavour or colour), and when song leaders make space for an-other's voice, then congregational song begins to become liberating.

The key to these initial rubrics for liberating song leading practices is to be aware of issues of power and privilege. By being contextual and accountable, leaders take into account the people who are singing and the people from whom the song came. Liberating practices also include interrogating colonizing behaviours and issues of power that are inherent in song leading—an action which is especially crucial when a dominant culture leader leads music from marginalized communities. But they also take care to witness to people's concrete lived reality, not only by honouring the contexts of the songs but also by seeking partnership in leadership, especially

---

[34] The notion of accompaniment will be developed in more detail in the last chapter. See Roberto Goizueta, *Caminemos con Jesús: Toward a Hispanic/Latino Theology of Accompaniment* (New York: Orbis Books, 1995).

[35] Michael Hawn, *Gather Into One*, 250.

[36] Ibid.

from among the most marginalized. In other words, when an embodied participatory approach is rooted in community, lifts up the experience of the people, and sides with and draws from leadership from the marginalized, it can actually begin to become liberating.

Song leaders—and other liturgical leaders—embrace practices of liberating congregational singing when they open out through self-emptying, allowing themselves to be re-formed, to be transformed, to be converted, by encounters with other people, especially those from the margins, along with their songs, cultures, and contexts. Song leaders function sacramentally to enable this transformation of themselves and of their communities by connecting the congregation to the Divine through song. The people can then accompany each other and together experience an irruption of the Divine in singing in which the liberating action of the Holy Spirit can be felt. Rooted in relationship and community, in the everyday life of the people, this singing invites nothing less than a profound epistemological and theological re-orientation. It unsettles the status quo and has the potential to incite the stirrings of ecclesial and theological transformation.

This is not easy work; it calls us to take risks—and be ready to fail. Building upon the initial rubrics articulated above, the following chapters will propose a more detailed series of complex processes for liberating congregational singing. These praxical processes include: rigorously interrogating power in ourselves, our relationships, our communities, and our churches; vigorously contesting the status quo in our canons of hymnody; and finally, making a deep commitment to accompaniment, whether by song-leading, by joining with others who are singing, or by listening more carefully. To enable this work, it is crucial to interrogate the ways in which coloniality has infected our very being; it is paramount to interrogate empire within ourselves. To this task we now turn.

BIBLIOGRAPHY

Bell, John L. 2000. *The Singing Thing: A Case for Congregational Song*. Chicago: GIA Publications.

———. 2007. *The Singing Thing Too: Enabling Congregations to Sing*. Chicago: GIA Publications.

Calvin Institute of Christian Worship. Nairobi Statement on Worship and Culture. https://worship.calvin.edu/resources/resource-library/nairobi-statement-on-worship-and-culture-full-text. Accessed 16 Apr 2018.

Chopp, Rebecca S. 1986. Toward Praxis: A Method for Liberation Theology. In *The Praxis of Suffering: An Interpretation of Liberation and Political Theologies*, 134–148. Maryknoll: Orbis.

Christian Congregational Music. Homepage. https://congregationalmusic.org/. Accessed 8 Mar 2020.

DeAnda, Neomi. 2015. Jesus the Christ. In *The Wiley Blackwell Companion to Latino/a Theology*, ed. Orlando O. Espín, 155–171. Hoboken: John Wiley & Sons.

Freire, Paulo. 1971. *Pedagogy of the Oppressed*. Trans. Myra Bergman Ramos. New York: Herder and Herder.

Global Ministries. Global Praise. https://www.umcmission.org/Find-Resources/Global-Praise. Accessed 27 Oct 2015.

Goizueta, Roberto. 1995. *Caminemos con Jesús: Toward a Hispanic/Latino Theology of Accompaniment*. New York: Orbis Books.

Haig-Brown, Celia. 2009. Decolonizing Diaspora: Whose Traditional Land Are We On? *Cultural and Pedagogical Inquiry* 1 (1): 4–21.

Hall, Stuart. 1992. The West and the Rest: Discourse and Power. In *Formations of Modernity*, ed. Stuart Hall and Bram Gieben, 185–227. Cambridge: Polity Press in Association with the Open University.

Hawn, C.Michael. 2003. *Gather Into One: Praying and Singing Globally*. Grand Rapids: Eerdmans Publishing.

Ingalls, Monique, Carolyn Landau, and Tom Wagner. 2013. *Christian Congregational Music: Performance, Identity, and Experience*. Farnham: Ashgate Publishing.

Isasi-Díaz, Ada María, and Eduardo Mendieta, eds. 2012. *Decolonizing Epistemologies: Latina/o Theology and Philosophy*. New York: Fordham University Press.

Keller, Catherine. 2004. In *Post-Colonial Theologies: Divinity and Empire*, ed. Michael Nausner and Mayra Rivera. Danvers: Chalice Press.

Kimbrough, S.ed. 2007. *Music and Mission: Toward a Theology and Practice of Global Song*. New York: GBGMusik.

Lim, Swee Hong. 2008. *Giving Voice to Asian Christians: An Appraisal of the Pioneering Work of I-To Loh in the Area of Congregational Song*. North Charleston: VDM Verlag.

Maduro, Otto. 2012. An(Other) Invitation to Epistemological Humility: Notes Towards a Self-Critical Approach to Counter-Knowledges. In *Decolonizing Epistemologies: Latina/o Theology and Philosophy*, ed. Ada María Isasi-Díaz and Eduardo Mendieta, 87–103. New York: Fordham University Press.

Maldonado-Torres, Nelson. 2007. On the Coloniality of Being. *Cultural Studies* 21 (2–3): 240–70. http://www.decolonialtranslation.com/english/maldonado-on-the-coloniality-of-being.pdf. Accessed 25 July 2018.

Medina, Néstor. 2018. *Christianity, Empire and the Spirit: (Re)Configuring Faith and the Cultural.* Leiden: Brill.

———. 2008. Jürgen Moltmann and Pentecostalism(s): Toward a Cultural Theology of the Spirit. In *Love and Freedom: Systematic and Liberation Theology in the Canadian Context*, ed. David John C. Zub and Robert C. Fennell. Toronto: Toronto School of Theology.

Nekola, Anna, and Tom Wagner. 2015. *Congregational Music Making and Community in a Mediated Age.* Farnham: Ashgate.

Plaatjie, Gloria Kehilwe. 2006. Toward a Post-Apartheid Black Feminist Reading of the Bible: A Case of Luke 2.36–38. In *Voices from the Margin: Interpreting the Bible in the Third World*, ed. R.S. Sugirtharajah, 463–483. Maryknoll: Orbis Books.

Poling, James. 2013. Postcolonial Theologies. *Roundtable Response, International Academy of Practical Theology.* Victoria University, University of Toronto, April 13.

Pope Paul VI. Constitution on the Sacred Liturgy. *Sacrosanctum Concilium.* http://www.vatican.va/archive/hist_councils/ii_vatican_council/documents/vat-ii_const_19631204_sacrosanctum-concilium_en.html. Accessed 27 Oct 2017.

Porter, Mark. 2017. *Contemporary Worship Music and Everyday Musical Lives.* Abingdon/New York: Routledge.

Seeger, Pete. 2009. *Where Have All the Flowers Gone? A Singalong Memoir.* Pennsylvania: Sing Out Corporation.

Small, Christopher. 1998. *Musicking: The Meanings of Performing and Listening.* Hanover: Wesleyan University Press.

Spivak, Gayatri Chakravorty. 1988. Can the Subaltern Speak? In *Marxism and the Interpretation of Cultures*, ed. Cary Nelson and Lawrence Grossberg, 271–313. Urbana: University of Illinois Press.

Stokes, Martin. 2012. Globalization and the Politics of World Music. In *The Cultural Study of Music: A Critical Introduction*, ed. Martin Clayton, Trevor Herbert, and Richard Middleton, 107–116. New York: Routledge.

Taylor, Timothy D. 2007. *Beyond Exoticism: Western Music and the World.* Durham: Duke University Press.

World Council of Churches. Member Churches. *World Council of Churches.* https://www.oikoumene.org/en/member-churches/wcc-regions. Accessed 11 Feb 2018.

CHAPTER 3

Untangling the Threads of Our Stories

INTRODUCTION

The crucial question we must now address is how liberating congregational singing can flow out of the personal commitment of a song leader to a lived liberating praxis. Such a praxis becomes the source and motivation for liberating congregational singing. To enact a genuinely liberating *praxis*—reflection *and* action *for* transformation—we need to go beyond mere lip service, radically moving into liberating action. Liberating thus means enabling and empowering political, economic, and social liberation from systems and structures that continue to exclude and marginalize people because of how they look, how they move, who they are, who they love, how much money and wealth they have, where they live, what documents they carry, or what language they speak.

My own liberating approach includes an acknowledgement that these excluding and marginalizing systems and structures are part of the broader phenomenon of coloniality, the Eurocentric epistemological construct which is the result of colonialism. It also includes a commitment to liberating *for* the modelling of another way of living—modelling God's beloved community—particularly by lifting up and celebrating the voices and contributions of those from the underside who have been excluded. My praxis is inspired by liberationist theologies from multiple contexts, particularly the Americas; they follow the revolutionary heart of the gospel and Jesus' ministry that calls us to love our neighbours as ourselves and "bring good

© The Author(s) 2020   35
B. Whitla, *Liberation, (De)Coloniality, and Liturgical Practices*,
New Approaches to Religion and Power,
https://doi.org/10.1007/978-3-030-52636-8_3

news to the poor … bind up the broken-hearted … proclaim liberty to the captives … [and open] the prison to those who are bound" (Isaiah 61:1). Above all, singing cannot become liberating—and we cannot liberate congregational singing—if mechanisms that leave power systems intact are unaddressed, beginning with ourselves.

Seeking to enact a liberating praxis therefore requires adopting a self-critical stance, highlighting the social spaces that nurture our singing. To state the obvious, congregational singers are each marked by their own lived journey; we bring our complex stories together when we sing and when we lead singing. In Canadian contexts, as in many other places, our singing is further complicated by the reality of polyculturality. Describing both cultural and other intermixtures *in* people and *in-between* people is therefore central to my project. It is important to narrate these processes of identification—how we are formed as subjects and navigate our multiple selves—in order to understand, deconstruct, and ultimately develop strategies that will enable us to move toward liberating praxes. Such self-examination also entails an exploration and dismantling of the ways in which song leaders can abuse their power and suggests moments when they may choose to relinquish it. By so doing we can then work toward enacting our agency *as* a liberating praxis, whether in song leading, in singing, or simply by living.

In this spirit, I begin with myself. First, I narrate the circumstances, the identities, the relationships, and the communities which shape(d) me. I begin with my family origins and briefly describe the ethno-cultural mixtures that are in me. This will enable me to problematize facile notions of Canadian history which are reduced to binaries: colonizer/colonized or settler-immigrant/first peoples. Second, I consider the inter-mixtures that have shaped me through my relationships with other people, including through my vocation as a musician and community song leader. I rearticulate the boundaries of my own identities as fluid and unfixed, in a constant state of fluctuation, continually shaped by my relationships and the communities of which I am part. Of course, I do not focus here on myself to draw undue attention to me, per se, but to attempt to model a methodology of a liberating praxis of congregational song that takes singers and song leaders seriously as people who are historically, geographically, and culturally located.

Drawing on liberationist and post/decolonial insights and suggesting a number of techniques to help untangle these issues, I locate and interrogate my own identities in relation to intersecting discourses about "whiteness," multiculturalism, and intermixture in Canada. These discourses continue to shape and re-shape me. I continue to negotiate them within myself since I am not satisfied with a static and demarcated status quo. Finally, these analyses will be situated in the denominational contexts where congregational singing happens, using the Canadian Anglican and United Church contexts of my own heritage as examples. I write from the particularity of my own Canadian context, but the analysis and methodology could easily be adapted and applied elsewhere.

PART ONE: SINGING MY STORY

I have been asked to help lead the music at a seminary chapel service to celebrate Indigenous ministry in the United Church of Canada.[1] I have suggested that we sing "Confession," a hymn based on the Anglican apology for residential schools. As a Euro-Anglo-settler, I believe that the "we" of the hymn makes a powerful statement of repentance, asks for forgiveness, and imagines reconciliation. The rustic, aching lament of the tune WONDROUS LOVE makes the words come alive for me as I take them into my body. I feel I am soulfully expressing my shame for what my people did to the first peoples of Canada. I have taught the song to a group of singers so that the original shape-note setting now rings out, plaintive and palpable. As the song leader, I invite others to join me in the "we" of the song: "We're more than we can say. We have not shown God's love, caused suffering instead. We ought not to have done what we did." I feel the power of what we are doing. I can tell by the weight of the air in the room that people are moved.

For one person—a close friend—the singing seems disingenuous. As an Indigenous person, she is not part of the "we" of the song. I was trying to build solidarity and community. Instead, I excluded and hurt my friend, who, when I corner her after the service, has the courage to confront me despite her own emotional vulnerability. I feel terrible, like I have personally betrayed her as well as my own principles. Through my leadership, the community has forsaken her and her people in their singing (Fig. 3.1).

[1] The service occurred on Wednesday, October 17, 2012 at Emmanuel College chapel in Toronto.

Confession

American Folk Hymn - Wondrous Love: James Christopher, 1840
words: adapted by Christopher Lind 2008

We're   sor - ry   more   than   we,   we   can   say,   we   can   say.
We   are   ash - amed   to   say   what   was   done,   what   was   done.
First   Na - tions   of   this   land,   we   have   failed,   we   have   failed.
We   praise   a   God   who   can   raise   the   dead,   we   raise   the   dead.
As   soon   as   we   are   home,   we   shall   tell,   we   shall   tell,

We're   sor - ry   more   than   we,   we   can   say.
We   are   ash - amed   to   say   what   was   done.
First   Na - tions   of   this   land,   we   have   failed.
We   praise   a   God   who   can   raise   the   dead.
As   soon   as   we   are   home,   we   shall   tell,

We   have   not   shown   God's   love,   Caused   suf - fer - ing   in - stead.
The   Sac - red   was   pro - faned.   It   was   done   in   Christ's   Name.
Your   child - ren   left   too   young.   Your   lan - guage   was   not   wrong.
We'll   op - en   up   our - selves.   We'll   op - en   up   our   wounds.
All   peo - ple   of   our   hope,   Of   whole - ness   yet   to   come.

We   ought   not   to   have   done   what   we   did,   what   we   did.
We   need   God   to   for - give,   we   con - fess,   we   con - fess.
Your   sto - ries   we   de - nied   in   God's   name,   in   God's   name.
We'll   lay   them   out   be - fore   God   who   heals,   God   who   heals.
We'll   urge   them, Come   a - long!   On   this   path,   on   this   path

We   ought   not   to   have   done   what   we   did.
We   need   God   to   for - give,   we   con - fess.
Your   sto - ries   we   de - nied   in   God's   name.
We'll   lay   them   out   be - fore   God   who   heals.
We'll   urge   them,   Come   s - long!   On   this   path.

Words adapted by Christopher Lind, 2008, from the apology delivered by the then-Primate of the Anglican Church of Canada, Archbishop Michael Peers, to the National Native Convocation in Minaki, Ontario, Friday, August 6, 1993.

The version the choir sang was in traditional three-part shape-note harmony, with melody (tenor, shown here), soprano and bass.

Fig. 3.1   "Confession," hymn by Christopher Lind

Our identities are circumscribed by the issues that result from the legacy of colonialism and include a system of racialization which positions "white" people at the top of the food chain.[2] The colonial matrices that define our identities also determine how those identities impact what power we have in relation to other human beings. These complexities need to be accounted for in order for relationships and practices to credibly strive to be liberating. When we sing, our individual and collective voices, the subject(s) that is/are implied in the "I/we" of community and congregational singing, express our personal and collective agency. But these voices can be impeded by issues of representation and power. In fact, my own life and relationships have been significantly hemmed in and restricted by these issues. Uncomfortable in the dominant "white" middle-class spaces that are prescribed for me, I have often navigated restlessly between spaces, in a syncopated movement that has flourished when accompanied by others who are similarly resisting hegemonic structures, working to actualize a liberating praxis.

The first step in navigating these dynamics is to tell our stories, to disclose our autobiographical narratives. This is not a simple process of socially locating ourselves by re-stating identity markers (e.g., in my case: I am a university-educated, Anglo-Euro-Canadian settler, middle-class, cisgender, able-bodied, adult woman, and a mother). Rather, it includes the many complex factors and processes that influence how identities are represented, perceived, and felt—in other words, how we understand ourselves and each other as subjects. Stuart Hall argues that these factors are brought together in a process of identification that is "becoming rather than being: not 'who we are' or 'where we came from,' so much as what we might become, how we have been represented and how that bears on how we might represent ourselves."[3]

---

[2] The term "white" is problematic, as are other categories which essentialize people according to "race," itself a constructed category. It points to a false homogeneity, reducing the multiplicity of ethno-cultural groups to a single category, removing their differences, histories, particularities, and struggles. I am intentionally using it and unmasking it throughout this chapter. However, because it is an elusive term, I often use it with quotation marks. "Whiteness" is similarly problematic. The notion that there are such categories as "race," "white," and "whiteness" evokes stereotypical ideas of what it means to be "white." It connotes the racialization of colour; it refers to stereotypical cultural behaviours associated with being white and establishes "whiteness" as normative against which all "others" are measured. It thrives in the creation of alterity, in a via *negativa* which measures all those who are not white through these criteria of "whiteness."

[3] Stuart Hall, "Introduction: Who Needs Identity?" in *Questions of Cultural Identity*, ed. Stuart Hall and Paul Du Gay (London: Sage Publications Ltd., 1996), 4.

This "becoming rather than being" is an ongoing process that is continually in flux. Hall proposes a "concept of identity [which] does *not* signal that stable core of the self, unfolding from beginning to end through all the vicissitudes of history without change."[4] Rather, he writes that "identities are never unified and, in late modern times, increasingly fragmented and fractured; never singular but multiply constructed across different, often intersecting and antagonistic, discourses, practices and positions. They are subject to a radical historicization and are constantly in the process of changes and transformation."[5] In other words, a simple telling and fixing of the story of who we are, where we are, and how we got here, is insufficient. I am not suggesting that people are so capricious as to be endlessly malleable—we are some combination of nature and nurture, to cite the old adage. Yet, identification processes are fluid, complex, and unfixed—"always 'in process'"—operating discursively across difference, and undertaken in relation to an exterior, an-other.[6] Our stories therefore need to take into account our multiple and changing contexts as well as the fluidity of our identities, our lives, and our relationships and their ongoing impact on how we understand ourselves in relation to those contexts.

To begin, we must remember and retell the histories that have formed us; we are all embodied people that are historically located in a concrete time and place, in some kind of family grouping, within a variety of communities, within a culture or cultures, and in relation to other people. A process of autobiographical narrative is not in and of itself liberating, but a liberating praxis of living does mean that we must make sense of those histories in relation to our changing contexts and to the systems of power and privilege that continue to govern our lives.

I engage the autobiographical narrative of my own story by acknowledging that its fabric is woven together by people who came to Canada to find a better life. They were the working poor, carpenters, weavers, farmers, preachers, and teachers. My parents passed on an interlaced texture of ethnicity and circumstance to me through blood and culture. The lives of my grandfather's Irish immigrant family fleeing poverty fused with that of the destitute eight-year-old English child shipped across the ocean as a "Church of England Boy," to work as an indentured servant until

---

[4] Ibid., 3.
[5] Ibid., 4.
[6] Ibid., 2, 3.

adulthood.[7] This blood on my father's side intermingled in turn with the blood of the Welsh separatists on my mother's side. Cut from that rebellious cloth, my great-grandfather preached to the workers and the poor, anticipating the Canadian Social Gospel movement of which he would become part, and immigrated to Canada with his young family because his pacifist stance in World War I was seen as a betrayal of the British Empire. The fabric of my story is interwoven on all sides with the strands of the lives and struggles of farmers who settled the traditional land of Indigenous peoples. And it also includes missionaries who participated in the colonial project of Christianizing the world, however enlightened and respectful they may have been.[8] My maternal great grandfather was one of the earliest Moderators of The United Church of Canada (the sixth), a position that came with power. Whatever critique I may bring to bear on the history of the role of Christianity in Canada, I am also complicit in it through these bloodlines.

This brief autobiographical sketch leaves out many details which would certainly weave a richer story. My point is to use myself as an example of how every person has a unique and rich set of circumstances they bring with them—marked in their bodies and expressed as they relate to the world—when they come together to sing in community. Yet the structures of colonialism which are still intact in systems which privilege certain groups ("white," male, educated, wealthy, Anglo, heterosexual, able-bodied, etc.) over certain other groups (racialized, female, working class, poor, accented, queer, dis/abled, etc.) function to essentialize identity

---

[7] My father's father immigrated to Canada with his seven siblings and his parents to escape poverty in Ireland. His wife's father was given to the "Church of England Society for Waifs and Strays" to be shipped to Canada to become a farm labourer under a binding agreement of indenture. An article from "The Canadian," dated April 17, 1891 is entitled "From All Such, God Lord Deliver Canada" and reads in part "These 'waifs and strays' are tainted and corrupt with moral slime and filth inherited from parents and surroundings of the most foul and disgusting character. ... There is no power whatever that can cleanse the lepers to fit them to become desirable citizens of Canada." See the video documentary from the same website, "British Home Children in Canada: Born of Good Intentions." See British Home Children in Canada, "Sherbrooke, Quebec, Church of England Waifs and Strays," accessed July 25, 2018, http://canadianbritishhomechildren.weebly.com/church-of-england-waifs%2D%2Dstrays-4468.html

[8] The fact that my mother and her father were born in Japan meant that I grew up with the use of some Japanese words and customs in my family, as well as stories about life in Japan. I certainly don't claim any Japanese-ness, but this cultural influence shaped some of my ways of understanding the world and how to behave in it.

categories. In my case, a rich autobiographical narrative problematizes and complexifies this kind of categorization, "unbleaching" the ways in which I am essentialized simply as "white."

Celia Haig-Brown addresses the complexity of identification processes in Canada when she asserts that the "simple binary distinctions of colonizer/colonized or Indigenous/immigrant fail to address the range of ways that people are a part of this country."[9] She notes that all immigrants are implicated in processes of colonization, but they are not all implicated in the "same ways as those who came with the clear intention of exploitation and profit."[10] Like my family, she notes that "many people came for better lives, to escape war and famine, to seek freedom, to start anew."[11] She also rightly advocates locating our stories in relation to the traditional Indigenous lands which we inhabit so that we connect our personal stories to the colonial reality that is at the heart of Canadian history.

For example, my father grew up in Cambridge, Ontario (formerly Galt) on the banks of the Grand River, called "O:se Kenhionhata:tie" or "Willow River," in *Kanienkeha* (Mohawk.) The land was inhabited by Iroquoian-speaking nations before Europeans arrived. Six Nations of the Grand River (the Iroquoian Confederacy of Six Nations), the largest reserve in Canada, is still on the banks of the Grand River, south of Galt. As I map my own family's story, I acknowledge the reality that none of my ancestors settled in empty land or *terra nullius*. Each place in which they settled had been home for Indigenous peoples with distinct cultures and ways of life.[12]

Haig-Brown calls this narrative process "decolonizing autobiographies" and claims it is necessary in order to "historicize and complicate any notions of what it means to be part of a colonized country," in this case, Canada.[13] But as Eve Tuck and Wayne Yang note, "the metaphorization of decolonization makes possible a set of evasions, or 'settler moves to innocence', that problematically attempt to reconcile settler guilt and

[9] Celia Haig-Brown, "Decolonizing Diaspora: Whose Traditional Land Are We On?" *Cultural and Pedagogical Inquiry* 1, no. 1 (2009): 14.

[10] Ibid., 9.

[11] Ibid.

[12] Six Nations of the Grand River, "Community Profile," accessed March 9, 2020, http://www.sixnations.ca/CommunityProfile.htm; Wikipedia, "Grand River (Ontario)," accessed May 3, 2018, https://en.wikipedia.org/wiki/Grand_River_(Ontario)

[13] Haig-Brown, "Decolonizing Diaspora," 14.

complicity, and rescue settler futurity."[14] There are times when the language of decolonizing may be appropriate, but here I am advocating a process which lays the groundwork for a personal liberating praxis, so I am not prepared to run the risk of suggesting something which could allow people to evade their responsibility to be accountable for their ongoing power and privilege. Moreover, the notion of autobiography is more static. It assumes completion, as in: we write our autobiography. Rather, the process of autobiographical narrative is ongoing. It can also be characterized as predominantly oral in nature, even though for the purposes of this argument, I have written some of my narrative down.[15]

Of course, our stories—our autobiographical narratives—like our identities, are continually constructed and transformed as we tell our stories in ongoing interactions and relationships with other people. We are not some one thing; we are continually engaged in relationships and processes that change how we are seen, how we see ourselves, and who we become. Our narratives are therefore not static, but fluid; they change in relation to who we tell our stories to and where and when we tell them. Likewise, identity can be understood as strategic and positional and not as fixed or essentialist.[16] In other words, and to state the obvious, our sense of self changes through our relationships and circumstances and we understand who we are (or who we could become) differently as a result. Our processes of identification, both internal and those imposed on us by others, are constantly mutating through relationship and in community.

I learned early on that my family had class and race privilege. My Indigenous, immigrant, and racialized friends shared their stories with me and together we learned about prejudice and privilege as we accompanied each other in our growing up. In relationship, we worked out "which strands to discard, which strands to preserve, which to weave into a new fabric" as we forged new identities and matured as people, accompanying

---

[14] Eve Tuck and Wayne Yang, "Decolonization Is Not a Metaphor," *Decolonization, Indigeneity, Education & Society* 1, no. 1 (2012): 1, accessed July 25, 2018, http://www.decolonization.org/index.php/des/article/view/18630/15554. For Tuck and Yang, decolonization means nothing less than giving stolen land back.

[15] Singing is also always expressed orally. Even when songs are written down or fixed in their oral performance, their very orality also opens them to the possibility of expressive interpretation and transformation over time. Also, orality privileges "other ways of knowing," a concept articulated by Latin American decolonial thinkers, to which we return later.

[16] Alberto Moreiras, "Hybridity and Double Consciousness," *Cultural Studies* 13, no. 3 (1999): 373.

each other and allowing ourselves to be shaped by each other.[17] I turned to my friends to hear them "tell it like it is." They helped me stay account-able to myself and others and to understand the privilege of my family of origin. I welcome the ongoing gift and challenge of intercultural relation-ships as I continue to cross linguistic and cultural barriers to navigate friendships in languages other than English and often from very different social, political, and economic contexts.

I don't mean to romanticize my own journey or to idealize my capacity for relationship. At times, I don't see how my Euro-Anglo and other privi-leges work for me and against some of my friends. At other times, I allow myself to be smug about my ability to transcend systems of oppression, forgetting that I can never step outside the systems of privilege that name me "white." This dilemma is crucial because I cannot challenge "white-ness" except from my own vantage point as "white." Since "whiteness" is like an infection that prevents me from seeing things as they are because I am conditioned by it, I depend on my friends to help me see. My friend-ships thus take me to liminal spaces that make me uncomfortable and can even hurt me. They share their most intimate fears and terrors, feelings that come out of their experiences of oppression, hatred, violence, and even torture. At times like these, I question myself and our "multicul-tural" Canadian context. I become confused and unsettled: I question who I am and who I am supposed to be. Yet a commitment to autobio-graphical narrative as part of an ongoing liberating life praxis requires me to stay in this liminal space between the safety of my own privileged "white" Euro-Anglo spaces and the painful and disempowering reality of discrimination in the spaces of my friends and colleagues.

To return to the opening story as an illustration, a commitment to a liberating praxis meant not being paralyzed by the fact that I had hurt my friend through my song leading. I could have claimed that my intentions were good. After all, I had enabled the ("white") people/settlers in the room to offer a symbolic confession and repentance to Indigenous peo-ples. Or, I could have wallowed in my own insufficiencies (and I have

---

[17]Wenh-In Ng, "Lands of Bamboo and Lands of Maple," in *Realizing the America of Our Hearts*, ed. Fumitaka Matsuoko and Eleazar S. Fernandez (St. Louis, MO: Chalice Press, 2003), 106.

certainly done this at times!) bemoaning my individual short-comings, caught in what Crista Lebens calls a "white guilt trap."[18]

Instead, I made a commitment to work on my relationship with my friend. This was not something I had the power to do on my own, though it certainly required my commitment and agency. She graced me with the trust to continue our conversation. We both became more aware of the impact of coloniality in the way that it advantages me and disadvantages her, circumscribing our identities and separating us from each other. Rejecting this separation, we are now both committed to ongoing conversations, including lots of listening, and an awareness of power differentials. In her openness to a conversation with me about my (unintentional) misuse of power, I experienced the gift of a theology of repentance and forgiveness and a sign of eschatological hope. She helped me to better embody the liberating praxis I sought. Our gentle conversations over time in the space of the everyday gives us the opportunity to embody right(er) relationships.[19]

A fecund liminal space-between, often found in the everyday, is a place where people clash, encounters occur, attitudes are redefined, and power differentials become conspicuous. Homi Bhabha writes about the challenges of inhabiting such relational in-between places. He notes that borderline negotiations at "culture's in-between"—in what he calls elsewhere the "third space" and "culture's undecidability"—are threatening for dominant culture proponents of (European colonial) liberalism.[20] It is in this space, he argues, that the "construction of cultural authority within conditions of political antagonism of inequality" and the emergence of an "'interstitial' agency" are possible, where "hybrid agencies find their voices in a dialectic that does not seek cultural supremacy or sovereignty."[21]

But Bhabha's articulation of culture's in-between is problematic because it is premised on the idea of a "partial culture" which is the "contaminated yet connective tissue between cultures."[22] It may expose the

---

[18] Crista Lebans, "On not Making a Labor of It: Relationality and the Problem of Whiteness," in *White Criticality Before Anti-Racism: How Does It Feel to Be a White Problem?* ed. George Yancy (London: Lexington Books, 2015), 78.

[19] My conversations with Susan Beaver continue. I am deeply grateful for our ongoing friendship. I have shared this account of these events with her.

[20] Homi K. Bhabha, "Culture's In-Between," in *Questions of Cultural Identity*, ed. Stuart Hall and Paul Du Gay (London: Sage Publications Ltd., 1996), 53–60.

[21] Ibid., 58.

[22] Ibid., 54.

limits of fraught liberal "principles of 'tolerance'" and the "sharing of equality" which do not recognize subaltern historical and contextual reality. But, the idea of a partial culture risks consigning subaltern culturality to a state of incompleteness, to the "outside of the inside" as a "part of the whole" as if there were a complete and fixed overarching Culture to which subaltern partial cultures could belong.[23] Néstor Medina argues instead that the

> phenomena of cultures must be understood as a series of dynamic, open-ended, interminable processes. It is these series of dynamic processes of culturalization that operate as people engage in the construction of cultures and draw on cultures to understand reality, live life, construct societies, interact with their immediate environment and each other, make sense of the world around them, and engage the divine.[24]

Above all, the cultural is not partial but is the "very essence of humanity."[25]

Alberto Moreiras offers another stance; he proposes moving beyond current categories of hybridity and identity, which he claims are constructed through discourses of colonialism and capitalism, to what he calls a relational or perspectival subalternism which is strategic and positional. Through relationality—a concept which is arguably less static than hybridity, being less fixed and more dynamic by definition—he argues that human beings may interact in a counterhegemonic praxis that holds the possibility to "find ways to articulate subaltern resistance against the terror of dominant identities more effectively within a larger commitment to economic justice."[26] The liberating praxis I am articulating here, with autobiographical narrative as a foundational methodological step, can be understood, along these lines, as a relationally oriented strategy. His frame helps make sense of the importance of relationship to my formation as a subject, to my evolving understanding of processes of identification, and to the praxis I seek to build on an ongoing basis.[27] My commitment to a

---

[23] Ibid., 54, 56.

[24] Néstor Medina, *Christianity, Empire and the Spirit: (Re)Configuring Faith and the Cultural,* (Leiden:Brill, 2018), 49.

[25] Ibid., 13.

[26] Alberto Moreiras, "Hybridity and Double Consciousness," *Cultural Studies* 13 (3) (1999): 373.

[27] I emphasize that I am not relinquishing my responsibility to continually examine the complex dynamics of identification and their connection to power and privilege, to which we shall turn shortly.

liberating praxis of living and singing is rooted in relationships, in community, and with a wide range of artistic and scholarly collaborators who work together with me to challenge structures of oppression by addressing these unjust mechanisms in what we do together, including in the very relationships we work to embody.[28] It is the doing, not only what we say or think, that makes this commitment praxical.

Committing to an ongoing process of narrating our lives begins to unmask, disentangle, and render complex the processes of identification that form us as subjects in relation to our histories, the lands we inhabit, our communities, and the relationships we have. I thus locate the genealogy of my project in my familial, relational, geographical, cultural, and ecclesial contexts and histories. Located on colonized treaty lands, springing from Canadian social gospel roots, nourished in churches and communities in solidarity with the marginalized, it has flourished in the diverse and constantly changing contexts of urban Toronto. However, while we are born into a specific location, "constituted by class, caste, gender, race, religion, economy, nation, etc.," what we *do* with ourselves, how we *enact* our own agency, including in relation to other people, also shapes who we are. It helps us to move from liberal rhetoric that does not always lead to liberating action, to actual liberating praxis.[29]

The Broader Context: Coloniality in Canada

Categories and systems which delimit human beings according to socially constructed identity markers are by-products of what decolonial scholars call "coloniality." I have described coloniality, along the lines of Latin American decolonial thinking, as follows:

> The concept of coloniality describes the all-encompassing residual web of colonizing processes, tendencies, and practices and its ongoing manifestation, especially in present capitalist, globalizing, neoliberal systems. Decolonial scholars argue that coloniality brings together the axes of colonialism, modernity and capitalism. They insist that "modern" history must

---

[28] My primary vocational focus has been to invite and encourage people to sing in community. For details, see Becca Whitla, "From the Heart of Song to the Heart of Singing," *Touchstone* 33, no. 1 (2015): 53–58.

[29] Paul Bramadat and David Seljak, "Charting the New Terrain: Christianity and Ethnicity in Canada," in *Christianity and Ethnicity in Canada*, ed. Paul Bramadat and David Seljak (Toronto: University of Toronto Press, 2008), 21.

be read from the perspective of the conquest of the Americas [with modernity beginning in 1492 and not with the Enlightenment]. Coloniality affects who we are, regulates how we understand the world, and conditions all our relations. Coloniality also unmasks the ideology of superiority in which the church, the empire, and notions of what was "civilized" were understood to be inseparable; this ideology permeated the European and Euro North American colonial projects.[30]

By further deciphering, dissecting, and deconstructing how identity markers essentialize us into categories and systems which either advantage or disadvantage us, we can confront the ways in which coloniality still permeates our lives. Such a confrontation is enabled by a number of techniques to which we turn shortly. But first, let us examine the dynamics of coloniality more fully.

One of the pillars of the lived experience of coloniality is the construction of various identity markers, especially the notion of race; it is/was a key mechanism for the production of cheap or free labour and has serious ongoing implications for how people continue to be racialized/identified. Affirming the ideological construction of the notion of race, Medina writes that "since we can no longer claim the presence of races based on the biological record and DNA evidence, we necessarily have to conclude that racialized differences are by definition culturally and socially constructed."[31] For Nelson Maldonado-Torres, "coloniality of being" best describes this lived experience and the ways in which coloniality impacts our intersubjective relations, as we come to grips with the "effects of coloniality in lived experience and not only in the mind."[32]

[30] Becca Whitla, "Coloniality in 'Glossary of Key Terms'," in *Decoloniality and Justice: Theological Perspectives*, ed. Jean-François Roussel (Saõ Leopoldo: Oikos: World Forum on Theology and Liberation, 2018), 22.

[31] Néstor Medina, Email correspondence with the author (22 January 2016).

[32] Nelson Maldonado-Torres, "On the Coloniality of Being," *Cultural Studies* 21, no. 2–3 (March/May 2007): 242, accessed July 25, 2018, http://www.decolonialtranslation.com/ english/maldonado-on-the-coloniality-of-being.pdf. Maldonado-Torres particularly emphasizes the suffering of "primarily Blacks and indigenous peoples, as well as all of those who appear as colored." Ibid., 255–56. I note that decolonial thinker Enrique Dussel emphasizes the indigenous underside of Western European "modernity" while others, like cultural theorist Paul Gilroy, argue that Anglo Euro-North American modernity and its capitalist systems must acknowledge the essential centrality and barbarity of plantation slavery in modernity's inception and fabric. See: Enrique Dussel, *The Invention of the Americas: Eclipse of "the Other" and the Myth of Modernity* (New York: The Continuum Publishing Company, 1995); Paul Gilroy, *The Black Atlantic: Modernity and Double Consciousness* (London: Verso, 1993).

Canada, as an invader/settler colony/nation is a product of what decolonial thinkers call the "modern-colonial capitalist world-system" and has, therefore, at the centre of its imaginary, an indisputable coloniality along with its constitutive apparatuses of identification.[33] In the wake of the Truth and Reconciliation process in what is now Canada, many have been confronting Canada's ugly history, beginning with the reality that Canada is part and parcel of the formation of the modern-colonial capitalist world-system which began 500 years ago with the conquering of the Americas.[34] Canada's evolution as a nation, understood along the lines of Latin American decolonial scholars, may be re-conceived to be part of this story of the "discovery" of the Americas as a result of the co-constitutive factors of modernity, coloniality, and capitalism.[35]

Indigenous activists and scholars in Canada have been insisting for a long time on telling this history along similar lines. For instance, Thomas King writes that he "cannot let post-colonial stand—particularly as a term—for, at its heart, it is an act of imagination and an act of imperialism that demands that I imagine myself as something I did not choose to be, as something I would not choose to become."[36] King's insistence to reframe the question outside the imaginary of coloniality is echoed by Lee Maracle, who argues that what is needed is a kind of re-creation. She

---

[33] Decolonial scholars use Immanuel Wallerstein's notion of the modern world-system, expanding it to include the reality of coloniality and capitalism. See Walter D. Mignolo, *Local Histories/Global Designs: Coloniality, Subaltern Knowledges, and Border Thinking* (Princeton: Princeton University Press, 2000), 18.

[34] Truth and Reconciliation Commission of Canada, "Reports of the Truth and Reconciliation Commission" (2105), accessed May 3, 2018, http://nctr.ca/reports.php. For an analysis of Canada's colonial legacy using a decolonial optic, along the lines of Latin American decolonial thinkers, see Néstor Medina and Becca Whitla, "(An)Other Canada is Possible: Rethinking Canada's Colonial Legacy," *Horizontes Decoloniales/Decolonial Horizons* Volumen V.1, 13–42, 2019. We argue that Canada ought to be re-situated historiographically in relation to the American Continental colonial experience.

[35] For a detailed discussion of the doctrine of discovery and terra nullius, see Néstor Medina, *On the Doctrine of Discovery* (Toronto: Canadian Council of Churches, 2017). Medina writes that "the doctrine of discovery and notions of *res nullius* (later *terra nullius*) constituted the initial ideological construct by which Western Europeans justified the seizing of the lands, territories, and resources of the (non-Christian) indigenous peoples of the Americas and other continents. The year 1492 marks a momentous point in the history of Western European imperialism as Western Europeans went out of themselves to conquer, invade, and colonize the rest of the world." Ibid., 7.

[36] Thomas King, "Godzilla Vs. Post-Colonial," in *Unhomely States: Theorizing English-Canadian Postcolonialism*, ed. Cynthia Sugars (Toronto: Broadview Press Ltd., 2004), 190.

makes the case that "Canadians must get out of the [colonial] fort and imagine something beyond the colonial condition—beyond violence, rape and notions of dirty people. We must move beyond what is—re-enter our dreamspaces and recreate ourselves."[37] These kinds of decolonizing approaches offer great possibility for a further work analyzing Canadian contexts and the implications for a decolonizing/liberating of ourselves, our songs, and our ways of singing.[38]

Given the reality of coloniality, we can insist that the complexity of Canadian subjectivities, "whether we have inherited identities as First Nations, Métis, Québecois, invader-settler, immigrant, or 'ethnic'" and our different relationships to Canada's invader-settler history renders a postcolonial—and I would now argue decolonial—analysis essential.[39] There is no doubt that at the heart of European colonialism was an ideology in which the church, the empire, and notions of what was "civilized" were inseparable and were dependent on constructing a "sense of identity as Christian, civilized, and superior."[40] In Canada, as elsewhere, this ideology was enshrined in the hymns sung by colonizers and imposed on Indigenous peoples and others.

Liberating congregational singing requires coming to terms with the pervasive impact of coloniality in the songs we sing and how we sing them, a task to which we return in the next chapter. It must also include grappling with the impact of these factors on processes of identification so that

---

[37] Lee Maracle, "The 'Post-Colonial' Imagination," in *Unhomely States: Theorizing English-Canadian Postcolonialism*, ed. Cynthia Sugars (Toronto: Broadview Press Ltd., 2004), 206.

[38] Several recently published volumes offer substantive critiques and methodological approaches. See for example: Glen Sean Coutlhard, *Red Skin, White Masks: Rejecting the Colonial Politics of Recognition* (Minneapolis: University of Minnesota Press, 2014); Arthur Manuel, Grand Chief Ronald M. Derrickson, *Unsettling Canada: A National Wake-up Call* (Toronto: Between the Lines, 2015); Arthur Manuel, Grand Chief Ronald M. Derrickson, *The Reconciliation Manifesto: Recovering the Land, Rebuilding the Economy* (Toronto: James Lorimer & Company Ltd., Publishers, 2017); Leanne Simpson, *Dancing on Our Turtle's Back: Stories of Nishnaabeg Re-Creation, Resurgence, and a New Emergence* (Winnipeg: Arbeiter Ring Publishing, 2011); *Marie Battiste, Decolonizing Education: Nourishing the Learning Spirit* (Saskatoon: Purish Publishing Limited, 2013). For a settler perspective on these issues, see Paulette Regan, *Unsettling the Settler Within: Indian Residential Schools, Truth Telling, and Reconciliation in Canada* (Vancouver, UBC Press, 2019).

[39] Dianne Brydon, "Reading Postcoloniality, Reading Canada" in *Unhomely States: Theorizing English-Canadian Postcolonialism*, ed. Cynthia Sugars (Peterborough, ON: Broadview Press Ltd., 2004), 171. See also Medina and Whitla, "(An)Other Canada is Possible: Rethinking Canada's Colonial Legacy."

[40] Medina, *Christianity, Empire and the Spirit,* 100.

we can acknowledge and understand the coloniality of our beings, our contexts, and how it influences our human interactions.

Multiculturalism as a Linchpin of Coloniality in Canada

Grappling with these issues is complicated by the fact that notions of race, ethnicity, culture, and religion blur in hotly contested Canadian discourses about multiculturalism. Approaches to multiculturalism have ranged from what Sneja Gunew calls "multiculturalism as a set of government policies designed to manage cultural diversity and multiculturalism" to the "attempt by various groups and individuals to use these policies to achieve full participatory cultural democracy."[41] In fact the range of analytic approaches is often opposing and contradictory, even from the same people. For example, Paul Bramadat and David Seljak admit that "for most of this country's history, Canadian policies related to race, ethnicity and culture were solidly colonialist and exclusionary."[42] Yet they still celebrate the tradition of multiculturalism when they point out that "the formal policy grew out of a combination of daring political insight and shrewd political calculation."[43]

The tendency to see multiculturalism as utopic in the Canadian context—as "daring political insight," despite the "shrewd political calculation"—is resoundingly critiqued by Himani Bannerji. At its most basic,

---

[41] Sneja Gunew, *Haunted Nations: The Colonial Dimensions of Multiculturalisms* (New York: Routledge, 2004), 5.

[42] Paul Bramadat and David Seljak, "Charting the New Terrain: Christianity and Ethnicity in Canada," in *Christianity and Ethnicity in Canada*, ed. Paul Bramadat and David Seljak (Toronto: University of Toronto Press, 2008), 21.

[43] Ibid. In Canada in 1971, the federal government under Prime Minister Pierre Elliot Trudeau declared multiculturalism to be an official government policy. The policy was and is supported by numerous programs across the country and has been taught in schools as distinct from the USA melting pot (or assimilationist) approach. To this day, the federal government continues to encourage citizens to "discover the significance of multiculturalism in Canada—ensuing that all citizens keep their identities, take pride in their ancestry and have a sense of belonging." Government of Canada, "Multiculturalism", accessed, February 3, 2020, https://www.canada.ca/en/services/culture/canadian-identity-society/multiculturalism.html See also: Canadian Museum of Immigration at Pier 21, "Canadian Multiculturalism Policy, 1971" accessed February 3, 2020, https://pier21.ca/research/immigration-history/canadian-multiculturalism-policy-1971 and Howard Schneider, "Canada: A Mosaic Not a Melting Pot" in *The Washington Post, July 5, 1998,* accessed February 3, 2020, https://www.washingtonpost.com/archive/politics/1998/07/05/canada-a-mosaic-not-a-melting-pot/8a4998ed-b04b-491e-b72e-1ef4d8e96d84/

she argues that official government-instituted multiculturalism (and "elite" multiculturalism) in Canada sets apart the "so-called immigrants of colour from francophones and the aboriginal peoples ... posing 'Canadian culture' against 'multicultures.'"[44] Bannerji notes that this multiculturalism depends on a process of "racialized ethnicization, which whitens North Americans of European origins and blackens or darkens their 'others' by the same stroke."[45] This whitening—or bleaching—"establishes Anglo-Canadian culture as the ethnic core culture while 'tolerating' and hierarchically arranging others around it as 'multiculture.'"[46] For Bannerji, multiculturalization reinscribes "colonial/racist discourses of tradition and modernity, civilization and savagery."[47] In the language of decolonial scholar Enrique Dussel, it perpetuates "the modern myth," that Europe's modernity succeeded in a vacuum because of the inherent superiority of European "civilization."[48] It does not account for the fact that any so-called success was made possible because of the enslavement, oppression, and conquering of Europe's "others," which in the Americas disproportionately includes Indigenous peoples and people of African descent. In this reading, multiculturalism then contributes to the maintaining of this myth of Europe's (in Canada, "white" Anglo) success with its feel-good mechanisms which keep everyone in their cultural/ethnic place.

But even for Bannerji, ambiguity remains, as she admits that there could be another possible way, a different Canadian imaginary. For her, the kind of radical change necessary would "emerge only from those who have been 'othered' as the insider-outsiders of the nation. ... They serve to remind us of the Canada that could exist."[49] Arun Mukherjee anticipates this possibility when she writes: "the old Canadian nationalism(s), founded on racial purity and cultural duality are being challenged by those who have long been excluded from the tables of dealmakers and dice rollers. Canada needs a new nationalism, a nationalism whose grounding

[44] Himani Bannerji, *The Dark Side of the Nation: Essays on Multiculturalism, Nationalism and Gender* (Toronto: Canadian Scholars' Press Inc., 2000), 10.

[45] Ibid., 6.

[46] Ibid., 78.

[47] Ibid., 6.

[48] Enrique Dussel, *The Invention of the Americas: Eclipse of "the Other" and the Myth of Modernity*. New York: The Continuum Publishing Company, 1995.

[49] Himani Bannerji, "Geography Lessons: On Being an Insider/Outsider to the Canadian Nation," in *Unhomely States: Theorizing English-Canadian Postcolonialism*, ed. Cynthia Sugars (Peterborough, ON: Broadview Press Ltd., 2004), 297.

premise will be Canada's heterogeneity."[50] Such a heterogeneous Canada built on this other kind of multiculturalism, or polyculturalism, requires a concerted and ongoing effort. Those living in Canada need to be account-able in this process in part by narrating our lived experiences as peoples, uncovering our histories, and problematizing the notion of Canada as a nation state. In other words, it would include both an acknowledgement of our colonial history and of the fact that the very notion of nation state remains contested by some in the Canadian context. Among other things, we would name the violence genocidal impetuses at the heart of the founding of the nation, along with the serial exploitation of waves of immigration.[51] For those from the dominant culture, what is needed is a "*continuous* effort on the part of whites to forge new ways of seeing, knowing, and being" that includes the process of autobiographical narra-tion described above, along with other techniques to which we now turn.[52]

PART TWO: MAKING SENSE OF OUR STORIES

At my first rehearsal with the newly formed Hotel Employees and Restaurant Employees (H.E.R.E.) Local 75 Choir, in the fall of 1998, I arrive with my fancy musical warm-ups and scores thinking we would get down to work when the rehearsal begins at 4 pm. The singers trickle in and mostly sit there staring at me like I am an alien from another planet. A couple of them oblig-ingly sing along with me as I try to teach. Finally, at the end of the rehearsal at 5 pm, worn-out and discouraged, I declare that the rehearsal is over. At that point, the women who had gathered really start to sing. Some of the spiri-tuals I had tried to teach now come alive. They stay until six, swapping songs and stories.

---

[50] Arun Mukherjee, "Canadian Nationalism, Canadian Literature and Racial Minority Women" in *Postcolonialism: Living My Life* (Toronto: TSAR Publications, 1998), 83.

[51] See: Medina and Whitla, "(An)Other Canada is Possible: Rethinking Canada's Colonial Legacy." See also: Thomas Peace "The Nation-State is not what we think it is: Teaching Canadian History for a non-national perspective," in *Active History*, accessed March 9, 2020, http://activehistory.ca/2014/12/the-nation-state-is-not-what-we-think-it-is-teaching-canadian-history-from-a-non-national-perspective/

[52] Barbara Applebaum, "Flipping the Script … and Still a Problem: Staying in the Anxiety of Being a Problem," in *White Criticality Before Anti-Racism: How Does It Feel to Be a White Problem?* ed. George Yancy (London: Lexington Books, 2015), 11 n52.

It is December and we are gathered again on Wednesday evening. We are celebrating our success because we sang at the first-ever official Toronto "Hotel Workers' Day." The choir would like to keep going; that is a good thing—they are energized and empowered. But I am keenly aware of the fact that I am the middle-class Euro-Anglo leader of this choir of women mostly from the Caribbean. Also, my contract is over and I think my work is done. So, I tell them that I have decided to leave as their leader to make space for a "woman of colour" to lead the choir. Linette, one of the singers in the group, says, matter-of-factly, "You can't leave. We broke you in!"

The techniques described in this section are not exhaustive or airtight. Rather, they are offered tentatively as possibilities for the ongoing process of autobiographical narrating as part of a liberating praxis. They involve reorienting the self/subject. For those who have been marginalized by the modern-colonial capitalist world-system, these techniques, along with some others, may involve reclaiming and recovering stories, cultures, and human dignity. In my case, they offer ways of coming to terms with being complicit with white supremacy as part of coloniality. No doubt there are and will be other techniques and ideas that will enrich what is suggested here. The very openness to the ever-changing nature of these processes is also part of a liberating praxis.

These adaptable methodologies need to confront and unmask the arbitrary nature of the notion of insider/outsider, a notion which undergirds socially constructed identity categories and essentializes people as one thing or another, disallowing the multivalency that is the reality of human existence. Gloria Anzaldúa describes this kind of identity multiplicity as *mestiza* consciousness, as a mode which transcends subject-object duality—or insider-outsider—based on "convergent thinking, analytical reasoning that tends to use rationality to move towards a single goal (a Western mode)"[53] It offers instead "divergent thinking, characterized by movement away from set patterns and goals and toward a more whole perspective, one that includes rather than excludes."[54] Her own experience of inhabiting more than one culture, of walking "out of one culture and into another, because I am in all cultures at the same time" is a "struggle of borders," "an inner war," a "cultural collision," and a "source of

---

[53] Gloria Anzaldúa, *Borderlands/La Frontera: The New Mestiza* (San Francisco: Aunt Lute Books, 2007), 102.
[54] Ibid., 101.

intense pain," though she also sees it as potentially transformative, in a positive sense.[55]

Expanding W. B. DuBois's oft-cited "double consciousness," which always looks "at one's self through the eyes of others," Medina similarly moves beyond binaries by arguing that a triple consciousness better describes human identity experience and opens up the notion of gazing to include the way you look at people, the way people look at you, and the way you look at yourself.[56] For me these notions of multiple or triple consciousness uncover the shifting and unstable nature of identity spaces. They illuminate the kind of syncopated rhythm of moving between spaces that is crucial for my liberating praxis. To repeat my earlier description, a syncopated rhythm interrupts the "normative" beat of the status quo and responds to the heartbeat of life with its provocative offbeat interjection that transforms the overarching rhythmic structure. Conscious, but never fully in one space and often simultaneously in more than one, my very being is dislocated and reconfigured. Though I am not forced to navigate these spaces as a racialized person, like Anzaldúa or Medina—this is a movement I can choose by virtue of my white privilege—I nonetheless limp from one space to another, necessarily questioning each next step.

Unbleaching

For a White Anglo dominant culture person like me, coming to terms with my "coloniality of being" involves unravelling and disentangling (my) whiteness, one of the most insidious outgrowths of coloniality. Drawing on Haig-Brown, Emily Lind argues for an opening up of whiteness as a "contingent, partial, or even a hybrid element of the storyteller's identity," instead of reinscribing white domination by essentializing whiteness.[57] She cautions that confessional feminist autobiographical stories which focus on white racism risk "positioning whiteness as a reified subjectivity (something one is or isn't) [which] necessarily de-historicizes its presence, and

---

[55] Ibid., 102, 107.

[56] William Edward Burdhardt Du Bois, *The Souls of Black Folks: Essays and Sketches* (Chicago: A.C. McClurg & Co., 1904), 3; Medina, Email correspondence with the author (25 October, 2016).

[57] Emily R. M. Lind, "I Once Was Lost but Now I'm Found: Exploring the White Feminist Confessional," in *Unveiling Whiteness in the Twenty-First Century: Global Manifestations, Transdisciplinary Interventions*, ed. Veronica Watson, Deirdre Howard-Wagner, and Lisa Spanierman (London: Lexington Books, 2015), 239.

limits intersectional readings of its construction."[58] Instead, Lind argues that it is necessary to "move beyond a coherent, singular sense of self ... [so that whiteness] ... can be explored as a category of analysis mediated through broader social and political structures that conspire to produce racism and white privilege."[59] Following decolonial thinkers, the broader structures which produce racism and white privilege are best described as coloniality.

Moving beyond a singular coherent self involves unmasking the complexity of biological, cultural, and relational identities which form all subjects as polyvalent human beings, as we have seen. In whatever ways a person is essentialized—whether through race as White, Black, Asian, Latino, Indigenous, and so on, or by other markers like gender, class, education, sexual orientation, or ability—the process unsettles clearly defined air-tight categorical silos and re-constitutes human identity as embodying multiple intertwined spaces. For the "white" self—or the multiple selves that form a "white" person—such a process may be described as "unbleaching."[60] Unbleaching moves beyond notions of pigmentation to include ethnic and cultural diversities and the reality of multiple situatedness that Lind refers to above. In my case, unbleaching is integral to the story I tell about my inheritance from the Welsh, the Irish, the "Church of England Boy," and the missionaries in Japan, as these cultural particularities take prominence over singular monosemic "whiteness."

Unbleaching is particularly helpful for Euro-Anglo women whose subjectivity has been circumscribed by gender in particular ways in the Canadian colonial context. Himani Bannerji notes that white women were forced into the role of "reluctant breeders" because "they are of the majority culture and are thus held responsible for counterbalancing the 'unassimilables' (i.e., non-whites) among us."[61] What Bannerji calls "womb hostage" was part of the colonial inheritance from Victorian England. Gender roles and values included rigid notions about virtue and womanhood which meant that "white" women "lived within a distinct and limited sphere of domesticity."[62] The cultural impact of such roles and values

---

[58] Ibid., 239–40.

[59] Ibid., 243.

[60] Néstor Medina suggested the notions of bleaching and unbleaching. Medina, Email correspondence with the author (22 January, 2016).

[61] Bannerji, *The Dark Side of the Nation*, 69.

[62] Wendy Fletcher, "Canadian Anglicanism and Ethnicity," in *Christianity and Ethnicity in Canada*, ed. Paul Bramadat and David Seljak (Toronto: University of Toronto Press, 2008), 154.

continue to be felt. Unbleaching then can also involve a "de-linking" from the domains of Victorian virtue, domesticity, and morals which circumscribe all women according to their reproductive and domestic functions.[63]

Even more importantly, unbleaching encourages me to move between different spaces in which I navigate relationships in familial, social, and vocational settings. Restless in "white" spaces which circumscribe my relationships and behaviour, it invites me to appreciate the gaze of an-other that welcomes me into a different space, like the choral space of Caribbean hotel workers in which I had been "broken in." Unbleaching thus encourages me to syncopate as I make myself vulnerable to an-other. When I worked with the H.E.R.E. Local 75 Choir, the praxis of opening myself unbleached me because it unhinged me from my inherited white privilege. By allowing the Spirit to move me to open myself, I was liberated toward the redemptive action of letting others lead me, allowing them to free me from the ways in which whiteness has limited me. I opened myself up to become the kind of choir director members of the choir wanted. It meant abandoning the Euro-Anglo liberal notion of a gentle, consultative choir director, taking on the role the choir gave me, and being accountable to them in community. They wanted a proper, traditional choir director, replete with church choir robes in union colours. I was not entirely comfortable with the role, but they were clear about what was appropriate for the particular choral space we inhabited together.

Unsuturing

It bears repeating that by complexifying my own story, especially by unbleaching whiteness, I am not trying to get out of my complicity with systems of white domination. George Yancy asserts that "as they [whites] move through the world, having been claimed by whiteness, their lives are complicit with a white supremacist system of interpellation, a system that they help to perpetuate and, by extension, a system that diminishes the

---

[63] Bannerji notes that the "the fact that the state seeks to hold white woman's womb hostage has profound repercussions for non-white women. Caught in the same legal labyrinth as their white counterparts, their motherhood is by implication also regulated." Bannerji, *The Dark Side of the Nation*, 70. "Delinking" is a term used by Latin American decolonial thinkers to indicate the severing of ties to European ways of thinking and being.

humanity of black people and people of color."[64] Yancy advocates an ongoing process of what he calls unsuturing in order to ensure that whites uncover and open themselves in a continuous effort to confront the "suturing of white history" and supremacy and to avoid narrative closure by claiming to be beyond racism.[65] For him, being unsutured is "dispositional and aspirational, involving a continuous process of renewal and commitment."[66] Indeed, the goal of avoiding narrative closure in a "continuous process of renewal and commitment" is an important part of autobiographical narrative.

But the notion of unsuturing is problematic on three fronts, however much it may illuminate the ways in which white supremacy claims white lives, allowing whites "to come to terms with the realization that their embodied existence and embodied identities are always already inextricable linked to a larger white racist social integument or skin which envelops who and what they are."[67] First, it overly relies on fragmentary postmodern paradigms which obscure the larger superstructures which need dismantling, like coloniality. Issues can remain at the level of black and white, drawing on US binary construction, and preclude working together, joining in solidarity across differences; unsuturing as a deconstructive move doesn't offer a reconstructive methodology or possibility. Second, it depends on a voluntary self-infliction of violence; unsuturing means undoing a wound with the risk of opening it up to infection, pus, and life endangerment, a process which is unrealistic and perhaps even a little perverse or masochistic.[68] Third, it is individualistic. It still rests with the individual "white" person's willingness to change, impeding the opportunities for change to be understood as something that comes out of relationship and in community with those who are not racialized as white.

---

[64] George Yancy, "Introduction: Un-Sutured," in *White Criticality Before Anti-Racism: How Does It Feel to Be a White Problem?* ed. George Yancy (London: Lexington Books, 2015), xxv.

[65] George C. Yancy, "White Suturing, Black Bodies, and the Myth of a Post-Racial America," *SARTS: Society for the Arts in Religious and Theological Studies,* accessed April 7, 2018, http://www.societyarts.org/white-suturing-black-bodies-and-the-myth-of-a-post-racial-america.html

[66] George Yancy, "Un-Sutured," xvi.

[67] Ibid., xvii.

[68] Certainly, the initial move of "suturing" also has inherent in it a violence, both in the meaning of the metaphor and the reality of the entrenchment of systems of white supremacy. The implications of this violence are worthy of further consideration.

It is certainly appropriate to establish particular processes for people racialized as white as part of broader collective strategies of resistance against oppressive structures. Such processes certainly ought to refuse to claim to have arrived at a place beyond the reaches of white supremacy and must confront the violence inherent in it. At the same time, without relinquishing responsibility to confront white supremacy, it is also important to affirm that "whites" are not a homogeneous group; the fallacy behind "whiteness" as an essentializing category needs to be unmasked, along with other essentializing categories like Asian, black, "people of colour," and so on. Furthermore, a liberating praxis moves beyond individual identities, inviting those who are racialized as white to become allies who chose to work together across differences to dismantle structures, systems, and ideologies that perpetuate coloniality, allowing themselves to be unbleached by the process. By so doing, in the words of Gloria Anzaldúa, "they [white allies] will come to see that they are not helping us but following our lead."[69] Unsuturing misses this important reality of community context.

Despite these significant shortcomings in the notion of unsuturing, it nevertheless offers language for unpacking the insidiousness of "whiteness." The starkness and even violence of the language are appropriate for the magnitude of the task at hand—confronting white supremacy as a key component of coloniality. At the same time, my own grappling with and critique of the language of unsuturing illustrates that a self-reflective and self-critical "continuous process of renewal and commitment" also includes a deep critical engagement with the very techniques and language we choose.

Mestizaje-Intermixture

To make sense of identity struggles in the North American context, let us turn to the work of LatinaXo scholars who have been wrestling—for a long time and substantially—with the reality and category of *mestizaje*.[70] *Mestizaje* is a discourse rising out of the LatinaXo experience that grapples with notions of intermixtures between race, ethnicity, and culture. Medina writes that *mestizaje* "names identities forged in the conditions of

[69] Anzaldúa, *Borderlands*, 70.
[70] I include Mexico, the USA, and Canada in "North America."

historical liminality," a liminality which is ubiquitous throughout the Americas.[71] He explains that *mestizaje* is a multivalent term which encompasses biological intermixture, cultural intermixture, the "dynamic contested nature of identities," and "the complex socialized processes of code-switching ... between two, three or more cultures and traditions."[72] Medina is clear that the discourses of *mestizaje* are "rooted in the numerous, messy, violent, bloody, and often painful historical human exchange" between Indigenous, African, and European peoples in the Americas.[73]

At the same time, he notes that "there is no one thing called *mestizaje*; rather, there are multiple spaces of ethnocultural and identity negotiation, exchange and cross fertilization that lead to the further proliferation of identities and ethnocultural affiliations."[74] He argues that "*mestizaje* gives us a glance into human history as marked by the violence of empire, colonization, and migration, in the form of violent results of cultural intermixture and miscegenation."[75] It helps to articulate what he describes as the "global shift toward the racialized culturalization of peoples" by marking the "point of redefinition of our understanding of human cultural and identity boundaries."[76] In a Canadian context, *mestizaje* can help problematize fixed identity categories and illuminates the risk of multiculturalist discourses which perpetuate coloniality in Canada through the ethnicization, racialization, and fixing of Canadian "multi" cultures over and against normative "Canadian" culture.

Mestizaje can thus shed light on how we understand ourselves through what Medina names as the "construction of identities away from rigid identity labels and paradigms ... render[ing] ineffective rigid monocultural essentialist notions."[77] Even for those who are identified as "white," notions of *mestizaje*-intermixture offer rich insight, illuminating the particularity, complexity, and fluidity of identities. The stories that have remained hidden or silenced, the ways in which our stories connect to the

---

[71] Néstor Medina, "(De)Cyphering Mestizaje; Encrypting Lived Faith: Simultaneous Promise and Problem," in *The Preferential Option for Culture*, ed. Miguel Diaz (Minneapolis: Fortress Press, Forthcoming).

[72] Ibid.

[73] Ibid.

[74] Ibid.

[75] Ibid.

[76] Ibid.

[77] Néstor Medina, *Mestizaje: (Re)Mapping Race, Culture and Faith in Latina/o Catholicism* (Maryknoll, NY: Orbis Books, 2009), 113.

history of conquest, and the ways which we wrestle with identity markers—whether they be connected to race, gender, sexual orientation, ability, or class—are potentially unmasked, remembered, and reconfigured as people identify with the experience of *mestizaje* richly articulated by LatinaXo scholars.

Though *mestizaje* emerged out of the particularities of Latin American and LatinaXo experiences, and perhaps in part because it did, it offers wisdom for conversation about interculturality and intermixture in a Canadian context which could lead to fruitful interrogation and collaboration in solidarity in a variety of ways. In particular, it accounts for the violence in the colonial encounter between Europeans and Indigenous peoples which continues to play out in our relationships, in our discourses, and in the ongoing reality of white supremacy in Canada. It also affirms the complexity of processes of ethno-racial and cultural intermixing as "ambiguous, plurivocal, polysemic, and heterogeneous," including in bodies racialized as "white."[78] This rich intellectual history and the ongoing engagement of *mestizaje* as a category in the Americas, helps make sense of autobiographical narratives in the Canadian context, particularly in coming to grips with notions of intermixture.[79]

As we have seen, processes of identification are multiple, richly interwoven, and fluid. My aim is to suggest a number of possible (but not exhaustive) modes to unpack these dynamics. To be sure, the kaleidoscope of identities and the complexity of identification processes, including issues of representation and power, have an impact on the way we understand ourselves as subjects. They also have a profound impact on the way we understand our agency as people who can act on desires to liberate or not. Congregational singing as an embodied collective action tilts us toward agency rather than subjectivity and identity, toward "doing" rather than "being." These issues are central for—and handled differently by—post and decolonial scholars. Let us briefly consider some of their insights.

---

[78] Ibid., 110. The notion of *mestizaje* is not without its problems and critics. Medina notes, for instance, the erasure of Indigenous and African-descended experiences and identities in some notions of *mestizaje*. See Medina, "(De)Cyphering Mestizaje."

[79] Another similar category that is distinctly and only Canadian is *Métis*. However, the term *Métis* refers specifically to people of Indigenous and French descent. The Métis people form a distinct people group, "the Métis Nation." See "Métis Nation," accessed May 3, 2017, http://www.metisnation.ca; "The Métis," in *Canada's First Peoples*, accessed May 3, 2017, http://firstpeoplesofcanada.com/fp_metis/fp_metis1.html

From Being to Becoming

In *Orientalism*, Edward Said exposes the imperial agenda of Europe's mis-representation and exteriorizing of the Orient as Europe's Other, as a means to claim authority and power over the Orient. By naming, pointing to, and fixing the identity of the Oriental Other as "irrational, depraved (fallen), childlike, 'different'," Said argues that the European "subject" is thus rendered its binary opposite, as "rational, virtuous, mature, 'normal'."[80] This objectification of an "other" is evident in the discourses of white supremacy and multiculturalism discussed above, and it is at the heart of coloniality.

Given the reality of colonialism/imperialism and its sweeping cultural influence, Gayatri Chakravorty Spivak asks if the one identified and objec-tified as the most marginalized—the female subaltern—has the power to speak for herself. Concluding that she cannot, Spivak argues that she loses her agency through an act of epistemic violence which forecloses the very "possibility of collectivity itself ... through the manipulation of female agency."[81] Her conclusion is echoed in decolonial views of subjectivity and its relationship to the European imaginary. For instance, Enrique Dussel argues that an erasure of the humanity of the Other, a "negated alterity," was part and parcel of the conquering of the Americas—though decolonial scholars do not argue that the subaltern cannot speak.[82]

In fact, and despite this grim assessment, decolonial scholars propose a number of strategies for reclaiming agency, a project which Spivak herself also recognizes as essential.[83] They begin by dismantling the notion of "the" subject as a European construct. This subject is/was the wealthy, educated, cisgender, European male, whose individualistic, capitalistic, colonialist/imperialist desires have served to misrepresent, misrecognize, ignore, erase, or dispose of all Others. Interrogations of notions of subjec-tivity have led decolonial thinkers to seek other epistemological pathways. As such they move beyond the postcolonial focus on deconstructing the

---

[80] Edward Said, *Orientalism* (New York, London: Penguin Classics, 2003), 72, 40.

[81] Gayatri Chakravorty Spivak, "Can the Subaltern Speak," in *Marxism and the Interpretation of Cultures*, ed. Cary Nelson and Lawrence Grossberg, 280. 283.

[82] Dussel, *The Invention of the Americas*, 66.

[83] Spivak commits herself to subject-restoration as a crucially strategic task, identifying "subaltern consciousness as emergent *collective* consciousness" for subaltern studies. Gayatri Chakravorty Spivak, "Subaltern Studies: Deconstructing Historiography," in *Selected Subaltern Studies*, ed. Ranajit Guha and Gayatri Spivak, (Oxford: Oxford University Press, 1988), 18.

colonial gaze.[84] For instance, for decolonial scholar Walter Mignolo, the enactment of the decolonial option involves an epistemic disobedience which intertwines decolonial thinking *and* doing.[85]

Decolonial approaches thus prioritize agency over subjectivity by emphasizing "doing" and "relating" rather than "categorizing." They resonate with an emphasis on the relationship and community forces which shape us, rather than focusing on fixed identity markers. In other words, people have the agency to de-link themselves from systems of domination that have circumscribed how they are represented as subjects. Along these lines, the practices enumerated above—autobiographical narrative, unbleaching, unsuturing, and engaging *mestizaje/*intermixture— are concrete options, epistemically disobedient possibilities, for reshaping how we understand ourselves and our contexts. They also provide a bedrock for undergirding the work of liberating congregational singing.

PART THREE: CHURCH AND COLONIALITY

"So then you are no longer strangers and sojourners but you are fellow citizens with the saints and members of the household of God." Ephesians 2:19, quoted on the website of the Diocese of Toronto, Anglican Church of Canada in 2018.

To state the obvious, singing as an embodied activity is indisputably spatial and temporal—it always happens at a specific place and time. Building toward a liberating praxis by engaging with questions of power and privilege, as we have been doing, also requires a reckoning with these factors in our ecclesial contexts. Stuart Hall argues that "precisely because identities are constructed within, not outside, discourse, we need to understand them as produced in specific historical and institutional sites within specific discursive formations and practices, by specific enunciative strategies."[86] In other words, we must look at how these issues play out in specific ecclesial and denominational sites—in this case, the Anglican and

---

[84] Agency, or lack thereof, is also a concern for postcolonial scholars, as we saw with Spivak. But their focus tends to prioritize the reframing of issues of subjectivity by deconstructing the colonial gaze.

[85] Walter D. Mignolo, "Epistemic Disobedience, Independent Thought and Decolonial Freedom," *Theory, Culture & Society* 26, no. 7–8 (2009): 173–74. Accessed July 25, 2018, http://waltermignolo.com/wp-content/uploads/2013/03/epistemicdisobedience-2.pdf

[86] Hall, "Who Needs Identity?" 4.

United Churches of Canada—reading their histories, practices, and processes of identification as enunciative strategies.

As numerous scholars have established, Christianity was/is an intrinsic
part of the modern-colonial capitalist world-system. Colonizers understood themselves to be embarking on a legitimate civilizing/Christianizing
mission.[87] Canada was no exception; "the Christian churches have played
an integral role in the colonization of this land and its evolution into a
complex society."[88] In the English-speaking Canadian context, "British
culture and politics, Protestantism, and a belief in modern political, economic, and scientific 'progress' formed the three pillars of Canadian
nationalism."[89] In turn, the Anglican, Presbyterian, and United churches
were the "three pillars of Canada's Protestant establishment" with long
histories in Canada, including "their active involvement in Canadian public policy, as well as their ties to Canada's political and economic elite."[90]
The spectre of the historical colonial mission project—of Christianizing
Canada—haunts the nation. In very tangible ways, such as in the recent
Truth and Reconciliation process, Canadians are reminded that "for most
of this country's history, Canadian policies related to race, ethnicity and
culture were solidly colonialist and exclusionary."[91] The role of the
churches is inextricably linked with this history.

The Anglican Church of Canada, the church I have attended much of
my life and the church in which my father is an ordained priest, was
interwoven with the colonial project of the British Empire.[92] It is historically the most established and powerful church in the country, having

[87] For a detailed account of the multiple ways in which Christianity was used to promote
European imperialism and the resulting coloniality, see Medina, *Christianity, Empire and
the Spirit*.

[88] Bramadat and Seljak, "Christianity and Ethnicity in Canada," 6. Bramadat and Seljak
provide an excellent short history of churches in Canada in their introduction to this volume,
with particular attention to their connection to colonization and ethnicity. As to the initial
impetus of the churches in Canada, they further note that "Until very recently, the European
colonization of Canada has always occurred under the sign of the cross; that is, the Europeans
who first created Canada imagined it always as a Christian project," 6.

[89] Ibid., 10.

[90] Ibid., 32. Prior to the formation of the United Church of Canada in 1925 (uniting
Methodists, Congregationalists, and some Presbyterians), the founding denominations were
also part of the edifice that connected political and ecclesial power and influence.

[91] Ibid., 22.

[92] I consider myself bi-denominational, belonging to both the Anglican and United
Churches of Canada.

developed, "as did much of the larger global Anglican community, from the colonial activity of the British Crown, which sought to disseminate this uniquely English religion, along with English economic, political, and cultural power around the world."[93] As such, its civilizing agenda included: (1) the domination of other British ethnicities—the Irish, Scottish, and Welsh—carried over from Britain as an "institutionalized discrimination [which] engendered hostilities within the larger Anglican community that migrated with them wherever they travelled"; (2) the "Canadianizing"— and Christianizing—of new immigrants through urban social mission which embodied "both charity and advocacy for new immigrants in their social dislocation, as well as political action that attempted to introduce and then inculcate ethical norms reflective of British dominant culture"; and most heinously, (3) the attempted erasure of Indigenous cultures through the government-sponsored residential school system.[94] As Wendy Fletcher affirms, "the Anglican Church understood its role to be a former and framer of culture as well as religion," with the English monarch as both the head of the church and the titular head of the Canadian parliamentary system.[95]

Today, the Anglican Church of Canada, like the Anglican Communion worldwide, is a diverse church, having incorporated into itself the people it once colonized. It now wrestles with its history and struggles toward reconciliation with those who have suffered by its hand, attempting to truly welcome all as citizens in the household of God. This commitment is voiced, for example, by the Anglican Diocese of Toronto, in its desire to become an "inclusive and intercultural church."[96] The website for the diocese proclaims the desire to build a church "that reflects our cultural diversity ... [fosters] understanding, creating mutual respect and building a strong sense of shared community across cultures, races, and ethnic

---

[93] Wendy Fletcher, "Canadian Anglicanism," in *Christianity and Ethnicity in Canada*, ed. Paul Bramadat and David Seljak (Toronto: University of Toronto Press, 2008), 138. Although it could rightly be argued that after the United Church of Canada was formed in 1925 it became a competitor with the Anglican Church in terms of its political and social influence, the ties between the Anglican Church and the ruling elite in Canada before and after that date are indisputable.

[94] Ibid., 141, 144, 160.

[95] Ibid., 144. I note that this is still the case today.

[96] Anglican Church of Canada, Diocese of Toronto, "Diversity Resources," accessed February 4, 2017, http://www.toronto.anglican.ca/parish-life/diversity-resources

groups."[97] But the fact that the Anglican Church of Canada remains a "denomination imbued with historic privilege" means that "the threads of dominant culture and marginalized 'other' [continue to] weave themselves around each other in historically complicated ways."[98]

The United Church of Canada, the church of my mother's family, was also enmeshed with power structures in English/Anglo Canada, both since its inception in 1925 and before, through the influence of its founding members, the Methodist, Congregationalist, and Presbyterian churches.[99] According to Wenh-In Ng, it was a relationship in which the "dominant Anglo elements of the church only reluctantly allowed themselves to be challenged after 1967 [the centenary of Canadian Confederation] by the gradual emergence of a country characterized by immigration policies more favourable to prospective citizens from non-European home countries."[100] Ng documents the development of intercultural approaches in the United Church as genuine, if at times reluctant, responses to the changing face of Canada and the United Church itself. She notes that the church has increasingly made it a priority to stress

> several features of the new [intercultural] relationships it envisioned: justice, mutuality, and equity, as well as the expectation that traditional dominant Anglo-Celtic members (the 'ethnic majority constituencies' who usually do not see themselves as being 'ethnic groups') will recognize the need to foster these mutual and equitable relationships envisioned for the broader church.[101]

Despite the fact that it is making great efforts to address these issues by formally adopting an anti-racism policy in 2000, for instance, Ng wonders how the United Church will be able "to address both the systemic or institutional racism inherent in its structures and culture as well as the 'white privilege' that accompanies it."[102]

---

[97] Ibid.

[98] Fletcher, "Canadian Anglicanism," 139.

[99] The Anglican church of Canada's ties to "the Church of England," as the Mother Church, whose titular head is still the Queen of England to this day, make the colonial connections more conspicuous.

[100] Greer Anne Wenh-In Ng, "The United Church of Canada: A Church Fittingly National," in *Christianity and Ethnicity in Canada*, ed. Paul Bramadat and David Seljak (Toronto: University of Toronto Press, 2008), 206.

[101] Ibid., 218–19.

[102] Ibid., 219.

At the heart of this struggle to be a truly intercultural church, there is an unreconciled aspect in the tension between the "open and tolerant spirit" which the United Church has fostered, incorporating a "radical vision that tolerated and welcomed people of different ethnicities, races, and even religions" on the one hand, and the universalizing implication of Christianizing the social order that was central to the founding ethos of the United Church, on the other.[103] Like the undeniable link between the Anglican Church and the British Empire, the Christianizing impulses in the founding of the United Church are associated with the colonial project. There were those who sought to forthrightly convert, or even erase other cultures by establishing a more "universal" Canadian culture (read English Protestant), patronizingly Christianizing newcomers and making them "good Christians *and* good Canadians."[104] Others worked to establish the Kingdom of God as a commonwealth based on solidarity, mutuality, and radical love, along the lines of the Fellowship for a Christian Social Order (FCSO).[105] However much the first approach may seem to be obviously imperious and the second noble and politically progressive, both were predicated on the narrow-minded notion that English Protestant Christianity was the best way to Christianize/civilize the country. This viewpoint still undergirds many attitudes and practices in the United Church despite the commendable attempt in some quarters to genuinely grapple with increasingly complex cultural landscapes and discourses.

There is no doubt that the history of these two churches in Canada includes their incontrovertible role as "civilizing/Christianizing" forces of the British contingent of the modern-colonial capitalist world-system, a role which continues even today. As such, any dismantling of coloniality is no small task because they acted as "specific historical and institutional sites" for the dissemination of practices and strategies that formed "an

---

[103] Phyllis Airhart, *A Church with the Soul of a Nation: Making and Remaking the United Church of Canada* (Montréal: McGill-Queens, 2014), 211.

[104] Ibid., 14.

[105] See: R.B.Y. Scott and Gregory Vlastos, eds., *Towards the Christian Revolution* (Chicago: Willet, Clark and Co., 1936); Roger Hutchinson, "The Fellowship for a Christian Social Order: A Social Ethical Analysis of a Christian Socialist Movement" (PhD Diss.: Toronto School of Theology, University of Toronto, 1975); Roger Hutchinson, "The Fellowship for a Christian Social Order: 1934–1945," in *A Long and Faithful March: "Towards the Christian Revolution" 1930s/1980s*, ed. Harold Wells, Roger Hutchinson (Toronto: United Church Publishing House, 1989), 17–29.

ideological state apparatus."[106] As Fletcher asserts, "ethnicity must be brought into conversation with issues of geography, race, class, culture, ethics, theology, the history of missionary activity overseas, regional specifics, and globalization, since all of these forces work together."[107] It is true that both the Anglican and United Churches have begun to confront this legacy in their own history through participation in activities like the Truth and Reconciliation processes; working toward interculturality as a goal; and mustering prophetic voices in opposition to the dehumanizing forces of wealth and greed. These are crucial steps in a commitment to interrogate institutional history and practices. However, the churches and their leaders also have a responsibility to recognize, come to terms with, and begin to transform their ongoing role in perpetuating systems of domination and white supremacy as part of coloniality. Let me suggest two theoretical frameworks to that end.

First, since questions of land are paramount in the Canadian context because of the terrible impact of the colonial legacy on Indigenous peoples, we can make a commitment to always acknowledge the traditional land which one inhabits. Such a practice, which acknowledges, with gratitude, the land and the Indigenous people who inhabit(ed) it, speaks to an awareness that "in North America, nations have been superimposed on indigenous lands and peoples through colonization and domination."[108] As part and parcel of the earliest colonization efforts, the churches played an integral role in this process. The use of land or territorial acknowledgements is becoming increasingly widespread in Canada in church and other contexts and the rite ranges from standardized acknowledgements that children in schools have memorized to heartfelt poetic recitations. Debates swirl about whether this rite has become an empty gesture, an obligation, or a genuine action. Still, there seems to be a general consensus that an acknowledgement of the traditional land is a minimal first step.[109]

---

[106] Hall, "Who Needs Identity?" 4; Bannerji, *The Dark Side of the Nation*, 6.

[107] Fletcher, "Canadian Anglicanism," 163.

[108] Haig-Brown, "Decolonizing Diaspora," 5.

[109] Lee Maracle and others have criticized Indigenous acknowledgements for potentially becoming empty gestures. Actual reconciliation is more than reciting a statement; it must be accompanied by tangible actions. For her "reconciliation is economic equality, access to territory, all of those things that are in the 94 calls to action. ... No more taking our kids. Like stop right now. Take care of the missing and murdered women. Stop killing us. None of those things have ended." See Patty Winsan, "Are Indigenous Acknowledgements a Step Forward or an Empty Gesture?" (The Toronto Star, 27 December 2017), accessed April 10,

Second, Alexis Shotwell's notion of "unforgetting" could be an effective collective strategy for the churches.[110] She argues that a "central feature of white settler colonial subjectivity is forgetting; we live whiteness in part as active ignorance and forgetting."[111] Shotwell's tactic of unforgetting unmasks notions of identity and it complexifies the way we understand history, along the lines of engaging in autobiographical narrative. She argues that it must begin with an acknowledgement of "the historical context of the founding and grounding violence of the Canadian state— violence directed toward many immigrant and enslaved peoples, as well as toward indigenous peoples."[112] Unforgetting also includes resistance against what Shotwell calls the "social organization of forgetting [which] means that our actual histories are lost, and it means that we have a feeling of acceptance and normalness about living with a lie instead of an unforgetting."[113] In reality, histories are buried rather than lost and a process of unforgetting allows them to be unearthed.

For Shotwell, unforgetting is also deeply praxical. Not only does it involve the "acknowledgment—the coming into knowledge—of things that threaten the colonial status quo," but it also involves "a shift from *knowing about* particular things to *taking action* in particular ways

2018, https://www.thestar.com/news/insight/2017/12/27/are-indigenous-acknowledgements-a-step-forward-or-an-empty-gesture.html. See also: Kiara Rudder, "Hayden King and Others Question the Effectiveness of Land Acknowledgements" (The Eye Opener, 29 January, 2019), accessed May 19, 2019, https://theeyeopener.com/2019/01/hayden-king-and-others-question-the-effectiveness-of-land-acknowledgemenets/

[110] Shotwell is drawing on the notion of "unforgetting" originally coined by Roxanne Dunbar Ortiz. See Alexis Shotwell, "Unforgetting as a Collective Tactic," in *White Criticality Before Anti-Racism: How Does It Feel to Be a White Problem?* ed. George Yancy (London: Lexington Books, 2015). In *Outlaw Woman: A Memoir of the War Years 1960–1975* Ortiz writes that "Now more than ever, we must un-forget the past as the very survival of ourselves and humanity depends on it—from an honest un-forgetting of the long history that has led us to this point, to a revaluation of our immediate past." Quoted in James R. Tracey, "The Weather Underground and the Future of Memory: An Interview with Sam Green," *Contemporary Justice Review* 6, no. 4 (2003), 397.

[111] Alexis Shotwell, "Unforgetting as a Collective Tactic," 58.

[112] Ibid., 65.

[113] Ibid., 61. Shotwell uses the story of the conflict at Oka, Quebec in 1990 to exemplify unforgetting. She argues that it is not enough to go beyond the racist colonial versions of the story that stereotype indigenous peoples through a simple reversal/flipping. The complexities in the stories involved in the "unforgetting approach would need to go deeper: How do we tell a resistant, anti-colonial story without using colonial frameworks?" 63.

informed by that understanding."[114] It must be noted that the practice of territorial acknowledgements also needs to be leavened with this action orientation so that it doesn't become an empty gesture. As Shotwell argues, the stakes are high since "the colonial status quo involves truly vast apparatuses and histories [and] the point of reckoning with the social organization of forgetting is, if it is anything, to craft a future different than the horrific past we have inherited and live in the present."[115]

When the churches face their complicity with coloniality in these and other ways, they may become places where the "multiplicity of voices will [or could] remind us that there are many ways to be Christian and to be human ... [as we strive towards] a society in which social inclusion and open dialogue will replace the Eurocentric cultural and religious mono- logue that has marked Canada's history."[116] I suggest that a first step in this process is to admit that the churches, particularly the Anglican and United Churches, still fall woefully short of this goal on many fronts by perpetuating a coloniality of being in ongoing ecclesial structures and practices, including in and through congregational singing.

PART FOUR: CONGREGATIONAL SINGING IS A RISKY LIBERATING PRAXIS

I am leading the music for the first of two multi-faith services organized on the theme of ending human trafficking. My friend and conspiritor, Jani Lauzon, a Métis performing artist, is singing with me, along with my daugh- ter, Emma. The service is happening at St. James Anglican Cathedral in downtown Toronto. The three of us meet in a room near the entrance of the church to rehearse. One of the organizers comes in to tell us something and says "sorry to interrupt your little pow wow." As she leaves, Jani wryly says, under her breath, "unfortunate choice of words." In the service itself, things seem disconnected and superficial. The Christian, Muslim, Jewish, and Buddhist leaders are lack-luster. We offer our best musical leadership, but no-one sings and we leave de-energized. I wonder if Jani will be willing to come back.

She does. And so do I. And so does Emma. The same multi-faith leaders speak. But this second service is totally different. We have adjusted and fig- ured out how to encourage a small crowd to sing in a huge, austere, and

---

[114] Ibid., 65.
[115] Ibid.
[116] Bramadat and Seljak, "Christianity and Ethnicity in Canada," 37.

forbidding place—some might call it an architectural embodiment of the heart of coloniality. At the end, we sing Jani's song "No Matter What," a powerful tribute to women everywhere and in memory of her own mother who said on her deathbed, "No matter what, I will always be with you." We lead everyone in a procession outside with the song, as the vocables in three-part harmony ring out. We keep singing even after everyone is outside. People are joining in. Somehow, this time, the service works—we feel the Spirit moving. Afterwards, over food at our house where Jani and her daughter have joined my family for supper, we talk about the feeling of Spirit we just experienced. We can't really say how it is different from the first time. We just feel it and know it.

At the service just described, a commitment to liberating praxis meant embodying intercultural relationships in song leadership and in the music we chose. As the story shows, this is a risky business. The first time, the lacklustre and disconnected service put a strain on the personal relationship between me and Jani as well as on the fragile leadership partnership we modelled. Yet, we had made a commitment to do the work and so we came back and took the risk again, a risk which arguably took a greater toll on Jani as an Indigenous person than it did on me, as a "white" person. All of the processes outlined in this chapter—autobiographical narrating, unbleaching, unsuturing, engaging intermixture, and unforgetting—are integral to a liberating stance so that this fragile work, this risky business of song leading, can be nurtured.

Sharon Fennema argues for what she calls "postcolonial" liturgical acts which require an openness to relationships and human interdependence. For her as a "white" practitioner, such a recognition is connected to a stance of "postcolonial whiteness" which includes a commitment to "being-with" as advocated by Alfred López.[117] According to Fennema, the resulting relationships "rely on a fundamental reorientation from positions of colonizer over colonized, oppressor over oppressed, to reciprocal relations between equal human beings."[118] She argues that "the moment of encounter with another, and the recognition of our interdependence, brings both a reckoning and a responsibility: reckoning with the realities of privilege and dominance; responsibility for transforming those reali-

---

[117] Sharon R. Fennema, "Postcolonial Whiteness: Being-with in Worship," in *Liturgy in Postcolonial Perspectives: Only One is Holy*, ed. Cláudio Carvalhaes (New York: Palgrave Macmillan, 2015), 282–83.

[118] Ibid.

ties … towards mutual flourishing that radically challenges and seeks to unravel white privilege, domination, and the assumptions about supremacy that undergird them."[119]

With agreeing with Fennema's overall approach, I caution that reciprocity, mutuality, and equality are aspirational rather than actual. There is a great risk of remaining stuck in a liberal paradigm, talking about changing—and even wanting to change—power structures without actually doing anything. The theological commitment to subvert the power relations she describes must be understood as profoundly eschatological and also proleptic as we continually work toward a *metanoia* of the systems of coloniality which circumscribe us. Roberto Goizueta's notion of *acompañamiento* (accompaniment), to which we will return in subsequent chapters, can be understood along similar lines as an urgent call to side with and enter into solidarity with the poor, self-consciously and intentionally "being with" and "walking with" the marginalized and excluded.[120]

Fostering "being-with" in liturgical acts can certainly be encouraged by song leaders, as I tried to model in my work with Jani, but it is not limited to them. Liberating congregational singing is also the responsibility of the people who sing, both at the community level and in larger institutional ecclesial structures. Recognition of the importance of relationships and the complexity of interculturality can be fostered with the approaches outlined in this chapter when there is time and willingness on the part of community members.[121] As Michael Jagessar notes, such work, the work

---

[119] Ibid.

[120] Roberto Goizueta, *Caminemos con Jesús: Toward a Hispanic/Latino Theology of Accompaniment* (New York: Orbis Books, 1995), 178.

[121] In church contexts, an ongoing practice of autobiographical narrating which is richly developed by remembering, reclaiming, recovering, and retelling stories, can reveal the complexity of the interwoven fabric of our lives and relationships. In addition, "unforgetting" could be used as a metaphor to guide conversations, Bible study, or book groups. Along these lines, another possibility is the blanket exercise, a tool to retell the story of the encounter and ongoing relationships between settlers and Indigenous peoples in Canada. See Kairos, "Blanket Exercise," accessed July 25, 2018, http://kairosblanketexercise.org/. Singing can also be an effective tool to both "ethnicize" colonial whiteness and celebrate diversity. Lim Swee Hong and I have led workshops in which we asked participants to choose favourite hymns/songs to represent themselves and their communities. We have found that when participants, including "white" participants, shared the reasons behind their choices, it was an invitational way to begin to unmask the complexity of the hymns/songs we sing in relation to our ethno-cultural identities. "White" participants began to recognize the ethno-cultural origins of their choices (e.g. German, Irish, Welsh, etc.)

of "liberating liturgical God-talk/practice" would take into account "the multilayered heritage of the worshipping community members, while accepting the multiplicity of inherited traditions."[122] Indeed, the people who sing together could include any number of complex mixtures of identity and story, as we sort out what Gloria Anzaldúa calls the inherited, the acquired, and the imposed.[123] To be liberating—and truly praxical—this work must move beyond simple awareness into transformative action. For some of us, such transformative action entails an intentional willingness to relinquish power.

Relationally rooted, all of these interrogations of personal, interpersonal, and contextual identification processes, with special attention to questions of power, invite us to the in-between-ness of the congregational singing space where our singing can become a place where our identities intermingle as we open ourselves up and make ourselves vulnerable to each other and to the work of the Spirit. Community members and congregational song leaders who commit to living a liberating praxis by working toward a dismantling of structures which perpetuate a coloniality of being, including by transforming liturgy, can thus contribute to the creation of a robust, embodied, and accountable liberating approach to congregational singing. For me, attending to these congregational singing spaces is interwoven with the rest of my life and my own syncopated movement between spaces. Such a praxis liberates us then to be open to the in-between, spirit-infused, intercultural space as a *locus theologicus*.

In fact, with Orlando Espín, I affirm that the messy and complex work of drawing diversity together in Christian expressions *is* none other than the work of the Spirit.[124] It follows then that the risk entailed in confronting coloniality and liberating congregational singing is ultimately made possible through faith and by the work and grace of the Holy Spirit, and invites an unapologetically pneumatological perspective, an open awareness of the mystery of the Holy Spirit's work. As such, singing can thus become an act which already announces the building up of new relationships and communities modelled on the life and work of Jesus of Nazareth, living out the same holy and subversive liberating action of the Spirit

---

[122] Michael N. Jagessar, "Holy Crumbs, Table Habits, and (Dis)Placing Conversations—Beyond 'Only One is Holy'," in *Liturgy in Postcolonial Perspectives: Only One is Holy*, ed. Cláudio Carvalhaes (New York: Palgrave Macmillan, 2015), 224.

[123] Anzaldúa, *Borderlands*, 104.

[124] Orlando O. Espín, *Grace and Humanness: Theological Reflections Because of Culture* (Maryknoll, NY: Orbis Books, 2007), 31.

which he incarnates. Still, despite our own best attempts to live out a liberating praxis, the very action of the Spirit is hindered when canons of hymnody perpetuate coloniality and congregational singing still embodies empire. In the next chapter we confront this problem and begin to expose and dismantle coloniality in hymnic canons.

Bibliography

Airhart, Phyllis. 2014. *A Church with the Soul of a Nation: Making and Remaking the United Church of Canada*. Montréal: McGill-Queens.

Anzaldúa, Gloria. 2007. *Borderlands/La Frontera: The New Mestiza*. San Francisco: Aunt Lute Books.

Applebaum, Barbara. 2015. Flipping the Script… and Still a Problem: Staying in the Anxiety of Being a Problem. In *White Criticality Before Anti-Racism: How Does It Feel to Be a White Problem?* ed. George Yancy, 1–19. London: Lexington Books.

Bannerji, Himani. 2000. *The Dark Side of the Nation: Essays on Multiculturalism, Nationalism and Gender*. Toronto: Canadian Scholars' Press.

———. 2004. Geography Lessons: On Being an Insider/Outsider to the Canadian Nation. In *Unhomely States: Theorizing English-Canadian Postcolonialism*, ed. Cynthia Sugars, 289–297. Peterborough: Broadview Press.

Battiste, Marie. 2013. *Decolonizing Education: Nourishing the Learning Spirit*. Saskatoon: Purish Publishing.

Bhabha, Homi K. 1996. Culture's In-Between. In *Questions of Cultural Identity*, ed. Stuart Hall and Paul Du Gay, 53–60. London: Sage.

Bramadat, Paul, and David Seljak. 2008. Charting the New Terrain: Christianity and Ethnicity in Canada. In *Christianity and Ethnicity in Canada*, ed. Paul Bramadat and David Seljak, 3–48. Toronto: University of Toronto Press.

British Home Children in Canada. Sherbrooke, Quebec, Church of England Waifs and Strays. http://canadianbritishhomechildren.weebly.com/church-of-england-waifs%2D%2Dstrays-4468.html. Accessed 25 July 2018.

Brydon, Dianne. 2004. Reading Postcoloniality, Reading Canada. In *Unhomely States: Theorizing English-Canadian Postcolonialism*, ed. Cynthia Sugars, 165–182. Peterborough: Broadview Press.

Canadian Museum of Immigration at Pier 21. 1971. Canadian Multiculturalism Policy. https://pier21.ca/research/immigration-history/canadian-multiculturalism-policy-1971. Accessed 3 Feb 2020.

Coutlhard, Glen Sean. 2014. *Red Skin, White Masks: Rejecting the Colonial Politics of Recognition*. Minneapolis: University of Minnesota Press.

Diocese of Toronto, Anglican Church of Canada. Diversity Resources. http://www.toronto.anglican.ca/parish-life/diversity-resources. Accessed 4 Feb 2017.

Du Bois, William Edward Burdhardt. 1904. *The Souls of Black Folks; Essays and Sketches*. Chicago: A.C. McClurg.

Dussel, Enrique. 1995. *The Invention of the Americas: Eclipse of "the Other" and the Myth of Modernity*. New York: The Continuum Publishing Company.

Espín, Orlando O. 2007. *Grace and Humanness: Theological Reflections Because of Culture*. Maryknoll: Orbis Books.

Fletcher, Wendy. 2008. Canadian Anglicanism and Ethnicity. In *Christianity and Ethnicity in Canada*, ed. Paul Bramadat and David Seljak, 138–167. Toronto: University of Toronto Press.

Gilroy, Paul. 1993. *The Black Atlantic: Modernity and Double Consciousness*. London: Verso.

Goizueta, Roberto. 1995. *Caminemos con Jesús: Toward a Hispanic/Latino Theology of Accompaniment*. New York: Orbis Books.

Government of Canada. Multiculturalism. https://www.canada.ca/en/services/culture/canadian-identity-society/multiculturalism.html. Accessed 3 Feb 2020.

Gunew, Sneja. 2004. *Haunted Nations: The Colonial Dimensions of Multiculturalisms*. New York: Routledge.

H.E.R.E. Local 75 Choir. 2004. Ain't You Got a Right. In *I Still Have Joy*. Compact Disk Recording. Toronto: Deep Down Productions, CD.

Haig-Brown, Celia. 2009. Decolonizing Diaspora: Whose Traditional Land Are We On? *Cultural and Pedagogical Inquiry* 1 (1): 4–21.

Hall, Stuart. 1996. Introduction: Who Needs Identity? In *Questions of Cultural Identity*, ed. Stuart Hall and Paul Du Gay, 1–17. London: Sage.

Hutchinson, Roger. 1975. *The Fellowship for a Christian Social Order: A Social Ethical Analysis of a Christian Socialist Movement*. PhD Dissertation, Toronto School of Theology, University of Toronto.

———. 1989. The Fellowship for a Christian Social Order: 1934–1945. In *A Long and Faithful March: "Towards the Christian Revolution" 1930s/1980s*, ed. Harold Wells and Roger Hutchinson, 17–29. Toronto: United Church Publishing House.

King, Thomas. 2004. Godzilla Vs. Post-Colonial. In *Unhomely States: Theorizing English-Canadian Postcolonialism*, ed. Cynthia Sugars, 184–190. Toronto: Broadview Press.

Lebans, Crista. 2015. On Not Making a Labor of It: Relationality and the Problem of Whiteness. In *White Criticality Before Anti-Racism: How Does It Feel to Be a White Problem?* ed. George Yancy, 69–83. London: Lexington Books.

Lind, Emily R.M. 2015. I Once Was Lost But Now I'm Found: Exploring the White Feminist Confessional. In *Unveiling Whiteness in the Twenty-First Century: Global Manifestations, Transdisciplinary Interventions*, ed. Veronica Watson, Deirdre Howard-Wagner, and Lisa Spanierman, 229–246. London: Lexington Books.

Maldonado-Torres, Nelson. 2007. On the Coloniality of Being. *Cultural Studies* 21 (2–3): 240–270. http://www.decolonialtranslation.com/english/maldonado-on-the-coloniality-of-being.pdf. Accessed 25 July 2018.

Manuel, Arthur, and Grand Chief Ronald M. Derrickson. 2015. *Unsettling Canada: A National Wake-Up Call.* Toronto: Between the Lines.

———. 2017. *The Reconciliation Manifesto: Recovering the Land, Rebuilding the Economy.* Toronto: James Lorimer.

Maracle, Lee. 2004. The 'Post-Colonial' Imagination. In *Unhomely States: Theorizing English-Canadian Postcolonialism*, ed. Cynthia Sugars, 205–208. Toronto: Broadview Press.

Medina, Néstor. 2009. *Mestizaje: (Re)Mapping Race, Culture and Faith in Latina/o Catholicism.* Maryknoll: Orbis Books.

———. 2017. *On the Doctrine of Discovery.* Toronto: Canadian Council of Churches.

———. 2018. *Christianity, Empire and the Spirit: (Re)Configuring Faith and the Cultural.* Leiden: Brill.

———. Forthcoming. (De)Cyphering Mestizaje; Encrypting Lived Faith: Simultaneous Promise and Problem. In *The Preferential Option for Culture*, ed. Miguel Diaz. Minneapolis: Fortress Press.

Medina, Néstor, and Becca Whitla. 2019. (An)Other Canada Is Possible: Rethinking Canada's Colonial Legacy. *Horizontes Decoloniales/Decolonial Horizons* V.1: 13–42.

Métis Nation. http://www.metisnation.ca. Accessed 3 May 2017.

Mignolo, Walter D. 2000. *Local Histories/Global Designs: Coloniality, Subaltern Knowledges, and Border Thinking.* Princeton: Princeton University Press.

———. 2009. Epistemic Disobedience, Independent Thought and Decolonial Freedom. *Theory, Culture & Society* 26 (7–8): 151–81. http://waltermignolo.com/wp-content/uploads/2013/03/epistemicdisobedience-2.pdf. Accessed 25 July 2018.

Moreiras, Alberto. 1999. Hybridity and Double Consciousness. *Cultural Studies* 13 (3): 373–407.

Mukherjee, Arun. 1998. *Postcolonialism: Living My Life.* Toronto: TSAR Publications.

Ng, Wenh-In. 2003. Lands of Bamboo and Lands of Maple. In *Realizing the America of Our Hearts*, ed. Fumitaka Matsuoko and Eleazar S. Fernandez, 99–114. Atlanta: Chalice Press.

Ng, Greer Anne Wenh-In. 2008. The United Church of Canada: A Church Fittingly National. In *Christianity and Ethnicity in Canada*, ed. Paul Bramadat and David Seljak, 204–246. Toronto: University of Toronto Press.

Peace, Thomas. The Nation-State Is Not What We Think It Is: Teaching Canadian History for a Non-National Perspective. *Active History.* http://activehistory.ca/2014/12/the-nation-state-is-not-what-we-think-it-is-teaching-canadian-history-from-a-non-national-perspective/. Accessed 9 Mar 2020.

Regan, Paulette. 2010. *Unsettling the Settler Within: Indian Residential Schools, Truth Telling, and Reconciliation in Canada*. Vancouver: UBC Press.

Rudder, Kiara. 2019. Hayden King and Others Question the Effectiveness of Land Acknowledgements. *The Eye Opener*, January 19. https://theeyeopener. com/2019/01/hayden-king-and-others-question-the-effectiveness-of-land-acknowledgemenets/. Accessed 19 May 2019.

Said, Edward. 2003. *Orientalism*. New York/London: Penguin Classics.

Schneider, Howard. 1998. Canada: A Mosaic Not a Melting Pot. *The Washington Post*, July 5. https://www.washingtonpost.com/archive/politics/1998/07/05/ canada-a-mosaic-not-a-melting-pot/8a4998ed-b04b-491e-b72e-1ef4d8e96d84/. Accessed 3 Feb 2020.

Scott, R.B.Y., and Gregory Vlastos, eds. 1936. *Towards the Christian Revolution*. Chicago: Willet, Clark.

Shotwell, Alexis. 2015. Unforgetting as a Collective Tactic. In *White Criticality Before Anti-Racism: How Does It Feel to Be a White Problem?* ed. George Yancy, 57–67. London: Lexington Books.

Simpson, Leanne. 2011. *Dancing on Our Turtle's Back: Stories of Nishnaabeg Re-creation, Resurgence, and a New Emergence*. Winnipeg: Arbeiter Ring Publishing.

Six Nations of the Grand River. Community Profile. http://www.sixnations.ca/ CommunityProfile.htm. Accessed 9 Mar 2020.

Spivak, Gayatri Chakravorty. 1988a. Can the Subaltern Speak? In *Marxism and the Interpretation of Cultures*, ed. Cary Nelson and Lawrence Grossberg, 271–313. Urbana: University of Illinois Press.

———. 1988b. Subaltern Studies: Deconstructing Historiography. In *Selected Subaltern Studies*, ed. Ranajit Guha and Gayatri Spivak. Oxford: Oxford University Press.

The Métis. In *Canada's First Peoples*. http://firstpeoplesofcanada.com/fp_metis/ fp_metis1.html. Accessed 3 May 2017.

Tracey, James R. 2003. The Weather Underground and the Future of Memory: An Interview with Sam Green. *Contemporary Justice Review* 6 (4): 397–400.

Truth and Reconciliation Commission of Canada. 2015a. Canada's Residential Schools: The History, Part 1, Origins to 1939. In *The Final Report of the Truth and Reconciliation Commission of Canada*. *Volume 1*. Canada. http://nctr.ca/ assets/reports/Final%20Reports/Volume_1_History_Part_1_English_Web. pdf. Accessed 28 July 2018.

———. 2015b. Reports of the Truth and Reconciliation Commission. http:// nctr.ca/reports.php. Accessed 3 May 2018.

Tuck, Eve, and Wayne Yang. 2012. Decolonization Is Not a Metaphor. *Decolonization, Indigeneity, Education & Society* 1 (1): 1–40. http:// www.decolonization.org/index.php/des/article/view/18630/15554. Accessed 25 July.

Whitla, Becca. 2015. From the Heart of Song to the Heart of Singing. *Touchstone* 33 (1): 53–58.

———. 2018. Coloniality in 'Glossary of Key Terms'. In *Decoloniality and Justice: Theological Perspectives*, ed. Jean-François Roussel, 22–24. Saõ Leopoldo: Oikos: World Forum on Theology and Liberation.

Winsan, Patty. 2017. Are Indigenous Acknowledgements a Step Forward or an Empty Gesture? *The Toronto Star*, December 27. https://www.thestar.com/news/insight/2017/12/27/are-indigenous-acknowledgements-a-step-forward-or-an-empty-gesture.html. Accessed 10 Apr 2018.

Yancy, George. 2015. Introduction: Un-Sutured. In *White Criticality Before Anti-Racism: How Does It Feel to Be a White Problem?* ed. George Yancy, xi–xxvii. London: Lexington Books.

Yancy, George C. White Suturing, Black Bodies, and the Myth of a Post-Racial America. *SARTS: Society for the Arts in Religious and Theological Studies*. http://www.societyarts.org/white-suturing-black-bodies-and-the-myth-of-a-post-racial-america.html. Accessed 7 Apr 2018.

CHAPTER 4

The Empire Sings

INTRODUCTION

Much of the repertoire and values of the church music inheritances in the Anglican and United Churches of Canada, along with the rest of the English-speaking world, come from the hymnic traditions of Victorian England. These inheritances have often been unquestioningly and proudly accepted as the core of hymnic canons in these church contexts. Of course, the post-reformation affirmation of the participation of the people in worship in their own language was embodied in hymnody, especially in England in the hymns of Isaac Watts and Charles Wesley in the eighteenth century; the people's singing became paramount. And yet, at the same time, the very rise of English language hymnody, this uplifting of the people's song, was enmeshed and coincided with—and became conditioned by—the ascendancy of the British Empire. As a result, congregational singing from this inheritance is imbued with (English) coloniality—the all-encompassing residual web of colonizing processes, tendencies, and practices.

As we saw in Chap. 3, coloniality affects all aspects of human existence: who we are, how we behave, how we understand the world, and all our relations. People continue to live with this legacy of colonialism in a lived coloniality of being. In Anglo-Canada, the particular flavour of coloniality stems from the British contingent of European colonialism. In multiple ways, hymnody from the Victorian era came to embody coloniality.

© The Author(s) 2020   79
B. Whitla, *Liberation, (De)Coloniality, and Liturgical Practices,*
New Approaches to Religion and Power,
https://doi.org/10.1007/978-3-030-52636-8_4

Corresponding with and contributing to the rise of the British Empire, this hymnody was exported and imposed in the Canadian context, throughout Britain's imperial realm, and by extension, even more widely throughout the world. I call this phenomenon coloniality of music or musicoloniality.[1] It infects the way music is understood, taught, composed, performed, and experienced.

One way to unmask these forces in congregational singing is to examine the socio-cultural factors that led to the rise of English hymnody in the Victorian era and how it was enmeshed with the ascendency of the British Empire. As we shall see, the economic, military, territorial, political, and cultural facets of this ascendency coalesced in the promulgation of "a" superior British culture; patriotism and a sense of citizenry in sync with the values of its Empire were part of British identity.[2] This superior British self-understanding was bolstered by the construction and then entrenchment of systems of racialized classification which placed Anglo Saxons at the top by establishing white supremacy as a key mechanism to enforce colonialism throughout the British Empire.[3]

By confronting and unmasking this legacy, this empire at the heart of congregational singing, the connection between the proliferation of Victorian hymnody and the rise of the British Empire is exposed. This unmasking productively disrupts the domination of Western European Anglo North Atlantic cultures in liturgy. Liberating congregational singing can only really be seriously undertaken when these hymnic traditions, exported as part of the British imperial and colonial project to the United and Anglican Churches of Canada, are interrogated. We can then ask: what are the implications of still "sounding empire?"[4]

This chapter is not intended to be an exhaustive analysis of Victorian hymnody. Ian Bradley, Richard Arnold, Jeffrey Richards, J.R. Watson, and

---

[1] Coloniality of music is related to the other aspects of the colonial power matrix and refers to the multiple ways in which coloniality has pervasively infected music, music-making, and discourses about music. Musicoloniality encompasses this notion and also refers to the interconnected overarching web of factors which contribute to making Eurocentric approaches to music dominant. These factors will be further explored in this and the subsequent chapter.

[2] I recognize that the terms "empire" and "imperial" are slippery. In this chapter, "empire" at the heart of singing and "imperial" refer specifically to the British Empire that defined the British contingent of the expansion of European colonial projects.

[3] See Robert J.C. Young, *Colonial Desire: Hybridity in Theory, Culture and Race* (London, New York: Routledge, 1995).

[4] Michael N. Jagessar and Stephen Burns, *Christian Worship: Postcolonial Perspectives* (Sheffield: Equinox, 2011), 52.

others have done extensive work in these areas and I draw appreciatively on their wide-ranging scholarship, along with work by church music scholars and ethno/musicologists.[5] There are also other significant influences on the Canadian hymnic canons of the United and Anglican Churches of Canada, including especially by hymn-writers from the USA, which are beyond the scope of the present chapter.[6] Rather, the focus is on English hymnody from the peak of the British Empire in the nineteenth and early twentieth centuries as a predominant source for these musical canons.

The pervasive authority given to this hymnody in congregational singing practices is still operative in the Canadian context (and beyond).[7] This "authority," this coloniality in music, continues to impede the full expression of complex cultural identities that are prevalent in many contexts, including Canada. It also continues to perpetuate theologies of empire, and specifically the British Empire, with its glorification of monarchy, militarism, triumphalism, xenophobia, racial superiority, and patriarchy.

Liturgical scholars Michael Jagessar and Stephen Burns, in their critical engagement with liturgical practices have argued that a postcolonial optic "will want to ask why 'conserve' even good poetry [in hymns] when the integrity of a text may be questionable because of its implicit or explicit arrogance, marginalization of peoples of groups, and the locating of Eurocentric Christianity above all else (especially that which is native)."[8] They make important claims about the ways in which hymns continue to be colonizing. Indeed, many in our congregations still experience the daily painful reality of exclusion due to the multiple constitutive exclusionary factors which go hand in hand with colonialism. This complex matrix of colonial ideologies, encapsulated in coloniality, is expressed and

---

[5] See: Ian Bradley, *Abide with Me: The World of Victorian Hymns* (London: SCM Press, 1997); Jeffrey Richards, *Imperialism and Music: Britain, 1876–1953* (Manchester: Manchester University Press, 2002); Richard Arnold, ed., *English Hymns of the Nineteenth Century: An Anthology* (New York: Peter Lang, 2004); J.R. Watson, *The English Hymn: A Critical and Historical Study* (Oxford: Oxford University Press, 1997).

[6] Of interest is also the influence of USA gospel hymnody on British hymns of the Victorian era. See Ian Bradley's chapter seven on the topic, "'Hold the fort for I am coming': American Imports and Gospel Songs" (169–189) in Bradley, *Abide with Me*, 169–89.

[7] I use the term "canon" to refer to the core of traditional hymns that are understood to be part of the inheritance in these churches. I also note that in surveys done in 1994 and 1995, Victoria hymns from the peak of British imperialism remain among the top ten hymns, especially, as Bradley notes, at weddings and funerals. Ibid., 231.

[8] Jagessar and Burns, *Christian Worship*, 61.

embodied in our hymns, among other places.⁹ As we shall see subsequently (see Chap. 5), a postcolonial optic does not go far enough to build up liturgical practices, including congregational singing. This chapter, however, focuses on the deconstructive task of unmasking the colonial legacy in Anglo-European hymnody and exposing empire at the heart of song. As Jagessar and Burns assert, "many European ecclesial traditions—their ethos, hymns, bibles, interpretations, liturgies and doctrines—went hand in hand with the colonial enterprise to affirm production, control, and domination consciously or unconsciously" and are still perpetuated in our practices today.¹⁰

THE RISE OF HYMNODY

European Christians found, in what is sometimes referred to as the 'Great Commission,' (Matt. 28:18–20) inspiration for conquering foreign lands and their peoples. ... Christianity, expansion and civilization went together. ... Christianizing and civilizing became euphemisms for enslavement, domination and exploitation and the theology that the established and historic churches sang underscore this.¹¹

Setting the Historical Context

The second wave of European colonialism, after the conquering of the Americas by the Spanish and Portuguese, was in full swing amid (and contributing to) the enormous complexity and instability of European political, social, and cultural forces at the end of the eighteenth century and the beginning of the nineteenth. Decades of internal religious and political conflict within European nations and between them, coupled with the

---

⁹ The distinction between colonialism and coloniality is helpfully described by Nelson Maldonado-Torres as follows: "Colonialism denotes a political and economic relation in which the sovereignty of a nation or a people rests on the power of another nation, which makes such nation an empire. Coloniality, instead, refers to long-standing patterns of power that emerged as a result of colonialism, but that define culture, labor, intersubjective relations, and knowledge production well beyond the strict limits of colonial administrations. Thus, coloniality serves colonialism. ... In a way, we breathe coloniality all the time and everyday." Nelson Maldonado-Torres, "On the Coloniality of Being," *Cultural Studies* 21, no. 2–3 (March/May 2007). 243, accessed July 25, 2018. http://www.decolonialtranslation.com/english/maldonado-on-the-coloniality-of-being.pdf

¹⁰ Jagessar and Burns, *Christian Worship*, 53.
¹¹ Ibid.

impact of industrialization, imperial expansion, and colonization, significantly destabilized many European societies and led to the American, French, and Haitian revolutions.

In intellectual circles, European thinkers counterbalanced this disequilibrium—and contributed to the justification for colonization—in part by asserting the individual, rationalist, positivist "subject," beginning with Descartes' cogito ergo sum and continuing in the work of Rousseau, Kant, Hegel, and Darwin, among others. For all intents and purposes this subject of the Enlightenment was an elite European heterosexual man. Those who did not conform to the paradigms of this biologically and culturally "superior" subject—women, the conquered peoples of Latin America, the victims of plantation slavery, the oriental "other," and all other "others"—were consigned to the outside as "others."[12]

In England, partly in response to these historical factors and intellectual climates, forces coalesced to build up a national culture by affirming a superior British identity which celebrated the ascendency of the British Empire as the great imperial power it was to become at its peak, by the mid-late nineteenth century and beyond. Jeffrey Richards describes the ideological web that underpins this coalescence:

> Together monarchy, empire and Protestantism defined Britain and the British. Their world-role was the historical fulfillment of the mission imposed on them by God to bring Christianity, civilization and justice to the unenlightened areas of the globe. In the first half of the nineteenth century, evangelicalism was the shaping force of Britain's national ideology and national identity. In the second half of the nineteenth century, it was imperialism, but an imperialism that embraced evangelicalism and was seen as the working out of God's purpose.[13]

He also notes that an English national cultural identity gradually expanded to become British and subsume "celtic mysticism, for it had to embrace England, Scotland, Wales and Ireland, as well as India, and the colonies, dominions and dependencies overseas."[14] British imperial expansionism transmogrified to include the conviction that a superior English, and then

---

[12] Discussions of subjectivity begun in Chap. 3 are further expanded upon in Chap. 5.

[13] Richards, *Imperialism and Music*, 367.

[14] Ibid., 14. As Robert Young has documented, the complex construction of systems of racialization in nineteenth-century Europe included a racial hierarchy which positioned the Saxons above the Celts. Young, *Colonial Desire*, 55–89. I recognize the slipperiness of the

British, identity would enlighten and civilize those who were part of the Empire, both at home and abroad. In fact, this "imperialism that embraced evangelicalism" was set against the backdrop of increasingly complex British imperial interests abroad, in India, Crimea, Egypt, Southern and Eastern Africa, and among the colonies.

At home in England, the nineteenth century had begun with the Napoleonic wars and the abolition of slavery. At the same time, there was increasing discontent among the restless working classes and the urban poor who were suffering due to industrialization and urbanization. There were growing movements of resistance in socialist circles, among the Chartists, in the fledgling union movement, and in movements for men's and then woman's suffrage.[15] There were also tensions between divergent denominational traditions: between Catholic and Protestant as the English Reformation became firmly established, on one hand, and between Anglican and nonconformist groups as the conflict over which branch of reforming tradition ought to prevail, on the other. These tensions were relocated, to varying degrees and in different ways, wherever British imperial interests went. In addition, there were ongoing pressures between England and the nations that formed Great Britain, especially Ireland, but also Wales and Scotland. Establishing a hegemonic culture, a strong British identity, was imperative in order to keep all of these complex simmering and potentially volatile forces at bay.[16]

terms "English" and "British." Prejudice against the non-English nations of Britain was certainly prevalent in the Victorian age and was exported with British colonialism.

[15] The Chartists, named after the People's Charter, published in 1838, advocated for the rights of the working classes. Especially interested in parliamentary reform and universal suffrage, their goals influenced the Parliamentary Reform Acts of 1867 and 1884 which increased voting rights and political accountability in parliament. Women finally achieved full suffrage in 1928 in Britain. National Archives, "'Chartists,' Power, Politics & Protest: The Growth of Political Rights in Britain in the 19th Century," accessed January 18, 2017, http://www.nationalarchives.gov.uk/education/politics/g7/

[16] I am arguing that the drive to establish a British cultural identity was indeed hegemonic. I use hegemonic following Néstor Medina who extends Gramsci's notion of hegemony to allow for the complexity and agency of voices and forces which simultaneously resist hegemony even from within hegemonic structures. Néstor Medina, *Christianity, Empire and the Spirit* (Leiden: Brill, 2018), 21–24. Medina helpfully describes Gramsci's notion of hegemony as "referring to the ideological construct deployed by the dominant class as a mechanism designed to manipulate (read lead) the masses in terms of how to perceive reality," 23. But he also argues that Gramsci does not go far enough, remaining circumscribed himself by the very "coloniality of the Western European intellectual tradition," with its dualistic approach which tends to demarcate the dominant class too neatly, disallowing "the fluid and

This is not to suggest that the establishment of a hegemonic culture and British identity was an intentional and organized strategy, per se. Recent scholarship in both Empire and Victorian studies asserts that the formation of the British Empire itself was not a planned affair but was rather the result of multiple interwoven complex events and factors in the realms of politics, international relations, and economics. Driven by equally multiple, interwoven, complex—and sometimes contradictory— interests in the military, mercantile, and religious arenas, the British Empire left its mark on territories throughout the world. The implications of these dynamics are in dispute and subject to different interpretations which are beyond the scope of this chapter.[17] A recent cultural turn in the study of the British Empire has appropriately emphasized the importance of a historiographical emphasis on social and cultural perspectives, notwithstanding the fact that all of the events, factors, realms, and interests listed above are culturally conditioned.[18] Of particular interest, for our purposes, are two recent shifts. First, there is an increased emphasis on the agency of conquered and subjugated peoples, with an acknowledgement

unfixed character of power relations" and the "the fluid character of human cultural agency which occupies different spaces at different times within the broad network of sociocultural dynamics and identities," 24.

[17] For example, Victorianism is increasingly concerned with emphases on: women's studies; gender studies; class affiliations, especially working-class studies; ethnographic studies, especially white-black relations; and the representation of all of these in newly assessed periodical literature. In the study of imperialism in Britain, the emphasis has shifted from narratives of imperial conquest and military conquest to distinctions between white settler colonies, long-established British possessions (e.g., India), and those territories conquered and acquired in the late nineteenth century, (particularly in West Africa). For a summary of the issues in studies of the British Empire, see Andrew Porter, "Introduction: Britain and the Empire in the Nineteenth Century," in *The Oxford History of the British Empire, Volume 3, the Nineteenth Century*, ed. Andrew Porter (Oxford: Oxford University Press, 1989), 1–28. For a summary of the relations between Christianity and the British Empire, see his chapter in the same volume: Andrew Porter, "Religion, Missionary Enthusiasm, and Empire," in *The Oxford History of the British Empire, Volume 3, the Nineteenth Century*, ed. Andrew Porter (Oxford: Oxford University Press, 1989), 222–46. The Wikipedia page on the historiography of the British Empire offers an excellent summary of the threads in contemporary scholarship on these issues. See Wikipedia, "The Historiography of the British Empire," accessed March 3, 2017, https://en.wikipedia.org/wiki/Historiography_of_the_British_Empire

[18] For an excellent overview of the contexts of Victorian England, see: "Part One: Contexts" in Victor Shea and William Whitla, eds.,*Victorian Literature: An Anthology* (Oxford: Wiley Blackwell, 2015), 19–179. Shea and Whitla lay out the complex web of interlocking factors in sections that deal with the following topics: the condition of England; gender, women, and sexuality; literature and the arts; religion and science; and empire.

of the multi-directionality in flow of influence and exchange between the metropolitan centre and the peripheries, to which we return in the next chapter. Second, there is now an acknowledgement of the central role of doctrines of racial superiority during the nineteenth century—though these doctrines were also operative prior to the nineteenth century—as justification for British imperial interests, colonial conquests, and evangelization.[19]

The Rise of Hymnody in Britain

In the late eighteenth century, most congregational singing in Protestant Britain still consisted largely of metrical psalm singing. West gallery bands abounded in both Anglican and nonconformist contexts, consisting of local musicians and singers who played and sang metrical psalms and other anthems, often in polyphonic settings from the west gallery of the church. By the mid-nineteenth century these practices were all but abolished in favour of congregational hymn singing from hymnbooks, led by the organ and choir. As the popularity of hymn singing increased, hymns were sung everywhere and began to embody a British identity which encompassed "monarchy, empire and Protestantism."[20] Hymns became "the most universally popular art form and the nearest thing to a cultural inheritance common to women and men, working class and middle class, old and young, the skeptical and the devout."[21] There were six key factors that contributed to this flourishing of hymn singing.

First, the musical manifestations of the English Reformation were expressed in the metrical psalms of Isaac Watts [1674–1748] and the hymns of Charles Wesley [1707–1788] which were sung in the Evangelical Revival in the second half of the eighteenth century. They contributed to an invigoration of congregational singing, especially in nonconformist settings, and paved the way for the exponential burgeoning of British hymnody in the nineteenth. The zeal for singing these hymns was contagious, especially in contexts where there were strong Methodist influences. There is much to be said about the intersection between Wesleyan

---

[19] In my opinion, Andrew Porter (see footnote 17) provides a good overview of the discursive stands in current historiographical studies of the British Empire but does not sufficiently account for the impact of colonialism which cast a veil of the entire project of modernity.

[20] Richards, *Imperialism and Music*, 367.

[21] Ibid, quoting Hugh McLeod, *Religion and Society in England, 1850–1914* (London: Macmillan, 1996), 100, 103–04.

hymnody and present day liberationist and decolonial currents, but such an engagement would take me outside the intended goal here. Suffice to say that, although the Wesley brothers worked among the poor and often adopted non-conformist attitudes and approaches, their views—along with Wesleyan hymnody—were still deeply shaped by the rising tides and emerging colonial structures of British imperial rule.[22]

Second, early in the nineteenth century, and coming from an opposite (conservative, high church) impulse, clergy from the Oxford movement in the Anglican Church abolished the often rowdy west gallery choirs and barrel organs in favour of more austere chanting and singing.[23] Reforming what were seen as unseemly, disorderly, and irreverent worship practices, these Tractarians sought a return to more authentic (ancient) liturgies in

[22] Much could be done to explore proto-liberationist themes in Wesleyan hymnody. For instance, S. T. Kimbrough has commented that Charles Wesley's hymns about the poor are an important and neglected body of work, albeit also relatively small in relation to his vast corpus of more than 6000 hymns. Writing about these hymns, Kimbrough notes that "while the hymns and poems do utilize language with which the outcasts of society could identify, and many of his hymns remind the church of its responsibilities to them, almost no current hymnals contain hymns by Wesley that challenge the church to specific tasks on behalf of social activity for the poor and dispossessed." S. T. Kimbrough "Charles Wesley and the Poor" in *The Portion of the Poor: Good News to the Poor in the Wesleyan Tradition*, ed. M. Douglas Meeks (Nashville: Kingswood Books, 1995), 160. Indeed, Wesleyan hymn singing, especially in the latter half of the eighteenth century, along with Methodism more generally, was associated with movements of the poor and disenfranchised. The hymns Kimbrough refers to above articulated codes of moral behaviour guided by Christian principles to act for the benefit of the poor and John Wesley was well known for his strong objection to the Atlantic slave trade. Their contestatory eighteenth-century views are important reminders of the complex historiographic reality that was at play in this era of the ascendency of the British Empire and they anticipate contestatory voices of the nineteenth as well. At the same time, the Wesleys' advocacy on behalf of the poor and disenfranchised was primarily driven by evangelism and not resistance to empire or colonialism per se. Their work did little to resist the structures that made people poor. As Kimbrough argues, "as Tories and supporters of the monarchy, Charles and John Wesley were not engaged in efforts to reform the governmental and societal structures which perpetuated oppression of the poor in the eighteenth-century England, but they did attack head-on the problems and results of such oppression in English society" (152). It could be even argued that in their focus on evangelism, the Wesleys were all the more complicit with the English imperial project as it was to emerge. For a description of the imperial patriotism of the work Methodist Mission Society as it developed, see Hilary M. Carey's chapter on nonconformist missions, "Colonial Missionary Societies: Nonconformists," *God's Empire: Religion and Colonialism in the British World, c.1801–1908*, (Oxford: Oxford University Press, 2011), 177–205.

[23] Bernarr Rainbow, *The Choral Revival in the Anglican Church (1839–1872)* (London: Barrie & Jenkins, 1970), 269.

part by improving the quality of singing in church by introducing chant and choirs.[24]

Third, this Oxford movement interest in chanting and singing contributed to "the choral revival" in churches, which swept England (and Britain), resulting in choral training for entire congregations so that they could fully participate in worship by singing hymns.[25] This commitment to congregational singing among Tractarians led to a number of initiatives which significantly altered liturgical practices, including more formalized surplice choirs and the installation of choir stalls and pipe organs. It also led to "improved" hymn tunes, new hymn texts, and newly translated texts by the likes of John Mason Neale.[26] For example, during the sixty four years of Queen Victoria's reign beginning in 1837, most churches acquired an organ, an instrument that was understood to be "more solemn and distinctively ecclesiastical and also richer in harmonic resources, encouraging the composers of Victorian hymn tunes to indulge in lush chromaticisms."[27] Ultimately, and ironically, the organ "won out against Gregorian chant and early plainsong melodies" so beloved by the Tractarians. It continues to dominate church music practices to this day in many contexts as the "king of instruments."[28]

The abolishment of west gallery bands with the perceived "dreariness of much metrical psalmody, the vulgarity of the florid gallery anthems with their instrumental accompaniments, and the practice of congregations sitting and for the most part remaining silent for the musical parts of services" was not simply the result of the unmitigated influence of the Tractarians, however.[29] Other catalysts included "urbanization, greater mobility, technological progress and other social factors."[30]

Our fourth key influence is included in these "other social factors." There was somewhat of a "clerical conspiracy" across denominations to

[24] Proponents of the Oxford movement were called Tractarians, named for their publications, "Tracts for the Times," published between 1833 and 1841. See The Episcopal Church, "Tracts for the Times," accessed January 3, 2017, http://www.episcopalchurch.org/library/glossary/tracts-times

[25] Rainbow, *The Choral Revival*, 266.

[26] Ibid., 282. In some settings this commitment to "high" church liturgy ironically resulted in a cathedral style worship which left little room for congregational singing, focusing instead on the performances of the choir and organ.

[27] Bradley, *Abide with Me*, 37, 38.

[28] Ibid., 38.

[29] Ibid., 28.

[30] Ibid., 40.

"stamp out a potentially anarchic popular culture and replace it with a more authoritarian and elitist form of worship."[31] Bradley finds the claim that "elements of class struggle and ideological conflict in the battles over the introduction of choirs, organs and hymn-books, with Oxbridge-educated clergymen seeking to impose high culture and individualist values on working people steeped in a populist and communitarian folk tradition of worship" to be overstated.[32] At the same time, he also notes that eradicating the west gallery tradition as a "communal working-class folk tradition" was "part of a wider movement to replace a democratic and populist musical culture with a much more élitist [sic] and regulated regime which was essentially high-brow and rather stuffy."[33] However complex the various elements that contributed to these changes were, the result was that church music became dominated by the clergy, the organ, the choir, and a profusion of new hymnody, from the mid-nineteenth century onward.

Fifth, this new, controlled, and standardized church music culture, though it varied somewhat between denominations and even between churches in the same denomination, was reinforced by the proliferation of hymnbooks. The enormous growth in the publication of hymnbooks not only encouraged congregations to sing hymns, it also encouraged writers and composers to create new hymn settings. Significantly, beginning in the mid-nineteenth century and continuing well into the twentieth, many hymnbooks were produced for children in schools and Sunday schools. Hymns were memorized at home and in the classroom, creating a strong shared oral culture which "reinforced their [the hymns'] central place in the Victorian cult of the home and the sanctification of the family and it also confirmed their role as carriers of moral values, and teaching aids to instruct the young in catechetical principles, and the basic doctrines of the Christian faith."[34] These hymnals ensured that British identity and a pride in the British Empire were enculturated through hymns among the young.

Sixth and finally, hand-in-hand with the colossal production of hymns and hymnbooks, was the development of and investment in musical education in Victorian England. The end of the eighteenth century saw an increase in community choral activity which was fostered by the choral revival of the Oxford movement and gained a full head of steam with the

[31] Ibid., 41.
[32] Ibid.
[33] Ibid., 39.
[34] Ibid., 50.

"burst of musical education and explosion of popular interest and involvement in choral singing unparalleled before or since" in the early years of Victoria's reign.[35] Musical reformers encouraged singing throughout Britain, forming choirs and choral societies in community settings and in churches.[36] Though choirs did not always encourage congregational singing in churches—they were separated from the congregation and were sometimes elitist and performance-oriented—the overall impact seems to have been to bolster congregational and community singing generally. The musical educators who led these initiatives were participating in broader movements for literacy and social improvement and "exemplified the Victorian passion for cultural improvement and popular participation ... and championed the ideal of full-blooded congregational hymn singing to organ accompaniment as the main musical feature of worship."[37]

One illustration of this exponential growth of hymnody can be gleaned through a brief comparison of the indexes in the first edition of the quintessential Victorian hymnal, *Hymns Ancient and Modern* (1861) and the second edition, the second supplement (1916).[38] The first edition contained 273 hymns and the 1916 edition, 638. In the 1861 edition, there is a much greater emphasis placed on the importance of meter, reflecting both the inheritance of the psalm tradition, eighteenth-century hymnody (e.g., in the hymns of Charles Wesley), and popular romantic verse, such as the lyrical ballads of Coleridge and Wordsworth (e.g., as in Wordsworth's

---

[35] Ibid., 33.

[36] Bradley notes that the tonic sol-fa system was invented during this period to encourage community singing by Sarah Ann Glover [1785–1867], a Norwich schoolmistress, in the early 1830s, and was developed and promoted by John Curwen [1816–80], who was a pastor at Paistow in Essex from 1844 to 1867. See Ibid., 34. The tonic sol-fa system was also used in South Africa and has been critiqued by Grant Olwage for its "choralism." We return to his critique later in the chapter. Grant Olwage, "Discipline and Choralism: The Birth of Musical Colonialism," in *Music, Power, and Politics*, ed. Annie J. Randall (New York: Routledge, 2005), 25–46.

[37] Bradley, *Abide with Me*, 28. Devon Lemire traces the complex matrix of factors which led to a similar rise in literacy. He notes that the rise of education, especially for the poor and working classes, emphasized reading the Bible. Devon Lemire, "A Historiographical Survey of Literacy in Britain Between 1780 and 1830," *Constellations*, Accessed January 18, 2017, https://ejournals.library.ualberta.ca/index.php/constellations/article/viewFile/18862/14652

[38] W. H. Monk, ed., *Hymns Ancient and Modern for the Use in the Services of the Church with Accompanying Tunes* (London: Novello and Co., 1861); W. H. Monk and Steggall, C., eds., *Hymns Ancient and Modern for the Use in the Services of the Church with Accompanying Tunes* (London: William Clowes and Sons, Ltd., 1916).

Lucy poems).[39] There are 48 long meter (LM, or 8888), 28 common meter (CM or 8686), and 10 short meter (SM or 6686) hymns.[40] The remaining hymns follow other meter patterns. Thus, almost a third of the most frequent meters are in the four-line stanzas so common at the time in congregational singing and popular poetry. In contrast, though the number of hymns increased significantly in the 1916 edition, the overall percentage of these meters in traditional four-line rhymed verse form dramatically decreased to only 168 out of 638.[41] The overall growth in hymnody is apparent, as is the expansion of musical forms to include a much greater variety of meters and tunes.[42]

The other significant difference for our purposes is the addition of a new table of copyrighted tunes and their owners, of which the vast majority are the proprietors of *Hymns Ancient and Modern*. This shift reflects the new economic reality (and advantage) of hymn ownership, especially the ownership of an individual composer, author, or arranger.[43] References are also far more historicized in general, with attention to specific sources and transcriptions, including their historical and geographical provenance, providing historical justifications for the accuracy of what is in the volume.[44]

All of these factors are set against the backdrop of broader socio-cultural trends and contexts in Victorian England which were enormously complex and diverse. These contexts ranged from rural to urban, from lower to middle to upper classes, and were influenced by rapid industrialization and movements for democracy. Socio-cultural attitudes were shaped by ideas about gender and race, among other things. Ultimately there was no

---

[39] Observations on Victorian popular romantic verse and poetry are based on William Whitla, personal conversation with the author (4 April 2017).

[40] Common meter (or measure) is the church name given to the ballad stanza: aba/cb (as in the long meter) but with a different syllabic count (CM 8686 or 4343 feet, iambic).

[41] There are 79 long meter, 64 common meter, and 25 short meter hymns.

[42] For instance, the meter 7676D increased from 5 in 1861 to 35 in 1916.

[43] The indexes in the 1916 edition indicate a far greater variety of usage and attention to composers, sources, and translations. It also includes additional indexes: a metrical index of tunes; an alphabetical index of tunes; an alphabetical index of authors and translators; an alphabetical index of composers; and comparison tables of hymns in the old and new editions. We return to the implications of this emphasis on individual compositional ownership later in the chapter with reference to classical or serious-music ideology.

[44] For example, ancient tunes were defined more specifically as "proper Mechlin melody," "proper Sarum melody," or "medieval Italian melody," and geographical sources were identified by reference to their original sources, as in for example, "*Geistliche Lider,* Magdeburg, 1540," and "Day, *Psalms,* 1563." Monk and, *Hymns Ancient and Modern,* v–xxvii.

single "culture" that was established, no single British identity. But the drive toward a national cultural uniformity was strong. This drive was represented by a "centralizing authoritarianism which eroded variety and spontaneity and sacrificed local and regional traditions on the altar of national uniformity," coalescing as mechanisms which could control the population through music, among other things.[45] As a result, hymns often epitomized a pride in British identity, superiority, and imperial appetite, romantically painting a picture of a genteel, "cultured," British "race" divinely positioned to "civilize" the world. Even when the texts were not explicitly imperial, the fact that hymn singing was so widespread as a practice, in and of itself, boosted the overall sense of (imperial) British cultural identity. W.T. Stead [1849–1912] encapsulated this sentiment in the foreword to his hymnbook, *Hymns that Have Helped,* in 1896, when he wrote:

> The songs of the English-speaking people are for the most part hymns. For the immense majority of our people today the only minstrelsy is that of the Hymn-book. And this is as true of our race beyond the sea as it is of our race at home. ... At this moment, on the slope of the Rockies, or in the sweltering jungles of India, in crowded Australian city, or secluded English hamlet, the sound of some simple hymn tune will, as if by mere magic spell, call from the silent grave the shadowy forms of the unforgotten dead, and transport the listener, involuntarily, over land and sea, to the scene of his childhood's years, to the village school, to the Parish church.[46]

Toward the end of the Victorian era then, hymns, as bearers of cultural power "were being sung not just in churches and chapels, in parlours and school classrooms, at street corners and in tents, but also at the gatherings of those who had rejected Christianity in favour of the new creeds of positivism and secularism."[47] In other words, hymns were instrumental in enculturating the population. On one hand this "elevating" of British culture through hymns and music, along with drives to improve education

[45] Bradley, *Abide with Me,* 73.

[46] Richards, *Imperialism and Music,* 370. Richards is quoting W. T. Stead from *Hymns that Have Helped* (London: Masterpiece Library, 1896), 2.

[47] Bradley, *Abide with Me,* 188. Bradley notes, for instance, that the South Place Ethical Society published *Hymns of Modern Thought* in 1900 and that the *Labour Church Record* "published a curious amalgam of Isaac Watts, the American social gospel tradition, and twentieth-century religious pluralism." Ibid., 189.

and literacy, arguably contributed to a greater involvement with and commitment to participation in the growth of democracy in Britain, as signaled by the parliamentary reform acts for male suffrage (1832, 1867, and 1884).[48] On the other, it could be argued that these forces also contributed to a cultural hegemonization in Britain which ultimately spread throughout the British Empire.[49]

The desire to establish "a" superior British culture, even with all of its variations and permutations, involved establishing a cultural benchmark by which everything cultural, including hymnody, could be measured. The unprecedented rise of English hymnody as a cultural force—as "the" English (and British) folksong—functioned to marginalize other non-church and working-class musical traditions, like the prior "unseemly" west gallery tradition, for example. It also enfolded into itself the hymns of Watts and Wesley from the previous century. Furthermore, as Robert Young and others have shown, because the construction of race as a system of classification was intrinsic to the notion of a British identity—as well as the justification for European imperialism generally—the result in hymnody was to "whiten" or "bleach" music traditions which were seen as inferior.[50] Nineteenth-century British hymnody also included explicitly racist language as well as references to enlightening the heathen "others," enshrined in texts that were exported throughout the world as part of the establishing of the "superior" culture of the British Empire.

Much of the hymnody at the core of Anglican and United Church canons in Canada was imported from this context, along with the complex socio-political-cultural settings in which it was birthed. These hymns perpetuate the hegemonic vision from Britain between the end of the eighteenth century and the beginning of the twentieth. As Britain expanded its imperial interests it entrenched its influence in part by imposing its

[48] See National Archives, "The Struggle for Democracy: Getting the Vote," accessed January 18, 2017, http://www.nationalarchives.gov.uk/pathways/citizenship/struggle_democracy/getting_vote.htm

[49] We return to the underside of notions of cultural improvement in a discussion of choralism later in this chapter.

[50] For example, non-English hymns (Welsh, Irish, and Scottish) were gradually subsumed as British hymnody. As the reach of the British Empire was entrenched in the nineteenth century, Celtic-racialized "others" gradually gave way to a focus on other "others" in the British Empire, in the colonies in North America and Australia as well as in India and Africa. See, for instance, "The Complicity of Culture: Arnold's ethnographic politics," in Young, *Colonial Desire*, 55–89.

culture(s) upon the subjects in its dominion. In Canada, this imperial culture and identity, ensconced in hymns, was disseminated by colonizers/ settlers and imposed upon Indigenous peoples, afro-descendants, and other people groups in subsequent layers of immigration, becoming a missionary hymnody which "itself subjugates; it disciplines and controls; it is a text inscribing the act of colonialism itself."[51]

CONFRONTING EMPIRE: HYMNIC COLONIALITY

Unforgetting: Imperial/Colonial Theology in Mission Hymns

The most obvious and most painful example of the promulgation of this imperial British culture and attitude of British superiority—of hymnic coloniality—is evident in the hymns that travelled with the British in their imperial and colonial pursuits: nineteenth-century mission-focused hymns.[52] These hymns express an imperial/colonial theology of evangelism which undergirded the relationship between missionary activity and British imperial interests. They promoted a theology which had at its heart the view that European, and in this case British, cultural expressions of Christianity, were the superior religious cultural expression known to humanity. They displayed notions of divine providential chosenness and were marked by racialized and gendered language, all of which was endorsed by "Christ the King."

John Bell exposes this blatant ugly racist inheritance in his final chapter of *The Singing Thing Too*, "God's Worldwide Church."[53] The hymns he cites, like "Do you see this penny?", would certainly be deemed culturally unacceptable by today's standards, and include verses like the following: "Do you see this penny?/It is brought by me/for the little children/far

---

[51] Philip V. Bohlman, "World Musics and World Religions: Whose World?" in *Enchanting Powers: Music in the World's Religions*, ed. Lawrence E. Sullivan (Cambridge, MA: Distributed by Harvard University Press for the Harvard University Center for the Study of World Religions, 1997), 71.

[52] For a more focused discussion on missionary hymnody see: Becca Whitla, "Hymnody in Missionary Lands: A Decolonial Critique," in *Hymns and Hymnody: Historical and Theological Introductions, Volume 2: From Catholic Europe to Protestant Europe*, 285–302, edited by Benjamin K. Forrest, Mark A. Lamport and Vernon M. Whaley (Eugene, OR: Wipf and Stock, 2019).

[53] John L. Bell, *The Singing Thing Too: Enabling Congregations to Sing* (Chicago: GIA Publications Inc., 2007).

across the sea/Hurry, penny, quickly/though you are so small;/to tell the heathen/Jesus loves them all."[54] When he describes the context of the singing of this missionary hymn for children, he notes that the pennies were dropped onto "Black Sambo," a "cast iron model of the head and shoulders of a [black or brown] human being. ... 'Sambo' has an arm and hand which is held, palm upwards just below his open mouth. One by one the children put their penny on his palm, twist his ear, and he swallows the penny."[55]

Similarly, William Williams's "O'er the Gloomy Hills of Darkness" [William Williams Pantycelyn (1717–1791)] displays a missiology that endorses earthly conquest and is intertwined with a doctrine of racial superiority, in the name of spreading the gospel from "Pole to Pole."[56] Written in 1772 and republished as late as 1933 in the *Baptist Hymnary,* it includes the following racist verse (two): "Let the Indian, let the Negro,/Let the rude Barbarian see/That divine and glorious Conquest/Once obtain'd on Calvary;/Let the Gospel,/Loud resound from Pole to Pole."[57] This missionary hymn is filled with the evangelistic tone of its era, which paints the picture of "other" kingdoms sitting in darkness only to be freed by the "glorious Light," presumably of imperial British Christianity. Verse six of the original (and the final verse of the version that appeared in 1933) describes the evangelistic task in the language of winning and conquering on behalf of the Dominion. Though it is clearly referring to the spreading of the Gospel and God's Dominion, it borrows the language of imperial conquest in *this* realm: "Fly abroad, eternal Gospel,/Win and conquer, never cease;/May thy eternal wide Dominions/Multiply, and still increase;/May thy Scepter,/Sway th'enlight'ned World around." If there was any doubt about how such an evangelization should take place, the final verse from the original version is clear: "O let Moab yield and tremble,/Let Philistia never boast,/And let India proud be scatt'red/With their numerable Host;/And the Glory,/

---

[54] Ibid., 125, 127. John Bell notes that hymns like this come from such books as Carey Bonner, ed., *The Sunday School Hymnary: A Twentieth Century Hymnal for Young People* (London: Novello and Company, 1905), accessed May 5, 2018, https://archive.org/details/sundayschoolhym00nsgoog

[55] Bell, *The Singing Thing Too,* 126. For an image of this "toy" see William & H. James Co, "Cast-Iron-Mechanical Banks Sambo Mechanical Bank," accessed March 18, 2017, https://www.historytoy.com/william-h-james-co-cast-iron-toy-sambo-mechanical-bank

[56] Richards, *Imperialism and Music,* 388.

[57] Ibid. Verses in what follows, also as quoted in Richards, 388.

Jesus only be to thee." The spread of the Gospel is to be accomplished through the conquest of the "other:" the Indian, the Negro, and the "rude Barbarian."

One hundred years after this hymn was penned by Williams, Britain was in the throes of celebrating its monarch's diamond jubilee and the establishment of the British Empire around the world. The 1897 festivities affirmed the triumph of the British Empire in hymns like Jackson Mason's "Arise O Church of England," which praised "the Anglican Church, God, Queen and Empire [and] ... explicitly connects the cross and crown."[58] In Williams's hymn from 100 years before, the spreading of the gospel—and the British Empire—was more of an aspirational task. Here, in contrast, there is a sense that it had been accomplished. The queen—who was explicitly made empress of India in 1874—the flag, and the gospel were intertwined in a celebration of her beneficent and divinely sanctioned gaze. The hymn text has her bestowing light from "her sixty summers" upon "dark Afric's shores" and "India's sons of freedom":

> Yes, peace in rich abundance
> Has flourished in her time,
> While with her flag, the Gospel
> Speeds on to ev'ry clime.
> Light from her sixty summers
> Dark Afric's shores have seen,
> And India's sons of freedom
> Give thanks for England's Queen.[59]

One might ask, why unearth these obvious and embarrassing vestiges of a bygone era, with language that we now understand to be arrogant, patronizing, racist, imperialist, and patriarchal? The answer is that by exposing this imperial underside in its explicit expressions in these hymns, we commit to a process of hymnic unforgetting.[60] In the Anglican and United Churches of Canada, and in most traditional English-speaking Protestant churches generally, these hymns, replete with racist and imperialist overtones, *were* sung, "sounding empire" at the heart of congregational singing.[61] This vision of the British Empire was indivisible from the

---

[58] Ibid., 405.

[59] Ibid.

[60] For an exploration of unforgetting in relation to church complicity with coloniality, see Chap. 3.

[61] Jagessar and Burns, *Christian Worship*, 52.

particular brand of Christianity with which it was intertwined and which it exported. By beginning with these painfully obvious examples, the racist and imperialist roots of our hymn singing traditions are unmasked. Dr. John Clifford in his volume *God's Greater Britain* sums up the prevailing attitude when he writes:

> For we are called with a high calling. ... We must march in step. Ours is a single aim, a single task, the regeneration of Man. Our place is in the ranks of the great Anglo-Saxon missionary race, to whom is given the grace of preaching amongst all peoples the unsearchable riches of Christ. We are going to all men. They are coming to us. The world is becoming *one*. ... God chose us His colonizers and missionaries.[62]

Deconstructing hymnic coloniality begins by unearthing these obvious examples, in a confessional move which admits that they *were* in fact, sung. If these historic hymns are not exposed, the mechanisms of power that they epitomize remain forgotten. Moreover, when we ignore them and consign them to an embarrassing moment when "they" sang them, we risk perpetuating historical amnesia. Instead, unforgetting reveals the ugly underside of a pervasive coloniality which was unabashedly and explicitly promoted through such hymns, first in Britain and then in its colonies, including in Canada. These imperial dynamics, part of hymnic coloniality, are also still at work today. Recalling them reminds us of the larger history of colonization, a history still being sung, as we shall see in the three examples in the following section.

Unsanitizing: The Legacy Continues

Isaac Watts's version of Psalm 72, "Jesus Shall Reign," was written in 1719, well before the peak of the British Empire.[63] He was nevertheless

---

[62] John Clifford, *God's Greater Britain* (London: James Clarke & Son, 1899), 167, 175 quoted in Richards, *Imperialism and Music*, 384.

[63] This one hymn by Watts is a clear example of the coalescing of imperial/colonial themes in hymnody in the eighteenth century, but I could have equally chosen a hymn by Charles Wesley. "O For a Thousand Tongues to Sing," for instance, displays a similar triumphalist and expansionist ("through all the earth abroad" in verse two) vision. Beloved as an emblematic Wesleyan hymn, it also contains the no longer sung verse (sixteen) with the image of washing (or perhaps bleaching) the Ethiop white: "Wake from guilty nature's sleep,/And Christ shall give you light,/Cast all your sins into the deep,/And wash the Ethiop white." Note also the conflation of nature with guilt and sin in this verse. Interestingly, Benjamin

expressing the growing coalescence between European, and especially English, imperial desire and a vision of God's reign flourishing across the globe. Also, Watts's hymns, along with those of Charles Wesley, were adopted into the body of hymns that became associated with the canon of the nineteenth century, representing the British Empire abroad. We have successfully and for a long time expunged the offensive verses and it is sung with vim and vigor in the Anglican and United Churches of Canada to this day. However, the omitted verses may haunt us still. We no longer sing verses two, three, or thirteen of the original, in which: Europe's ascendency is asserted (verse two); other nations—Persia, India, and the un-named "barb'rous nations"—submit and bow to the Christian Lord (verse three); and "the heathen lands" are characterized unflatteringly as being in the darkness (shade) of death, soon to be enlightened by Christ and Christianity (verse thirteen):

> Verse 2: Behold the islands with their kings,
> And Europe her best tribute brings;
> And crowds of Indian nations meet,
> To pay their homage at His feet.

> Verse 3: There Persia, glorious to behold,
> There India shines in eastern gold;
> And barb'rous nations at His word
> Submit, and bow, and own their Lord.

> Verse 13: The heathen lands, that lie beneath
> The shades of overspreading death,
> Revive at His first dawning light;
> And deserts blossom at the sight.[64]

Kolodziej writes that John Wesley removed "any hint of nationalism" when he edited the hymns of Isaac Watts, a move that could be said to be resisting Empire. But this choice was out of an evangelistic desire to appeal to those who were influenced by the rising tides of the American revolution, rather than a resistance against the British Empire per se. Benjamin A. Kolodziej, "Isaac Watts, the Wesleys, and the Evolution of 18th-Century English Congregational Song," in *Methodist History*, 42: 4 (July, 2004), 242.

[64] Ibid., 389. Verse three is printed in Richards. The other two verses are available in the complete version at Isaac Watts, "Jesus Shall Reign," accessed July 25, 2018, http://www.cyberhymnal.org/htm/j/s/jsreign.htm. I note that verse three has a different third line in the cyber hymnal: "From north to south the princes meet" rather than the more objectionable "And crowds of Indian nations meet."

Yet, the hymn as it is sung today still rings out with the majestic and triumphalist strains of a universal monarchy, Christian to be sure, but with a trace of earthly empire echoing in the background as Jesus' kingdom stretches from "shore to shore" (verse one).[65] It could be claimed, and rightly, that the language of kingship, monarchy, and empire, are biblical and we could easily and fruitfully get distracted with the task of engaging Psalm 72 from a liberationist or postcolonial perspective. But the hymn conflates Jesus' reign with Europe's ascendancy. It assumes that European Christianity, English/British Christianity particularly, has a stranglehold on what and how God's "universal sway," from verse nine, ought to be lived out.

Watts's original version of the psalm reflects the cultural imperial aspirations of the day and emphasizes divine entitlement for earthly European nations, rather than the proclamation of God's protection and love for the poor which is emphasized in the biblical text.[66] Michael Hawn notes this imperial residue in the hymn/psalm setting when he remarks that "this hymn certainly coincided with the rise of the British Empire, and it would have been likely that a congregation in England who sang this psalm paraphrase in the eighteenth century would have made a link—consciously or subconsciously—between the Empire and phrases like 'his kingdom spread from shore to shore' in stanza one."[67]

A process of unforgetting goes beyond simply removing these verses and singing a sanitized version of the hymn. By the same token, unforgetting does not necessarily mean that this hymn ought never to be sung again, though it might mean that for some communities. Rather, unforgetting entails grappling with a series of difficult questions. Can we redeem

---

[65] Today usually only four verses are sung (typically one, five, six, and eight).

[66] A liberationist or postcolonial critique of Psalm 72 would admit that it does describe the king's dominion from "sea to sea and from the River to the ends of the earth" in verse 8 (NRSV). At the same time, the psalmist writes in distinctly liberative language. The sentiments of verse four—"May God defend the cause of the poor of the people, give deliverance to the needy, and crush the oppressor"—are echoed in verses 12–14. The psalm proclaims the Divine announcement of God's protection and love for the poor. While Watts does write: "Blessings abound wherever He reigns;/The prisoner leaps to lose his chains" in verse six; "His justice shall avenge the poor,/And pride and rage prevail no more" in verse ten; and "With power He vindicates the just, And treads th'oppressor in the dust" in verse eleven—the emphasis on justice, especially for the poor and oppressed is not as strong as in the biblical version.

[67] Michael Hawn, "Jesus Shall Reign," accessed July 25, 2018, http://www.umcdiscipleship.org/resources/history-of-hymns-jesus-shall-reign

or reform the hymn by revising some verses or writing new ones? Should we? Or ought we to throw it overboard? How could we help a congregation wrestle with this legacy and its implications? What does unsanitizing look like? How do we grapple with the implied theological implications of superiority and conquest? How do we confront the historical meaning of the omitted verses? If we ignore or forget the hymn's genealogy and refuse to address these questions, the omitted dubious verses linger implicitly, infecting present-day singing and contributing to a kind of historical amnesia.

"Onward Christian Soldiers" is another example—albeit a more controversial one—of a hymn still sung which obviously perpetuates coloniality. Written in 1865 by Reverend Sabine Baring-Gould [1834–1924], with music composed by Sir Arthur Sullivan [1842–1900] in 1871, it evokes the long held metaphor of the cross as a (righteous) battle shield going back to Constantine. It also echoes the "popular military enthusiasm of the day" in the wake of the Crimean war and the general military imperial expansion of the British Empire.[68] Drawing its key military image from 2 Timothy 2:3 ("good soldier of Christ Jesus") and Ephesians 6:13–17 (images of battle and armour), this hymn emphasizes hierarchical images of Christ as royal Master (verse one) and triumphant King (verse five). The church is likened to an undivided, unquestioning ("one in … doctrine," verse three) army.[69] Bradley argues that its language is metaphoric and that "those who object to its supposed militarism are perhaps unaware of the fact that it was never intended for use in church."[70] No doubt contemporary interpretations like mine are somewhat anachronistic. Regardless of the circumstances of its origins, however, how it has and continues to be used and understood also bears considering.[71] Over the

---

[68] Sabine Baring-Gould, "Onward Christian Soldiers," accessed July 25, 2018, http://www.hymnary.org/text/onward_christian_soldiers_marching_as. See also: Shea and Whitla, *Victorian Literature*; Victor Shea and William Whitla, "Victoria Literature: Supplementary Web Resource," accessed March 23, 2017, http://higheredbcs.wiley.com/legacy/college/shea/140518874X/supp/web_contexts.pdf

[69] Baring-Gould, "Onward Christian Soldiers."

[70] Bradley, *Abide with Me*, 100.

[71] By the same token, Bradley problematically argues that "those missionary hymns that also cause such unease today because of their perceived racism and imperialism often belonged in a similar category, as in the case of 'From Greenland's Icy Mountains,' were not written to be sung at regular Sunday services." Ibid. We return to a discussion of this hymn in Chap. 5.

long history and popularity of this hymn, it *has* been used as a hymn to be sung *in* church, and in battle, for that matter.[72]

More to the point, the fact that it was originally written as a children's processional illustrates precisely—in this concrete example from the children's and school hymnals of the mid-nineteenth century—the hegemonic power of hymns fostered through these volumes. It not only contributed to the Christian formation of children as subjects of the British Empire, it also functioned to re-inscribe ideologies of colonial conquest, British imperialism, and British militarism, all ensconced in a triumphalist theology which was justified biblically. These hymns were instilled in the hearts and minds of children, taught orally by "mothers, grandmothers, nursemaids and teachers" and memorized at school.[73] In the present day, "Onward Christian Soldiers" functions to re-inscribe these ideologies in contemporary Canadian congregations, though its use is highly controversial. Because of this militaristic triumphalism, The United Church of Canada chose to omit it from its most recent hymnal, *Voices United,* though it does appear in the Anglican Church's *Common Praise.*[74] This controversy points toward the challenges of unsanitizing. Whichever decision is made—to omit or include the hymn—the stakes are high.

Finally, let us consider "Lift High the Cross" by George W. Kitchin [1827–1912], written in 1887 (altered by Michael R. Newbolt in 1909). The original first verse of the hymn combines the military and monarchical images so prevalent in imperialist English hymnody: "Come, brethren, follow where our Captain trod,/our King victorious, Christ the Son of God." The second and third verses continue along the same lines with "Led on their way by this triumphant sign,/the hosts of God in

---

[72] In fact, according to Ace Collins, Winston Churchill [1874–1965] described the singing of "Onward Christian Soldiers" at the church service marking the occasion of Atlantic Charter agreement between Britain and the USA in 1941 as "serving a cause for the sake of which a trumpet has sounded from on high. ... when I looked upon that densely packed congregation of fighting men of the same language, of the same faith, of the same fundamental laws, of the same ideals. ... it swept across me that here was the only hope, but also the sure hope, of saving the world from measureless degradation." Notwithstanding the highly charged context of WW II including the fight against expanding fascism, it is clear that the propagandistic potential of the hymn—for good or for ill—was fully exploited here. Ace Collins, "Onward Christian Soldiers" In *Stories Behind the Hymns That Inspire America: Songs That Unite Our Nation* (Grand Rapids, MI: Zondervan, 2003), 147–54.

[73] Bradley, *Abide with Me,* 50.

[74] United Church of Canada, *Voices United* (Etobicoke: United Church Publishing House, 1996); Anglican Church of Canada, *Common Praise* (Toronto: Anglican Church of Canada, 1998), #602.

conquering ranks combine" and "Each newborn soldier of the Crucified/ bears on the brow the seal of him who died."[75]

Between each verse the stirring chorus rings out: "Lift high the cross,/ the love of Christ proclaim/till all the world adore/his sacred Name." Written originally for a celebration of the Society for the Propagation of the Gospel, this processional, in which "the crucifer (cross-bearer) leads the stately procession down the long nave, lifting the cross high" celebrates the cross as a sign of the victory of the resurrection, based on John 12:32. The hymn also evokes Emperor Constantine's vision in which he is said to have seen the words "in this sign you will conquer" (*In hoc signo vinces*), the sign being the cross.[76] Hawn writes that the hymn also "expresses the understanding of the Church Militant (Ecclesia Militans), 'those Christians on earth who are engaged in a continuous war against evil and the enemies of Christ,' and the Church Triumphant (Ecclesia Triumphans), 'those Christians in heaven who have triumphed over evil and the enemies of Christ.'"[77] Still sung today, this hymn reinscribes the notion of a victorious Christianity which conquers "all the world." Even more problematic is the conflation of military and kingship language with evangelism, which expressed the triumvirate of evangelism, Christianity, and imperialism in Britain that was flourishing at the beginning of the twentieth century. This *cristus victor* mode in which Christ is victorious over all "Satan's legions" (verse 4) is problematic when coupled with the triumphalist, military, monarchical tenor of the text, because it implicitly reinforces the notion that "a superior group of people either ruling an inferior lot or a superior group of souls filled with chalky light [is] bringing enlightenment to natives in their natural state of ignorance."[78]

What is more, the emotional, stirring music (CRUCIFER) composed by Sir Sydney Nicholson [1875–1947] for the 1916 Supplement of *Hymns Ancient and Modern* compounds the effect. The triumphant setting of the chorus in C major consists of a unison melody with walking harmony parts underneath. The rhythmic emphasis in "lift high the cross" and "till all the world" falls on the words "high," "cross," and "world," since they are longer half notes and dotted half notes. Further emphasizing these words,

---

[75] George W. Kitchin, "Lift High the Cross," accessed January 10, 2017, http://www. oremus.org/hymnal/l/l118.html

[76] C. Michael Hawn, "Lift High the Cross," in *History of Hymns*, accessed July 25, 2018, http://www.umcdiscipleship.org/resources/history-of-hymns-lift-high-the-cross

[77] Ibid.

[78] Jagessar and Burns, *Christian Worship*, 55.

the melody rises up with a leap of fourth on "high" and "world." The verses modulate to the third of the scale, E minor, where the text is set to thick chromatic harmony which strides forward—with a walking bass underneath—toward the dominant chord, leading the singers back to the home/tonic key once again to affirm the victorious message of the text. The effect of the chromaticism and modulation to E minor in the verses is to emphasize a sense of (Christian) struggle which overcomes and triumphs each time the chorus repeats, reminding the singer again and again that Christ's dominion is firmly established.[79]

Many have rejected "Lift High the Cross" for its triumphalism and militarism. Yet in 1984 present day hymnwriter Shirley Erena Murray [1931–2020], a prominent voice among those who articulate contemporary social justice and theological concerns in hymns, wrote new verses to accompany the evocative chorus and music. It was published later in 1992.[80] Her commitment to issues of social justice and peace, and to her own context in New Zealand, makes her choice to re-write "Lift High the Cross" somewhat puzzling. True to her poetic voice, the verses she penned for the hymn are a compelling plea for compassion and peace and include the following: "Jesus, you wept to see our human strife, teach us compassion for each human life" (verse 2) and "Peace was your plea and peace your loving theme: let peace be our passport, peace a living dream" (verse 3). No doubt her re-write was an attempt to subvert the original, to reclaim stirring music and a beloved chorus for contemporary use. In fact, Colin Gibson writes that "rejecting the military imagery and what she describes as the 'now inappropriate theology' of Kitchen's text, her revision locates the emphasis on 'the Holy Week story, the cost of conflict and the Gospel imperatives of peace-making.'"[81] Yet, in between each of her

---

[79] Along similar lines, the walking bass line throughout the hymn is reminiscent of Vaughan Williams' setting SINE NOMINE (published in 1906), with a perpetual motion and drive that underpins the melody and text. The pattern of the composition—a unison melody, modulation to the 3rd of the scale in the minor, a moving bass line underneath—is also the same as the tune THORNBURY for "Thy Hand, O God, Has Guided."

[80] Colin Gibson writes that Erena-Murray's hymns "are distinguished by their inclusive language and their innovative use of Maori, their bold appropriation of secular terms, and their original poetic imagery drawn from nature and domestic life; but equally by the directness with which they confront contemporary issues." Colin Gibson, "Shirley Erena Murray," in *Canterbury Dictionary of Hymnology*, accessed July 25, 2018, https://hymnology-hymnsam-co-uk.myaccess.library.utoronto.ca/s/shirley-erena-murray?q=erena%20murray

[81] Colin Gibson, "Lift High the Cross (New Zealand Version)," in *Canterbury Dictionary of Hymnology*, accessed July 25, 2018, https://hymnology-hymnsam-co-uk.myaccess.

eloquent—and arguably subversive—verses, the original chorus rings out with Nicholson's triumphant music contradicting the poetry in her verses and evoking the "other" words which seem to lurk underneath.

A process of unsanitizing "Lift High the Cross," even in Erena Murray's rewrite, reveals the perpetuation and pervasiveness of coloniality in music. Her bold final verse—"Worlds to be born and children yet to be, come, take up this song into eternity"—leave the singer (this singer, at least) wondering which song is to be sung into eternity. I cannot sing "lift high the cross" without remembering those other words.

Unbleaching: The Pervasiveness of Hymnic Coloniality

Like the political, economic, and socio-cultural contexts in which they lived, the Victorians encompassed a multilayered, interwoven texture of complex relationships and people groups. For instance, there were significant socio-cultural differences between the urban and rural poor and the elite and working classes, and among the growing pool of labouring classes fed by industrialization throughout Britain. These differences also played out along denominational lines with many among the working classes being nonconformist. As the century progressed, the middle class was increasingly the centre of political and social power, and it was chiefly Church of England.

The militaristic, monarchical, triumphalist, xenophobic, racist, imperialist texts we have just examined—written it must also be noted in unabashedly patriarchal language—were certainly not the only views represented in hymnody in nineteenth-century Britain. Pastoral hymns were written which responded to the challenging and diverse circumstances in which ordinary people found themselves in the nineteenth century, with a "pastoral sensitivity ... and their consciousness of the many lives worn down by tiredness and cares."[82] Topics included: death, including of children; the family, including especially an idolization of the (middle-class) family home; sickness; and weariness/rest, especially among the working

---

library.utoronto.ca/l/lift-high-the-cross,-the-love-of-christ-proclaim?q=Lift%20high%20the%20cross,%20the%20love%20of%20Christ%20proclaim.

[82] Bradley, *Abide with Me*, 122.

classes.[83] As expected, the complexity of these Victorian social conditions and structures, including denominational differences, were also exported to the colonies.

Initial missionary impulses were dominated by Methodist and other nonconformist denominations. But as the century wore on, Anglicans went beyond the simple establishment of a colonial church in colonial outposts like Canada toward a more evangelical emphasis as is evidenced by their support for the Society for the Propagation of the Gospel, the London Missionary Societies, and the Oxford and Cambridge Missionary Societies.[84] Porter rightly argues that "there were no simple connections between this religious [missionary] expansion and a specifically British influence and Empire overseas."[85] Certainly, the web of interconnections was complex. However, he also argues that "missionary thinking was profoundly egalitarian ... [that] 'race' was immaterial," and that government institutions and the church were not intertwined in the common goals of Christianizing and civilizing.[86] These assertions fly in the face of reality. For example, the recent experience of the Truth and Reconciliation process in Canada affirmed that racially-based cultural genocide under the mission inspired mantle of Christianizing and "civilizing" was in fact actualized in the partnership between the church and the state in the establishment of Canadian Residential Schools.[87]

A detailed analysis of the breadth of themes in Victorian hymns, including how they were determined along class and denominational lines and how these in turn were exported to the colonies is beyond the scope of this chapter.[88] But let us consider three categories that will serve to

---

[83] See Bradley's chapter on the topic: "Tell me the old, old story: Themes in Victorian hymns." Ibid., 108–39. He also writes about a theological shift "from atonement to incarnation" and toward the Christ of faith and the Jesus of history, and pedagogically toward "instruction rather than conversion." Ibid., 109–10.

[84] Porter, "Religion, Missionary Enthusiasm, and Empire."

[85] Ibid., 229.

[86] Ibid.

[87] Truth and Reconciliation Commission of Canada, "Reports of the Truth and Reconciliation Commission," 2105. Accessed May 3, 2018, http://nctr.ca/reports.php

[88] For example, more "emotional" texts and music, in the tradition of the Wesleys were associated with nonconformists and more "objective," abstract texts and music with Anglicanism, especially of the high church variety. "High" and "low" church in contemporary usage refers to Anglo-Catholic and Evangelical strains of Anglicanism. Historically, those dubbed high Anglicans were opposed to Puritanism and became associated with the Oxford movement. Low Anglicans "placed great emphasis on preaching, personal piety and the authority of scripture" and were closer in liturgical style and theological approach to

illustrate the pervasiveness of coloniality. First, biblical literalism was more or less universal and all-pervasive, especially at the beginning of the nineteenth century. Hymns, as versified versions of biblical stories and theological aspirations, shared in that literalism and its power. The conferring of "dominion" over the animal and vegetable kingdoms was easily extended, as we have already seen, into a territorial imperative and justification for a divinely sanctioned dominion over the lands of the earth and its peoples.

Second, the trope of the servant/master which became increasingly prevalent in Victorian cultural expressions, including hymnody, illustrates how a kind of submissive theology can undergird textual coloniality in hymns. It was reinforced by the idolization of the family, along middle-class lines, which sentimentalized ideas of domesticity, characterizing normative relations between men and women. Evident in novels from the middle of the century (in the Brontes and early Dickens, for instance), this trope is reflected in hymns in the servant/master relations invoked between the individual believer and Jesus, Jesus and God, and the congregation and God, and has implications for the relationship between the pastor and the church congregation as well. Victorian attitudes about domesticity were instrumental in shaping colonial societies, including Canada.[89] For instance, Wendy Fletcher explicitly connects Victorian notions about gender to British ethnicity and to the Church of England in Canada; "Anglicanism in the modern era modelled its understanding of gender roles on the values and mores of Victorian England ... what we might call the 'gender project' of Canadian Anglicanism was fundamentally a colonial inheritance of British origin ... features of what we might call Victorian era British ethnicity."[90]

Interestingly, the submissive theology associated with the master/servant trope is often found in hymns by Victorian women hymn writers. For

nonconformist traditions. Anglican Church of Canada, "'High' and 'Low' Church," in *Frequently Asked Questions,* accessed January 21, 2017, http://www.anglican.ca/ask/faq/high-low-church/

[89] To recap from Chap. 3, "white" women not only served their husbands, but also the colonial project of Christianizing the nation, as they became breeders and bearers of culture. Racialized women and men also served the colonial project, but in a clearly understood hierarchy in which they were lower down the ladder.

[90] Wendy Fletcher, "Canadian Anglicanism and Ethnicity," in *Christianity and Ethnicity in Canada,* ed. Paul Bramadat and David Seljak (Toronto: University of Toronto Press, 2008), 154.

example, Francis Havergal [1836–1879] said "that her favourite name for Christ was Master because 'it implies rule and submission, and that is what love craves. Men may feel differently but a true woman's submission is inseparable from deep love.'"[91] This kind of submissive theology reinscribed colonial roles which were/are "steeped with the notion of submission, meekness and docility, proposed as the way of Jesus."[92] In "Take My Life and Let it Be," for instance, Havergal articulates a sacrifice of her whole life, her very self. In verses two to five, she gradually consigns each of her body parts in turn to the service of God, her "king"—her hands, feet, voice, lips—and then her other possessions and attributes—silver and gold, will, heart, and love. The last two verses epitomize the submissive stance of the hymn as the author completely submits to her Lord: "Take my will and make it Thine,/It shall be no longer mine./Take my heart, it is Thine own,/It shall be Thy royal throne" (verse five) and "Take my love, my Lord, I pour/At Thy feet its treasure store./Take myself and I will be/Ever, only, all for Thee" (verse six).[93]

Third, let us briefly examine a few contestatory voices who, though they expressed opposition to the status quo, nevertheless could not escape the reaches of coloniality.[94] Responding to the political, economic, and social circumstances of the times, these hymn writers agitated for a more inclusive society in which the values of the Gospel, as they saw them,

[91] Moffat and Patrick, eds., *The Handbook to the Church Hymnary*, London: Oxford University Press, 1927, 365, cited in Bradley, *Abide with Me*, 92. I note that the notion that "a woman's submission is inseparable from deep love" could certainly be understood as a form of internalized coloniality, or at the very least, patriarchy.

[92] Jagessar and Burns, *Christian Worship*, 55. Jagessar and Burns are writing about what they view as the problematic submissive theology in the hymns of Charles Wesley.

[93] Frances Havergal, "Take My Life and Let It Be," accessed January 4, 2018, https://hymnary.org/text/take_my_life_and_let_it_be. Study of the master/servant trope and its implications in relation to coloniality warrants future attention, which could include—though it may be anachronistic to suggest it—an examination of gender issues, including the exclusively male language used to describe God and humanity.

[94] Hymns in this section are drawn from my research into a song collection called *Awake and Sing! Songs for Singing Democracy*. Barbara Cass and Helen Freeman, eds., *Awake and Sing! Songs for Singing Democracy* (Toronto: Fellowship for a Christian Social Order, 1941). The FSCO was a Canadian organization which was active in the 1930s in the fight against the rise of fascism and sought to call the churches back to their true vocation, the cultivating of solidarity with the exploited and oppressed. It had an enormous influence on shaping Canadian polity, including universal healthcare and welfare, among other things. Essays by leaders of the FSCO were published as *Towards the Christian Revolution* edited by R.B.Y. Scott and Gregory Vlastos, (Chicago: Willet, Clark and Co, 1936).

included things such as pacifism, an end to racial discrimination, women's suffrage, and socialist values. They called the churches to live up to the gospel and to embrace a theological vision of the all-inclusive reign of God's radical love, in which peace reigns, slavery (both literal and metaphoric) is abolished, and workers are glorified.[95] For example, written just after the Victorian era, G. A. Studdert-Kennedy's [1883–1929] "When Thro the Whirl of Wheels," evokes a reign of God as incarnated in the labour of the worker. Verse three reads: "When in the depths the patient miner striving,/feels in his arms the vigour of the Lord,/strikes for a kingdom and his King's arriving,/holding his pick more splendid than the sword."[96]

Texts like this one certainly represent fissures in the hegemony of hymnic coloniality. Yet, even in many of these hymns there is an imperial residue. They evoke a longing for a different kind of British Empire to be sure, along more egalitarian and socialist lines, but they nonetheless long for a British Empire. That is the nature of coloniality. It is in the air! It is difficult if not impossible to get outside of it. Consider William Blake's [1757–1827] Jerusalem, for example. His poem, a critique of the "dark Satanic Mills" of the Industrial Revolution, nevertheless imagines Jerusalem being built on "England's green and pleasant lands."[97] Similarly, in "These Things Shall Be: A Loftier Race," John Addington Symonds [1840–1893] envisions a "loftier race" aspiring to arts in a "loftier mold," with "mightier music." This loftier race is committed to freedom and knowledge, peace and the arts, but the question of how it is loftier than which "other" is unaddressed. Here, a vision of humanity united to make

---

[95] These voices also included hymn writers from the USA from politically and culturally progressive circles; several of these hymns from found their way into the corpus of Victorian hymnody. See Bradley's Chapter 7: "'Hold the fort for I am coming': American Imports and Gospel Songs" in Bradley, *Abide with Me*. To choose just one example, Fireside poet, John Greenleaf Whittier's [1807–92] "O Brother Man, Fold to Thy Heart Thy Brother," evokes the eschatological vision of God's all-inclusive reign of radical love. Cass and Freeman, *Awake and Sing! Songs for Singing Democracy*, 37.

[96] Ibid., 31. The palpable, imminent vision of the God's realm is perhaps no more clearly expressed than in African-American James Weldon Johnson's [1871–1938] "Lift Every Voice and Sing," written in 1899, with music composed by his brother, in which the striving for the God's kin-dom is achieved through praxis in the very action of singing. Johnson's text is also an example of the subaltern/marginalized singing back against empire, to which we shall return in subsequent chapters.

[97] William Blake, "And Did Those Feet in Ancient Time," accessed January 4, 2018, https://hymnary.org/text/and_did_those_feet_in_ancient_time

the world better is a strong central image. In verse three of the original six verse hymn, the "pulse of one fraternity" is said to throb in every heart and brain: "Nation with nation, land with land,/Inarmed shall live as comrades free;/In every heart and brain shall throb/The pulse of one fraternity."[98] Certainly the pacifist, egalitarian, socialist-inspired values imagined in these hymns offer an alternative vision of society and a fissure over and against the more prevalent imperialist language of mainstream Victorian hymnody. Still, the emphasis on fraternity and nationhood is strongly reminiscent of "Jesus Shall Reign," "Arise, O Church of England," and "Lift High the Cross," in their expansionist and universalizing vision of evangelizing/Christianizing the world. Unbleaching these hymns entails confronting their incipient coloniality.

Unmasking: Musical Coloniality in Hymns

As we saw briefly in "Lift High the Cross," the forces that bolstered the British Empire and the colonial project were also at play in hymn composition. On one hand, these forces had a role in hierarchizing a more elite musical style over those which were more popular. On the other, they subsumed all Victorian hymnody to firmly establish the Victorian hymn in general as *the* benchmark for hymn composition. Let us consider these dynamics.

When texts began to be paired with and fixed to particular tunes in *Hymns Ancient and Modern*, cementing an association between the two, British composers turned their talents toward the task of writing tunes. Paul Westermeyer notes, for instance, that *Hymns Ancient and Modern* "left an indelible mark in its pairings of texts and tunes, which became unbreakable throughout the English-speaking world." Prior to this point, texts were sung to a limited pool of tunes.[99] The resulting proliferation of hymn tunes contributed to the general explosion of hymnody we have been examining and was nothing short of a major cultural shift.

The style of tunes varied greatly. Tunes in the more popular genre proved to be singable and durable, with a "particular aptness to the words

[98] John Addington Symonds, "These Things Shall Be a Loftier Race," accessed July 25, 2018, http://www.traditionalmusic.co.uk/hymn-lyrics/these_things_shall_be_a_loftier_race.htm

[99] Paul Westermeyer, *Te Deum: The Church and Music* (Minneapolis, MI: Augsburg Fortress, 1998), 279.

to which they are set," but many were (and are) criticized for their "vulgarity, sentimentality, emotionalism," and even effeminacy.[100] These types of hymns were generally meant to be sung in four-part harmony, often with lush chromatic settings and were strongly influenced by the popular part song and parlour ballad styles of the day.[101] They were associated with "lower" denominational contexts—nonconformists and low Anglicans who had nonconformist inclinations.

This criticism belies a snobbery against popular music styles and in favour of serious, rugged, majestic, "dignified" tunes typical of serious music composers at the end of the nineteenth and early twentieth centuries. It also exposes a classist and gendered bias against stereotypically feminine qualities of the more popular styles and toward the more masculinist approaches of later composers. Lush hymn settings were composed by the likes of Ralph Vaughan Williams [1872–1958], who was staunchly critical of his predecessors precisely for what he and others viewed as a sentimentality and vulgarity.[102] Vaughan Williams epitomized a kind of musical climax of a triumphant tenor typical of hymn writing in the late Victorian era with his majestic tune SINE NOMINE (which was published immediately after Victoria's reign in 1906).[103]

This preference for elite music rather than popular music reveals a haughtiness and pretension on the part of those schooled in European art music which is still operative. Composers like Vaughan Williams and Hubert Parry [1848–1918], composer of JERUSALEM, are regarded as the best in the tradition.[104] This tension between elite rather than popular music was also exported throughout the British Empire. For instance, it

---

[100] Bradley, *Abide with Me*, 163, 202.

[101] Bradley writes that those "well-schooled in setting drawing-room ballads also produced good hymn tunes. ... [since] they [both] require a close attention and sensitivity to the words, and especially to their mood and flow, and the ability to provide a strong and fresh melody which is eminently singable and yet does not grow stale with repeated use." Ibid., 165.

[102] Ibid., 222–25.

[103] Vaughan Williams was a strong advocate of congregational singing with unison melodies. His attitude is epitomized in the following: "the average congregation likes fine melody when it can get it, but it is apt to be undiscriminating, and will often take to bad melody when good is not forthcoming." See Vaughan Williams's Introduction to the *English Hymnal* of 1906 in: Music, *Hymnology*, 171.

[104] For instance, eminent church music scholar Eric Routley writes that "the overstatement we find in both kinds of music—the verbose anthem-hymn of Methodism and the succulent hymns and anthems of the second-flight Victorian Anglican composers—is an indication of

was present in the controversy surrounding the production of the first United Church of Canada hymn book, *The Hymnary*. Certainly, the musical/liturgical tensions between the denominations that had formed the United Church were evident in the pull between the more Presbyterian metrical psalms and Wesleyan texts and tunes. But there was an outcry because the proposed draft "almost completely ignored the gospel song tradition," the more "populist spirit of evangelical Congregationalism."[105] "Charges of elitism were levelled" and in the end the gospel section was the most popular, though it was "inserted at the eleventh hour to appease the populist hue and cry."[106] Having inherited the colonial prejudice against hymns written in more popular styles, gospel hymns were seen as inferior in theology, sensibility, and craft.

There remains substantial disagreement as to which hymns ought to rise to the top, which are the "better" hymns. Still, despite this internal hierarchy within Victorian hymnody, the fact remains that Victorian hymns in general continue to predominate in the hymnic canons in English-speaking contexts throughout the world. The influence of Victorian hymnic sensibilities, as diverse and complex as they are, reached back in time as well as forward. These sensibilities changed the way chant and pre-Victorian hymns were sung by arranging them in a Victorian style in four parts, with metered poetry, to be accompanied by organ in the harmonic language of the Victorian era. They also established these benchmarks for "good hymn writing" into the future. Congregational singing advocate Alice Parker notes how the former tendency to "modernize" a tune "locks it into a nineteenth-century harmonic framework where chromaticism and modulation are a way of life."[107] It propagated hymnic standards, embodying a kind of musical coloniality, which reached back to before the Victorian era and which still has a grip on what congregations sing today, promoting certain ideas of "good" hymns along Victorian lines, whether they are from the more popular or more highbrow traditions. This musical coloniality in hymns is part of the larger phenomenon of musicoloniality to which we now turn.

---

failure on the part of the artist." Eric Routley, *Church Music and the Christian Faith* (Carol Stream, IL: Agape, 1978), 86.

[105] William S. Kervin, ed., *Ordered Liberty: Readings in the History of United Church Worship* (Toronto: United Church Publishing House, 2011), 34–35.

[106] Ibid.

[107] Alice Parker, *Melodious Accord: Good Singing in Church* (Chicago: Liturgy Training Publications, 1991), 69.

MUSICOLONIALITY

In its most basic sense, musicoloniality refers to how the fundamental structures of and discourses about music-making became determined and defined by Europe, with European "art" music being understood as *the* superior mode. Musicoloniality also helps describe the ways in which music itself became an instrument for the colonization of peoples, knowledges, sounds, bodies, and so on. There are a number of factors that contribute to the broader phenomenon of musicoloniality from a musicological point of view. Let us consider four. To begin with, music production in Europe was dominated by an overarching "serious-music ideology" or "classical-music ideology." Tia DeNora argues that serious-music ideology hinges on the construction of the myth of the creative genius.[108] This myth privileges musical ability, virtuosity, and the European art music canon over and against people making music together in community and against repertoires that fall outside the canon. As we have seen, this emphasis on individual artistic creation is illustrated in the decision to include individual compositional copyright information in the 1916 edition of *Hymns Ancient and Modern.*

In a similar vein, Timothy Taylor writes that what he calls "'classical musical ideology' ... has as its two foundational tenets the concepts of 'genius' and 'masterpiece,' two concepts that arose in their present form in the first half of the nineteenth century."[109] Serious- or classical-music ideology also emphasized transcendence in music which in turn reinforced the perceived acultural, ahistorical nature of the creative genius, and of music generally, as what Richard Wagner called "absolute music."[110] All of these factors in serious- or classical-music ideology coalesced to establish the superiority of Western European art music over and against "other" musics both in European contexts and beyond.[111]

---

[108] De Nora connects the development of the canon of European Art Music (and its serious music ideology) with the ideology of genius in the person of Ludwig Van Beethoven, through the construction of his persona in the Vienna of the 1790s. Tia DeNora, *Beethoven and the Construction of Genius: Musical Politics in Vienna, 1792–180* (Oakland, CA: University of California Press, 1995), 35.

[109] Timothy D. Taylor, *Beyond Exoticism: Western Music and the World* (Durham, NC: Duke University Press, 2007), 3.

[110] Absolute music, a term coined by Richard Wagner [1813–83], was "seen as timeless, universal, transcendent, the product of individual genius." Richards, *Imperialism and Music*, 4.

[111] Taylor, *Beyond Exoticism.*

Second, as musicologist Susan McClary has shown, gendered language was inscribed in musical theory in notions like masculine and feminine cadence endings and the masculine and feminine themes/subjects of the sonata-allegro form. She also notes that this phenomenon was part of the musicological claim to "supremacy in European classical music."[112] McClary's primary contribution has been to scrutinize musicology with a feminist optic by interrogating the very language of musical theory for its sexism, noting, along the way, connections to other gaps in scholarship that have occluded issues of class, race, and ethnicity. Along these lines, Timothy Taylor appreciates and extends McClary's argument when he writes that:

> McClary's conception of heterosexual male desire, to the extent that we can situate it historically and culturally, could be put to other uses in the representation of ethnic and racial Others as well as women … [her] characterization of tonality as a musical structuring of heterosexual male desire thus needs to be understood with the added valence of expanding European colonialism and all the ideologies of otherness that came with it.[113]

All in all, her important contribution marked a paradigm shift in ethno/musicological thinking by redefining "European art music as [a particular] cultural practice;" historicizing it; and taking seriously issues concerned with the body and emotions, among other things.[114]

Indeed, McClary's insights help us to unmask how gendering was used in the dismissal of more popular-style Victorian hymn compositions—both text and music—as sentimental, emotional and effeminate. Indeed, this gendering of hymns is related to the sentimental portrayal of Victorian

[112] Susan McClary, *Feminine Endings: Music, Gender, and Sexuality* (Minneapolis, MN: University of Minnesota Press, 2002), 57. In her critical engagement with Bizet's *Carmen* she also notes that "several issues other than gender are engaged and brought to violent–if equivocal–closure in the opera, most notably the perceived 'threats' of the racial Other and of popular culture" (63). Ultimately, McClary notes that Don José does kill Carmen—the "colonial, non-white, non-Christian, lower-class female character," as a result of his "mind/body crisis" (66).

[113] Taylor, *Beyond Exoticism*, 29.

[114] McClary, *Feminine Endings*, xvi, xvii. In the forward to her 2002 edition of *Feminine Endings*, she sets her work in the context of similar shifts in the humanities represented by new criticism in literature, sociology, politics, and art history. She also explains how her work, along with the work of others in musicology who were challenging the status quo, was derogatorily described as "new musicology" by its detractors. Ibid., ix–xx.

(middle-class) domesticity. As we have seen, hymns that were understood to be powerful (read "masculine") continue to hold sway in the hymnic canon, representing the "best" of Victorian hymnody and a benchmark for composing "good" hymns. My comments on these hymns are in no way meant to diminish the experience of singing them or to undervalue them. I am simply pointing out the ways in which they have been used to reinforce coloniality.

Third is the concept of tonality. Tonality, according to Taylor is predicated on the notion that the "tonic—the 'home' or main key—came into being through its opposition to the 'nontonic.'" He argues that "early modern epistemology made a place for an idea and its negation; in music, this is the construction of a tonic key and its defining opposite nontonic."[115] Taylor proposes that tonality entails a teleological progression and spatialized conquest. He argues that it contains the notion of a "distant Other … that can be used to assert western European superiority over 'primitives' whose cultures do not seem to possess a similar concept of progress, or who are later thought to be far behind in a progressive march toward industrial and scientific modernity."[116] Tonality thus suggests a progression forward to the same end or telos as an assertion of European superiority, represented harmonically by the tonic or home key. Even when a harmonic movement deviates away from the tonal centre—and though the movement could be understood as circular since it moves through a chord progression in the harmonic cycle of fifths—it progresses eventually back to the tonal—and symbolic—centre most often by means of its strongest relative, the "dominant" chord (on the fifth degree of the scale). The feminized and racialized "other" is brought under the "control," both emotional and psychological, as well as physiological, of the gendered (male) tonality of the tonic, a musical dynamic that is also evident in hymnic sensibilities of the Victorian age in hymns by Vaughan Williams, Parry, and others, as we have seen.

In my opinion, Taylor does not sufficiently wrestle with the fact that the "other" of this tonic-dominant relationship is called the "dominant." It signifies, in the dominant-tonic, V-I, or "perfect" cadence, a strong relationship and masculine ending, to borrow from McClary. Perhaps it would be more fruitful to think of the notion of dominant as the key and chord most closely related to the tonic or home key. The dominant and

---

[115] Taylor, *Beyond Exoticism*, 27.
[116] Ibid., 28.

tonic together thus make the "strongest" cadence, a "perfect" cadence, a kind of relational power centre. The next key relationship in the circle of fifths is with the "subdominant" key and chord on the fourth degree of the scale, which is sounded in the plagal or IV-I cadence, and is understood to be a gentler ending and, interestingly, the "Amen" cadence. There is rich possibility here to further explore the histories and ideologies behind how scales and keys are articulated along the lines of power relationships in musical theory and how such terminology may influence how music is understood and experienced as a result.

Related to tonality, and along the lines of Edward Said's deconstruction of orientalization and otherization, is our fourth factor—exoticism. Taylor notes that the "term 'exoticism' in its standard musicological usage tends to cover up and gloss over the varieties of treatments of otherness in the last few hundred years."[117] He connects this ideological move to the rise of European supremacy in its imperial appetites, along the lines of decolonial scholars, writing that a "new conception of otherness was one result of the colonial encounter, and a crucial factor in the rise of modernity itself."[118] He explains that it "facilitated a concept of spatialization in music that provided for centers and margins, both geographically and psychologically, as margins that were 'natural, inevitable, stable, just as Europeans naturalized their selfhood vis-á-vis non-European Others.'"[119]

Taylor's effort to expose colonialism in musical practices and discourses contributes to the growing body of work in musicology and ethnomusicology which is concerned with prior overly-abstract and positivist approaches. These approaches problematize the study of music as an absolute art form riven from the socio-cultural and historical circumstances which bore it. Indeed, the very formation of ethnomusicology as a discipline was the result of forces of orientalization or otherization in the academy. The move to conflate the two disciplines as an ethno/musicology has the effect of ethnicizing Western European musics by way of

---

[117] Ibid., 9. See also Edward Said, *Orientalism* (New York, London: Penguin Classics, 2003). In *Orientalism*, Said was specifically referring to the relation between the Oriental and the Orientalist (i.e., the person observing/studying/objectifying/othering the Oriental). The rise of Orientalism as a field of study is part and parcel of the entrenchment of coloniality. Hymns like "O'er the Gloomy Hills of Darkness" and "Jesus Shall Reign," along with "From Greenland's Icy Mountains" (which we will analyze in the next chapter), could be fruitfully interrogated using Said's critical optic.

[118] Taylor, *Beyond Exoticism*, 9.

[119] Ibid., 25, 28.

nomenclature, disrupting their position of superiority above all "other" musics, and unsettling the neat divide between musicology and ethnomusicology or, to borrow Stuart Hall's dictum, "the West and the rest."[120]

Fifth, and finally, musicians, including especially church musicians, are trained to emulate a serious- or classical-music ideology. In my own training as a pianist, for instance, I was taught that my musical inheritance could be traced in a direct line back to Beethoven.[121] I was also trained to believe that each of my performances ought to be the most important, the most beautiful, the most transcendent. This training was in line with notions that first arose in the

> late eighteenth and early nineteenth centuries, and as a direct result of the rise of Romanticism, [in which] theorists began to argue that music was a fine art, transcending its surroundings and reaching to the sublime. Musicians were heroically individualist artists; their music free of outside associations. This doctrine was the ultimate expression of 'Art for Art's Sake' and the celebration of the solitary genius, alone and complete unto himself. It has continued to hold powerful sway.[122]

Such training encouraged me to believe in the superiority of my training, my talent (though I also never felt I could measure up!), and the kind of music I played. To counteract this kind of approach, Christopher Small advocates for a wholesale reconceptualization of music itself, insisting that the word "music" is a misnomer and recasting "music" as the verb "to music." He reorients discourses about music(king) toward what people do and hear (musicking), rather than toward music as an object—what is seen in the score and what is debated in discourses about music. At the centre of his argument is an interrogation of the "privileging of Western classical music above all other musics."[123]

---

[120] Stuart Hall, "The West and the Rest: Discourse and Power," in *Formations of Modernity*, ed. Stuart Hall and Bram Gieben (Cambridge, U.K.: Polity Press in association with the Open University, 1992).

[121] The line was traced from Beethoven to Carl Czerny (1791–1857) to Theodor Leschetizky (1830–1915) to Vasily Safonov (1852–1918) to Rosina Lhevinne (1880–1976) and to my teacher Claire Hoeffler.

[122] Richards, *Imperialism and Music*, 4.

[123] Christopher Small, *Musicking: The Meanings of Performing and Listening* (Hanover, NH: Wesleyan University Press, 1998). 3. Small challenges the fundamental paradigm of the discipline of musicology which "has always been cultivated by the holders of power, first in Europe and later in its colonies and outposts," with its Euro-centric gaze which consigned

Of course, the drive and passion to pursue artistic excellence in and of itself is not necessarily a bad thing and is not limited to Western European contexts. But doing so at the expense of "other" musics, peoples, and cultures perpetuates an attitude of Eurocentric superiority. It eclipses other musical traditions—folk, popular, and "world" musics—and instills a coloniality of music. In addition to factors already described, it also emphasizes: the "canon" of Western European Art Music and its superiority; the written score over and against orality and the actual music making itself (i.e., music becomes what is on the page and not what we hear); the importance of athletic and technically masterful performances rather than participation; and a disregard for the meaning-making aspect of music.

Choralism: An Example of Musicoloniality[124]

A closer scrutiny of choral activity in nineteenth-century Britain and its colonies exposes the ubiquity of musicoloniality. For instance, in South Africa in the late nineteenth century, at that time a British colony, choirs were celebrated for their remarkable potential to control what was called the "black peril" by (re)forming choir members—through what Grant Olwage calls "choralism"—into docile and obedient bodies as part of a collective body which was also docile and obedient.[125] He argues that singing was used first as a civilizing technique by the British at home, as internalized colonialism among the working classes and poor. It was then exported to the colonies and used among colonized (often non-White) subjects abroad, including in South Africa and Canada.[126] In my experience,

---

the study of any other music to the fields of ethnomusicology and popular music studies (220). He also notes that the idea of musicking destabilizes the elitist orientation of musicology, with its focus on Western European Art Music, by being *"des*criptive, not *pre*scriptive" and insisting on an inclusive and relational vision of musicking which allows for various modes of participation (9).

[124] Portions of the material on choralism have been revised from presentations at the World Forum on Theology and Liberation, Montréal, August, 2016, and the American Academy of Religion, San Antonio, November 2016 which were subsequently published as: Becca Whitla, "The Colonizing Power of Song," in *Decoloniality and Justice: Theological Perspectives*, ed. Jean-François Roussel (Saõ Leopoldo: Oikos: World Forum on Theology and Liberation, 2018).

[125] Olwage, "Discipline and Choralism," 138.

[126] Ibid., 33. See also Deanna Yerichuk, "Grappling with inclusion: Ethnocultural diversity and socio-musical experiences in Common Thread Community Chorus of Toronto," *International Journal of Community Music* 8, No. 3 (2015), 217–231.

a complex system of techniques that could be associated with "choralism" is still widely used: choral structures tend to be hierarchical with top-down, disciplinary leadership styles; repertoire often consists of European art music, or arrangements of "other" (colonized) musics in European art music styles; wide vocal ranges tend to be highly gendered and classically oriented most often in four-part harmony (soprano, alto, tenor, and bass); and vocal training is highly controlled.[127]

Canadian contexts were not immune to "choralism." For example, the photograph below, from the "Barnabas Indian Residential School at Onion Lake in Saskatchewan" shows bodies disciplined into the conformity of Anglican dress, Anglican ritual, and Anglican music. Music was part of the curriculum at residential schools, with a strong emphasis on hymn singing. Students "were given a constant drilling in English, and spent much of their time memorizing and reciting religious texts and hymns."[128] Christian ritual, including hymn singing, was used as a way to discipline and "civilize" the children as an intentional means to eradicate their sacred Indigenous practices and Indigenous culture.[129] The positive benefits of singing notwithstanding, learning to sing in this manner operated as part of the civilizing and colonizing machine/apparatus which sought to turn aboriginal children into white children in Canadian residential schools, part of the cultural-genocidal project of "taking the Indian out of the child."[130] In my view, it was a sinful use of singing because it violated the *imago dei* which resides in Indigenous peoples. In the words

[127] In choralism, the pseudo-scientific discipline of vocal physiology ensured that an emphasis was placed on controlling the body. Olwage writes that "any wrong tone—shouting, forcing, penetrating—was immediately audible" and that "soft-singing was a microdisciplinary technique. ... through which the voice was normalized as bourgeois, [and] through which the anachronistic 'rough voice' was remade." Olwage, "Discipline and Choralism," 33.

[128] Truth and Reconciliation Commission of Canada, *Canada's Residential Schools: The History, Part 1, Origins to 1939, The Final Report of the Truth and Reconciliation Commission of Canada. Volume 1* (Canada, 2015), accessed July 28, 2018, http://nctr.ca/assets/reports/Final%20Reports/Volume_1_History_Part_1_English_Web.pdf, 86.

[129] Sarah Johnson unpacks the complex roles of ritual in Residential Schools in Sarah Kathleen Johnson, "On Our Knees: Christian Ritual in Residential Schools and the Truth and Reconciliation Commission of Canada," in *Studies in Religion* 47, no. 1 (2018), 3–24.

[130] This phrase is attributed to Sir John A. MacDonald, the first Prime Minister of Canada. Sean Fine, "Chief Justice Says Canada Attempted 'Cultural Genocide' on Aboriginals," *The Globe and Mail* (2016), accessed July 25, 2018, http://www.theglobeandmail.com/news/national/chief-justice-says-canada-attempted-cultural-genocide-on-aboriginals/article24688854/

of former Anglican Primate, Archbishop Michael Peers, "we tried to remake you in our image, taking from you your language and the signs of your sidentity" (Fig. 4.1).[131]

Examples of liberating choral activity abound, in the civil rights movement in the USA or in the anti-Apartheid movement in South Africa, for instance, or in my own experience with community choirs in Toronto.[132] In addition, not all choral singing, even in residential schools, was necessarily experienced as oppressive. Nonetheless, it is clear that choirs could be and were used as a means to "civilize," assimilate, and "Christianize"

Fig. 4.1 Photograph of the Rev. H. Ellis and his choir at St. Barnabas Indian Residential School, Onion Lake, Saskatchewan, 1935, The General Synod Archives, Anglican Church of Canada, Photographs: P75-103-S6-156

[131] Anglican Church of Canada, "Apology to Native People," accessed April 22, 2020, http://www.anglican.ca/wp-content/uploads/2011/06/Apology-English.pdf

[132] For example, the same Tonic Sol-Fa system that was used to control the British working-class and the black South African population chorally in the nineteenth century was flipped to become a subversive and liberating choral expression among the dissenting voices of the anti-Apartheid struggle, giving voice to hope and strength in the face of violence and death. When asked what kept people going in the Apartheid era, Salvation Army Captain Timothy Mobaso said "we kept singing." Polokwane Choral Society, *We Keep Singing*, Compact Disk Recording (Toronto: Deep Down Productions, 2004).

"others," to establish European sovereignty, beyond a shadow of a doubt, by replicating the English choir model. Instilled in practitioners of Western European Art Music and disseminated broadly, this example of musicoloniality was part of the complex web of cultural factors and elements used in the colonization/assimilation of various people groups (Fig. 4.2).

This outline of a few critical engagements in ethno/musicology points to the broader phenomenon of musicoloniality. As we have seen, a complex web of factors—serious-music ideology, gendering, tonality, exoticism, musical training, and choralism, among others—coalesced to hierarchize European art music at the top, above other musics, including folk and popular music from Europe as well as other musics or "ethnic" musics from around the world.

We have also seen that British hymns were imposed as the benchmark for superior cultural and religious expression, marginalizing, silencing, and even erasing other practices and expressions and insisting upon a culturally and racially superior British identity, all justified as a means to

Fig. 4.2 Photograph, Girl's Choir of St. John's Indian Residential School in Wabasca, Alberta, 1963, The General Synod Archives, Anglican Church of Canada, Photographs: P7528-95

Christianize "others." Over time, these hymns have become mainstays of many congregational repertoires, cloaking congregational singing practices with distinctly Victorian—and imperial—sensibilities and theologies.

To be clear, I am not proposing that all hymns from nineteenth-century Britain be expunged from congregational repertoires. On the other hand, liberating congregational singing does require an interrogation of the texts, music, forms, and practices associated with the hymns we sing. This confronting and deconstructing of coloniality in hymnody is part of the process of liberating congregational singing.

At the same time, and though coloniality permeates much of our hymn singing even today, this musical inheritance also did entail a renewal and revitalization of congregational singing. The people were being encouraged to sing in church, joining their voices together in a range of collective expressions before God and with each other, expressions which could still carve a space for the irruption of divine disclosure and potentially even for our own liberating action, despite the pervasiveness of coloniality. There remains a troubling incommensurability between the elitist cultural drive to get people singing and the actual singing of the people, as well as between the people's singing and the forces of Empire which were always and already at work. But even hymns and songs which appear to embody empire beyond the shadow of a doubt can be ambiguous. There is no question that some hymns may be unsalvageable. But others, clothed in the garments of European hymnody, including Victorian poetry and musical vocabulary from the "high-noon" of the British Empire, are sometimes inverted (flipped) by those who are oppressed and can become instruments of resistance, or at the very least theological sources of forbearance, strength, and hope.[133]

BIBLIOGRAPHY

Anglican Church of Canada. 1998. *Common Praise: The Hymnal of the Anglican Church of Canada.* Toronto: Anglican Church of Canada.
———. Apology to Native People. https://www.anglican.ca/wp-content/uploads/2011/06/Apology-English.pdf. Accessed 22 Apr 2020.
———. 'High' and 'Low' Church. *Frequently Asked Questions.* http://www.anglican.ca/ask/faq/high-low-church/. Accessed 21 Jan 2017.

[133] I borrow the term "high noon" from Jagessar and Burns, *Christian Worship*, 57.

Arnold, Richard, ed. 2004. *English Hymns of the Nineteenth Century: An Anthology*. New York: Peter Lang.

Baring-Gould, Sabine. Onward Christian Soldiers. http://www.hymnary.org/text/onward_christian_soldiers_marching_as. Accessed 25 July 2018.

Bell, John L. 2007. *The Singing Thing Too: Enabling Congregations to Sing*. Chicago: GIA Publications Inc.

Blake, William. And Did Those Feet in Ancient Time. https://hymnary.org/text/and_did_those_feet_in_ancient_time. Accessed 4 Jan 2018.

Bohlman, Philip V. 1997. World Musics and World Religions: Whose World? In *Enchanting Powers: Music in the World's Religions*, ed. Lawrence E. Sullivan, 61–90. Cambridge, MA: Distributed by Harvard University Press for the Harvard University Center for the Study of World Religions.

Bonner, Carey, ed. 1905. *The Sunday School Hymnary: A Twentieth Century Hymnal for Young People*. London: Novello and Company. https://archive.org/details/sundayschoolhym00nsgoog. Accessed 5 May 2018.

Bradley, Ian. 1997. *Abide with Me: The World of Victorian Hymns*. London: SCM Press.

Carey, Hilary M. 2011. Colonial Missionary Societies: Nonconformists. In *God's Empire: Religion and Colonialism in the British World, c.1801–1908*, 177–205. Oxford: Oxford University Press.

Cass, Barbara, and Helen Freeman, eds. 1941. *Awake and Sing! Songs for Singing Democracy*. Toronto: Fellowship for a Christian Social Order.

Collins, Ace. 2003. Onward Christian Soldiers. In *Stories Behind the Hymns That Inspire America: Songs That Unite Our Nation*, ed. Ace Collins, 147–154. Grand Rapids: Zondervan.

DeNora, Tia. 1995. *Beethoven and the Construction of Genius: Musical Politics in Vienna, 1792–180*. Oakland: University of California Press.

Fine, Sean. 2016. Chief Justice Says Canada Attempted 'Cultural Genocide' on Aboriginals. *The Globe and Mail*. http://www.theglobeandmail.com/news/national/chief-justice-says-canada-attempted-cultural-genocide-on-aboriginals/article24688854/. Accessed 25 July 2018.

Fletcher, Wendy. 2008. Canadian Anglicanism and Ethnicity. In *Christianity and Ethnicity in Canada*, ed. Paul Bramadat and David Seljak, 138–167. Toronto: University of Toronto Press.

Gibson, Colin. Lift High the Cross (New Zealand Version). In *Canterbury Dictionary of Hymnology*. https://hymnology-hymnsam-co-uk.myaccess.library.utoronto.ca/l/lift-high-the-cross,-the-love-of-christ-proclaim?q=Lift%20high%20the%20cross,%20the%20love%20of%20Christ%20proclaim. Accessed 25 July 2018.

———. Shirley Erena Murray. In *Canterbury Dictionary of Hymnology*. https://hymnology-hymnsam-co-uk.myaccess.library.utoronto.ca/s/shirley-erena-murray?q=erena%20murray. Accessed 25 July 2018.

Hall, Stuart. 1992. The West and the Rest: Discourse and Power. In *Formations of Modernity*, ed. Stuart Hall and Bram Gieben, 185–227. Cambridge: Polity Press in association with the Open University.

———. 1996. Introduction: Who Needs Identity? In *Questions of Cultural Identity*, ed. Stuart Hall and Paul Du Gay, 1–17. London: Sage Publications Ltd.

Hawn, C. Michael. Jesus Shall Reign. http://www.umcdiscipleship.org/resources/history-of-hymns-jesus-shall-reign. Accessed 25 July 2018.

———. Lift High the Cross. In *History of Hymns*. http://www.umcdiscipleship.org/resources/history-of-hymns-lift-high-the-cross. Accessed 25 July 2018.

Jagessar, Michael N., and Stephen Burns. 2011. *Christian Worship: Postcolonial Perspectives*. Sheffield: Equinox.

Johnson, Sarah Kathleen. 2018. On Our Knees: Christian Ritual in Residential Schools and the Truth and Reconciliation Commission of Canada. *Studies in Religion* 47 (1): 3–24.

Kervin, William S., ed. 2011. *Ordered Liberty: Readings in the History of United Church Worship*. Toronto: United Church Publishing House.

Kimbrough, S.T. 1995. Charles Wesley and the Poor. In *The Portion of the Poor: Good News to the Poor in the Wesleyan Tradition*, ed. M. Douglas Meeks, 147–190. Nashville: Kingswood Books.

Kitchin, George W. Lift High the Cross. http://www.oremus.org/hymnal/l/l118.html. Accessed 10 Jan 2017.

Kolodziej, Benjamin A. 2004. Isaac Watts, the Wesleys, and the Evolution of 18th-Century English Congregational Song. *Methodist History* 42 (4): 236–248.

Lemire, Devon. A Historiographical Survey of Literacy in Britain Between 1780 and 1830. *Constellations*. https://ejournals.library.ualberta.ca/index.php/constellations/article/viewFile/18862/14652. Accessed 18 Jan 2017.

Maldonado-Torres, Nelson. 2007. On the Coloniality of Being. *Cultural Studies* 21 (2–3): 240–270. http://www.decolonialtranslation.com/english/maldonado-on-the-coloniality-of-being.pdf. Accessed 25 July 2018.

McClary, Susan. 2002. *Feminine Endings: Music, Gender, and Sexuality*. Minneapolis: University of Minnesota Press.

Medina, Néstor. 2018. *Christianity, Empire and the Spirit: (Re)Configuring Faith and the Cultural*. Leiden: Brill.

Monk, W.H., ed. 1861. *Hymns Ancient and Modern for the Use in the Services of the Church with Accompanying Tunes*. London: Novello and Co.

Monk, W.H., and C. Steggall, eds. 1916. *Hymns Ancient and Modern for the Use in the Services of the Church with Accompanying Tunes*. London: William Clowes and Sons, Ltd.

National Archives. 'Chartists,' Power, Politics & Protest: The Growth of Political Rights in Britain in the 19th Century. http://www.nationalarchives.gov.uk/education/politics/g7/. Accessed 18 Jan 2017.

———. The Struggle for Democracy: Getting the Vote. http://www.nationalar-chives.gov.uk/pathways/citizenship/struggle_democracy/getting_vote.htm. Accessed 18 Jan 2017.

Olwage, Grant. 2005. Discipline and Choralism: The Birth of Musical Colonialism. In *Music, Power, and Politics*, ed. Annie J. Randall, 25–46. New York: Routledge.

Parker, Alice. 1991. *Melodious Accord: Good Singing in Church*. Chicago: Liturgy Training Publications.

Polokwane Choral Society. 2004. *We Keep Singing*. Compact Disc Recording. Toronto: Deep Down Productions.

Porter, Andrew. 1989a. Introduction: Britain and the Empire in the Nineteenth Century. In *The Oxford History of the British Empire, Volume 3, the Nineteenth Century*, ed. Andrew Porter, 1–28. Oxford: Oxford University Press.

———. 1989b. Religion, Missionary Enthusiasm, and Empire. In *The Oxford History of the British Empire, Volume 3, the Nineteenth Century*, ed. Andrew Porter, 222–246. Oxford: Oxford University Press.

Rainbow, Bernarr. 1970. *The Choral Revival in the Anglican Church (1839–1872)*. London: Barrie & Jenkins.

Richards, Jeffrey. 2002. *Imperialism and Music: Britain, 1876–1953*. Manchester: Manchester University Press.

Routley, Eric. 1978. *Church Music and the Christian Faith*. Carol Stream: Agape.

Said, Edward. 2003. *Orientalism*. New York/London: Penguin Classics.

Scott, R.B.Y., and Gregory Vlastos, eds. 1936. *Towards the Christian Revolution*. Chicago: Willet, Clark and Co.

Shea, Victor, and William Whitla, eds. 2015. Part One: Contexts. In *Victorian Literature: An Anthology*, ed. Victor She and Willian Whitla, 19–179. Oxford: Wiley Blackwell.

———, eds. Victoria Literature: Supplementary Web Resource. http://high-eredbcs.wiley.com/legacy/college/shea/140518874X/supp/web_contexts.pdf, page 215–215. Accessed 23 Mar 2017.

Small, Christopher. 1998. *Musicking: The Meanings of Performing and Listening*. Hanover: Wesleyan University Press.

Symonds, John Addington. These Things Shall Be a Loftier Race. http://www.traditionalmusic.co.uk/hymn-lyrics/these_things_shall_be_a_loftier_race.htm. Accessed 25 July 2018.

Taylor, Timothy D. 2007. *Beyond Exoticism: Western Music and the World*. Durham: Duke University Press.

The Episcopal Church. Tracts for the Times. http://www.episcopalchurch.org/library/glossary/tracts-times. Accessed 3 Jan 2017.

Truth and Reconciliation Commission of Canada. 2015a. Canada's Residential Schools: The History, Part 1, Origins to 1939. In *The Final Report of the Truth and Reconciliation Commission of Canada. Volume 1*. Canada. http://nctr.ca/

assets/reports/Final%20Reports/Volume_1_History_Part_1_English_Web.
pdf. Accessed 28 July 2018.

———. 2015b. Reports of the Truth and Reconciliation Commission. http://
nctr.ca/reports.php. Accessed 3 May 2018.

United Church of Canada. 1996. *Voices United: The Hymn and Worship Book of the United Church of Canada.* Etobicoke: United Church Publishing House.

Watson, J.R. 1997. *The English Hymn: A Critical and Historical Study.* Oxford: Oxford University Press.

Watts, Isaac. Jesus Shall Reign. http://www.cyberhymnal.org/htm/j/s/jsreign.htm. Accessed 25 July 2018.

Westermeyer, Paul. 1998. *Te Deum: The Church and Music.* Minneapolis: Augsburg Fortress.

Whitla, Becca. 2018. The Colonizing Power of Song. In *Decoloniality and Justice: Theological Perspectives,* ed. Jean-François Roussel, 43–50. Saõ Leopoldo: Oikos: World Forum on Theology and Liberation.

———. 2019. Hymnody in Missionary Lands: A Decolonial Critique. In *Hymns and Hymnody: Historical and Theological Introductions, Volume 2: From Catholic Europe to Protestant Europe,* ed. Benjamin K. Forrest, Mark A. Lamport and Vernon M. Whaley, 285–302. Eugene: Wipf and Stock.

Wikipedia. The Historiography of the British Empire. https://en.wikipedia.org/wiki/Historiography_of_the_British_Empire. Accessed 3 Mar 2017.

William & H. James Co. Cast-Iron-Mechanical Banks Sambo Mechanical Bank. https://www.historytoy.com/william-h-james-co-cast-iron-toy-sambo-mechanical-bank. Accessed 18 Mar 2017.

Young, Robert J.C. 1995. *Colonial Desire: Hybridity in Theory, Culture and Race.* London/New York: Routledge.

CHAPTER 5

Singing Back Against Empire (or the Subaltern Sings Back)

Introduction

A facile unmasking of empire at the heart of hymnody needs to be prob-lematized because when empire sings, "other" voices which sing-along may actually be subverting the imperial agenda. This "flipping" of hymns can take the form of a subtle act of subversion or a direct act of defiance. Two case studies of hymns in the canon—"From Greenland's Icy Mountains" and "O store Gud" or "How Great Thou Art"—illuminate these issues and reveal how meaning-making is experienced in different contexts. Songs, like people, are bound and conditioned by specific social, historical, political, and cultural contexts with specific identity/identities and associations. Because they are socially constructed, we can speak of songs as having a character, lineage, and history, and changing through their relationships to "other" peoples, contexts, cultures, and traditions; they are polysemic. A third example, "El Espíritu de Dios," is not part of the "canon" of European hymnody but emerged from an oral community context in Latin America. Its journey beyond its context of origin reveals the complex matrix of coloniality that is at play.

© The Author(s) 2020
B. Whitla, *Liberation, (De)Coloniality, and Liturgical Practices,*
New Approaches to Religion and Power,
https://doi.org/10.1007/978-3-030-52636-8_5

BEYOND SUBJECTIVITY

Before we turn to our analysis of these hymns, the issue of subjectivity requires some further comment; the "who" that sings remains important. Both post and decolonial discourses offer insights, but decolonial thinking helps to assess the insights and categories of postcolonial theories, rather than the other way around. More specifically, a decolonial approach emphasizes the importance of intersubjectivity and collective agency in congregational singing rather than the deconstructive approach of postcolonial scholars which emphasizes subjectivity. It entails a commitment to affirm identity/ies and empower agency, both personal and collective, and to emphasize singing "with" each other and from our experience.

As we have seen, many hymns sung in the Victorian era—and which were exported with colonialism—embodied a coloniality of music which mis/represented "others" in hymns like William Williams's "O'er the Gloomy Hills of Darkness." This mis/representation is framed, according to Edward Said, "by a whole set of forces that brought the Orient [and the other "others" of Europe's colonial conquests in Africa and the Americas] into Western learning, Western consciousness, and later, Western empire" and which ultimately enabled "a white middle-class Westerner [who] believes it his human prerogative not only to manage the non-white world but also to own it, just because by definition 'it' is not quite as human as 'we' are."[1] It so often led beyond misrepresentation or misrecognition of an-other to ignoring, erasing, eradicating, or disposing of the "other." Ongoing legacies of colonialism are felt, in the Canadian context and elsewhere, and continue to negatively impact many peoples' daily lives—for example, the conquests of and genocides against Indigenous people groups; the legacy of plantation slavery; the ongoing mistreatment of and discrimination against immigrants, especially racialized immigrants; the marginalization of other "others" like women, LGBTQ+ communities and those stigmatized as disabled.

---

[1] Edward Said, *Orientalism* (New York, London: Penguin Classics, 2003), 203, 108. To recap, verse one reads: "Let the Indian, let the Negro,/Let the rude Barbarian see/That divine and glorious Conquest/Once obtain'd on Calvary;/Let the Gospel, Loud resound from Pole to Pole." Jeffrey Richards, *Imperialism and Music: Britain 1876–1953* (Manchester: Manchester University Press, 2002), 388.

Decolonial scholar Enrique Dussel describes the resulting eclipse of the "other" as a "negated alterity," an erasure of the humanity of the Other.[2] He demonstrates how the European subject—the "I-conquer" which is constitutive of Descartes' dictum *cogito ergo sum*—defined himself as discoverer, conquistador, and colonizer by "controlling, conquering, and violating the Other."[3] By challenging the Cartesian principle, Dussel strikes at the heart of European epistemology, shaking and dislocating its very foundations. Unlike Gayatri Chakravorty Spivak who documents how the female subaltern loses her agency and cannot speak,[4] Dussel refutes the self-claimed superiority of Europe and reclaims agency beyond European paradigms by re-telling the story of conquest from the perspective of the vanquished civilizations of the Americas.[5]

Postcolonial scholars do also recognize the problems inherent in notions of subjectivity, particularly in the European proclivity to objectify the "other," as noted in Said and Spivak. For Homi Bhabha, the colonial subject, discursively constructed under the colonial gaze and vulnerable to colonial power, is always ambivalent. It resists fixity, always being both split and doubled, known and disavowed, absent and present.[6] This ambivalence, as Bhabha describes it, helps to deconstruct some of the dynamics of congregational singing, as we shall soon see, especially through his notion of mimicry.

Yet, postcolonial scholars tend to remain circumscribed by their own emphasis on the subject and its relation to the colonial gaze. Analysis still revolves around the (white, male) European subject of *cogito ergo sum*. This subject—which is present in the subject/object binary at the heart of Said's unmasking of orientalism, in Spivak's subaltern subject who cannot speak, and in the ambivalent subject of Bhabha's colonial discourse—is the same subject of the "I conquer" identified by Dussel. In fact, Dussel actually argues that "I conquer" made "I think" possible and identifies

---

[2] Enrique Dussel, *The Invention of the Americas: Eclipse of "the Other" and the Myth of Modernity* (New York: The Continuum Publishing Company, 1995), 66.

[3] Ibid., 12.

[4] Gayatri Chakravorty Spivak, "Can the Subaltern Speak," *Marxism and the Interpretation of Cultures*, ed. Cary Nelson and Lawrence Grossberg (Urbana, IL: University of Illinois Press, 1988).

[5] Dussel, *The Invention of the Americas*. As we saw in Chap. 3, decolonial scholars also interrogate the very notion of subjectivity as a Eurocentric construct.

[6] Homi K. Bhabha, *The Location of Culture* (New York: Routledge, 1994), 96, 107.

Columbus as the first modern man.[7] He writes that the "experience not only of discovery, but especially of the conquest, is *essential* to the constitution of the modern ego, not only as a subjectivity, but as subjectivity that takes itself to be the center or end of history"[8] He continues, "the "I-Conquistador" forms the protohistory of Cartesian *ego cogito* and constitutes its own subjectivity as will-to-power."[9] Because of the association of "subject" and "subjectivity" with this *particular* European subject and its (his) individualistic, capitalistic, colonialist/imperialist proclivities of the last 500 years, "subject" and "subjectivity" as categories are tangled up with notions of power, and especially the power-over, of the European subject.[10] Walter Mignolo advocates a reorientation which dislocates this Cartesian formulation—"I am where I think" rather than "I think therefore I am."[11] For him,

> 'I am where I think' highlights the 'I'—not a 'new' universal 'I,' but an 'I' that dwells in the border and has been marked by the colonial wound. The 'I's' of the colonial wound, which dwells in the borders, provide the liberating energy from which border thinking emerges, in rebellion, all over the planet, beyond the red carpet of the spirit's road from East to West.[12]

In other words, Mignolo's notion of "I am where I think" reframes discourses of coloniality in active modes of resistance, drawing on alternative paradigms in which agency is affirmed and expressed.

It also emphasizes the *where* I think as epistemologically central. This praxical approach draws on lived concrete historically and geographically located reality to be the source for reflection, rather than abstract

---

[7] Dussel, *The Invention of the Americas*, 28.

[8] Ibid., 25.

[9] Ibid., 43.

[10] It is precisely these problems with notions of subjectivity that have led decolonial scholars and others to problematize subjectivity itself, preferring instead to reframe human relations in terms of intersubjectivity or resistant subjectivity. See, for example, Maria Lugones, "Methodological Notes Toward a Decolonial Feminism," in *Decolonizing Epistemologies: Latina/o Theology and Philosophy*, ed. Ada María Isasi-Díaz and Eduardo Mendieta (New York: Fordham University Press, 2012), 68–86.

[11] Walter D. Mignolo, *Local Histories/Global Designs: Coloniality, Subaltern Knowledge, and Border Thinking* (Princeton: Princeton University Press, 2000), xiv.

[12] Ibid. We return to the notion of border thinking below.

discourses about subjectivity.[13] It also resonates with Indigenous traditions throughout the Americas which insist on acknowledging and being grateful for the land and all the beings which inhabit the land.[14] The insistence on prioritizing context and agency over subjectivity enlivens an analysis of congregational singing because it considers what people do, where they're coming from, and how they relate to each other rather than who they are as fixed subjects.[15] The three hymns to be considered in this chapter will therefore be analyzed from the perspective of how they have been embraced by particular communities in particular places and sung by particular people as a means to express their faith and their identity.

MIMICRY AND EPISTEMIC DISOBEDIENCE IN "FROM GREENLAND'S ICY MOUNTAINS"[16]

I am sitting in the office of Bishop Mark MacDonald, National Indigenous Bishop for the Anglican Church of Canada. We have conversations from time to time about hymns. We share a love of congregational singing. It is a sunny June day. The light illuminates the art and sacred objects that adorn the room, softening the hard angles of the modern high-rise building that houses the national offices of the Church. I am feeling a little shy and awkward, surprised and delighted that Mark has once again set aside the time to talk with me. I tell him how I stumbled on "From Greenland's Icy Mountains" in the hymnal that was used in Residential Schools. "I know that hymn," he says

---

[13] We return to criticisms of Latin American decolonial scholars for being overly abstract in Chap. 7.

[14] For instance, Arturo Escobar writes about *sentipensar* (thinking-feeling) as the art of living learned in relation to the particular land which is inhabited by Afro-descendent Columbians as they think-feel with the territories, cultures, and knowledges (*conocimientos*) of their peoples. Arturo Escobar, *Sentipensar con la Tierra: Nuevas Lecturas Sobre Desarrollo, Territorio y Diferencia* (Medellín, Colombia: Ediciones UNAULA, 2014).

[15] As noted in Chap. 3, agency is also a concern for postcolonial scholars, especially Bhabha, but their focus tends to prioritize the reframing of issues of subjectivity by deconstructing the colonial gaze. Interestingly, Mignolo notes Bhabha's emphasis on "agency over representation." See Ibid., 119.

[16] Portions of the material in this section have been revised from presentations at the World Forum on Theology and Liberation, Montréal, August, 2016, and the American Academy of Religion, San Antonio, November 2016 which were subsequently published as: Becca Whitla, "The Colonizing Power of Song," in *Decoloniality and Justice: Theological Perspectives*, ed. Jean-Francios Roussel (Sao Leopoldo: Oikos: World Forum on Theology and Liberation, 2018).

and pulls out his well-worn copy of Psalms and Hymns in the Language of the Cree Indians. "How could it have been sung in Indigenous communities?" I ask, incredulous. At his puzzled look, I show him the English text. "That's bad," he says. "Yes," I say, "it's bad."

There is no doubt that "From Greenland's Icy Mountains" epitomizes the ideology of a superior salvific Christianity from the peak of the British Empire. It was penned reportedly in less than an hour by Anglican priest Reginald Heber in 1819 for an event to support the Society for the Propagation of the Gospel in Foreign Parts and went on to become one of the most popular missionary hymns of all time. Heber, who wrote 57 other hymns including "Holy, Holy, Holy, Lord God Almighty," became Bishop of Calcutta in 1823, where he was known for his advocacy with the East India Company on behalf of Indians who were overlooked for higher ranking positions within the company.[17] Yet the hymn still displays the colonialist values of his era, however noble his intentions were, and in spite of the vocational commitment he was to make to serve in India. In fact, John Julian reports that Heber had originally written "The savage in his blindness," at the beginning of verse two. It was later changed to "The heathen in his blindness."[18] This dualistic trope of the inferior "blind" heathen/savage and the superior European/English Christian, divinely ordained to rescue "others," is epitomized in verse three: "Can we, whose souls are lighted with wisdom from on high." The hymn is clothed in the evangelistic language of the Victorian era that envisions a global, triumphant Christianity. It perpetuates concepts like the civilizing mission which was used to justify European sovereignty over lands and peoples on a massive scale, in this case by establishing the domination of the British Empire in as many parts of the world as possible. In short, it embodies coloniality.

An easy target for those who want to expose coloniality in the heart of congregational singing, this hymn was no doubt forcibly imposed on conquered peoples in multiple contexts. For this reason, and in the wake of

---

[17] Derrick Hughes, *Bishop Sahib: A Life of Reginald Heber* (West Sussex: Churchman Publishing Ltd., 1986), 170–72. In fact, Hughes' biography of Heber reveals that he was a man of integrity who, in his short life, increasingly sought to advocate on behalf of those "less fortunate." Not afraid to keep his own council and make difficult administrative decisions, he nevertheless also did so within the structures of his church and his family of "old fashioned Tories, High Churchman, [who were] unsympathetic to radical doctrines or to any challenge to legitimate authority," 8.

[18] Greg Scheer, "From Greenland's Icy Mountains," in *Hymnary.Org*, accessed February 4, 2017, http://hymnary.org/text/from_greenlands_icy_mountains

the Truth and Reconciliation process and its exposure of cultural genocide in Canadian residential schools, I struggled to understand how "From Greenland's Icy Mountains" can remain among the hymns that Mark MacDonald turns to in his well-thumbed volume. But our understanding is reduced when we limit it to one single interpretation—as only oppressive and exploitative.

To that end, postcolonial scholar Homi Bhabha's concept of mimicry offers another way to understand the repetition of colonial hymns as potentially subversive. He goes beyond the popular understanding of mimicry as imitation for the purpose of satire, ridicule, or critique. For Bhabha, mimicry is a complex, ambivalent and "menacing" process, a double articulation, "at once resemblance and menace."[19] Imposed on the colonized, it can be flipped to become a threat or "menace" because the repetition can be "potentially and strategically an insurgent counter-appeal," a resistance against colonialism.[20] The singing colonized subjects can be understood to subvert the colonial agenda through their mimicry, just by being who they are through the very agency of their singing—which is, in his words, *almost the same but not quite"* or more sinisterly, in racialized terms, *almost the same but not white."*[21]

Mimicry thus offers a way to understand the repetition of colonial hymns as potentially subversive. It can be read as a threat to what Bhabha calls "normalized knowledges and disciplinary powers"; a challenge to hegemonic discourses or "the very discourse of civility"—the insidious "sly civility" at the heart of coloniality; and a challenge to colonial authority at its origins.[22] Yet it is already and always also circumscribed by the colonial discourses and the colonial gaze which define it. In other words, because of the fetters of the colonial gaze, interpreting hymns using Bhabha's notion of mimicry therefore limits the way we can understand what's going on.

However, the singing of "From Greenland's Icy Mountains" can be interpreted as more than the mere repetition of coloniality—more than an expression of mimicry. When sung by Indigenous communities, for instance, it goes beyond being "almost the same but not quite," in many ways becoming an entirely different hymn which embodies a subversive

---

[19] Bhabha, *The Location of Culture*, 123.
[20] Ibid., 122, 130.
[21] Ibid., 122, 128.
[22] Ibid., 136.

way of singing. Consider the fact that people never really accept imposition totally willingly or passively. Oppressed communities often outrightly invert or flip these colonial tools so that they become instruments of resistance, refusing the role of passive victims.

In Anglo North America, the hymn was translated into multiple Indigenous languages, including into Cree in the version that MacDonald knows. The hymn became something entirely different, as we shall soon see, despite the fact that missionaries were involved in translation and the tune was preserved to some extent. In other words, the power dynamics of colonization were certainly present, but the translation and the singing of the hymn embodied other ways of knowing outside the parameters of colonization and European modernity. It was sung, at least in part, outside the colonial gaze. The singing of the hymn thus both simultaneously resisted coloniality and embodied it, forming a kind of patchwork of musical relations to coloniality, however blurry the boundary between one and the other was, and despite the fact that the singing was not always necessarily self-aware or intentionally defiant.

Through translation, the original English meaning of "From Greenland's Icy Mountains" is flipped—from a triumphalist, expansionist vision of what was understood as a superior Christianity, with superior (European) Christians favoured with the task of evangelizing, into a vision which emphasizes a collaborative relationship between the Creator and all of humanity and focuses on living well in the here and now (Fig. 5.1).[23]

In verse one for instance, the line "They call us to deliver their land from error's chain" changes significantly in the Ojibwe translation, becoming "You who have heard us, have great mercy for that reason." In verse two, the production of an exotic other in the original version gives way to a humanizing affirmation of the people. In the original English, the vile heathen man is blind to the lavish kindness of God's gifts. But in the Ojibwe, "those who salute wood and stone live well; they are beautiful." Their beauty and living well is emphasized rather than the Eurocentric idea that they lack something because they are non-Christians. In this context God's mercy is described as the immediate and intimate act of a loving creator rather than as a remote, superior, beneficent mercy bestowed from on high.

---

[23] Michael McNally provides an excellent unpacking of the complexity of issues of translation, both in terms of text and culture. Michael McNally, *Ojibwe Singers: Hymns, Grief, and a Native Culture in Motion* (St. Paul, MN: Minnesota Historical Society Press, 2009).

From Greenland's Icy Mountains	Reginald Heber, 1819	
English Original	**Ojibwa Hymnal**	**Translation**
From Greenland=s icy mountains	Kiwedinong eyadjig,	Those who are in the North
From India=s coral strand,	Gaye >gu wabunong	And also in the East
Where Afric=s sunny fountains	Igiu endunukidjig	Those living there
Roll down their golden sand;	Iwidi kijateg,	There where it is hot
From many an ancient river,	Gaye patukizowad	And also those who harpoon
From many a palmy plain,	Palm inagawanjig,	[and those among] Palms that bend
They call us to deliver	Ki nundomigonanig	You who have heard us
Their land from error=s chain.	Che shawenimungwa	Have great mercy for that reason.
What though the spicy breezes	Anin su enabaduk	How they sleep
Blow soft o=er Ceylon=s isle;	Guanachiwuninig,	It is handsome/beautiful,
Though every prospect pleases,	Endunukiwad anind	Those who live there
And only man is vile:	Enamiasgog;	Those who would pray.
In vain with lavish kindness	Ano shawenimindwa;	Have mercy on them (?)
The gifts of God are strown;	Mino dunukiwad,	They live well there
The heathen in his blindness	O shugushkitanawa	They who salute
Bows down to wood and stone.	Mitig gaye asin.	Wood and also stone
Can we whose souls are lighted	Kinawind nebuakayung,	All of us who have wisdom,
With wisdom from on high;	Wayaseshkagoyung,	Who have light,
Can we to men benighted	Ki ga-shaguen=momin na	Will you be discouraged/afraid
The lamp of life deny?	Che widokageyung?	To help people?
Salvation, O salvation!	O bimadjiiwewin!	O restoration of *bimaadiziwin*
The joyful sound proclaim,	Mizi dibadjimon,	Tell the news everywhere,
Till each remotest nation	Nananj igo kakina	Until everyone
Has learnt Messiah=s Name.	Gi-minotumowad.	They have listened to you.
Waft, waft, ye winds, His story,	Nodin! sasueyasidon	Good wind! Scatter it
And you, ye waters, roll,	Iu minwadjimowin;	That good word;
Till like a sea of glory,	Mano su einashkag	Let it pierce through
It spreads from pole to pole:	Ta-iji-webaun,	In a certain way
Till o=er our ransomed nature,	Nananj igo Jesus Christ,	Until Jesus Christ,
The Lamb for sinners slain,	Au ga-nibotaged	That one who died for others
Redeemer, King, Creator,	Neyab aking duguishing,	Has reached/returned to that land,
In bliss returns to reign.	Che bi-ogimawid.	And come to be our boss here.

bimadjiiwewin: resuscitation, restoration, saving, or giving of life
from root *bimaadis* -- it lives, moves along

bimaadiziwin -- the recurring cycle of living things moving in relation
bimaadiziwin-bakwzhigan -- bread of *bimaadiziwin* (life)
anishinaabe bimaadiziwin -- AGood Life@, the ideal way of life that joins culture and nature
  (one missionary translates it as *savage life* because of attachment to a seasonal life-way)

**Re-translation into English from Ojibwe by the Late Larry Cloud Morgan
and Michael McNally. Used by permission.**

Fig. 5.1 Retranslation of "From Greenland's Icy Mountains"

The Ojibwe version of "From Greenland's Icy Mountains" could be described, following Walter Mignolo, as an act of epistemic disobedience, of "knowing, being, and doing decolonially," beyond the modern European epistemology of the English version, subversively expressing, affirming, and carrying Indigenous cultural ways.[24] Epistemic disobedience is part of a decolonial turn which seeks to de-link from the modern-colonial capitalist world-system. Mignolo says it involves "thinking in exteriority, in the spaces and time that the self-narrative of modernity invented as its outside to legitimize its own logic of coloniality … acts of epistemic disobedience are thus acts of resistance which are outside and resistant to ways of understanding 'modern' epistemology."[25]

Mark MacDonald affirms the importance of hymn singing as mode of resistance, as a way in which Indigenous language and culture were carried. He says that culture went underground through hymns.[26] MacDonald also says that the singing itself is just as important as the text. The slow fervent style of hymn singing in many Indigenous communities is appreciated and evaluated for its passionate commitment and expression rather than for the European valuing of technical proficiency and controlled vocal quality.

This kind of emphasis on passionate expression, read as a mode of epistemic disobedience, confronts and contests the "modern epistemology, which was able to subalternize other forms of knowledge, and build itself assuming a universal perspective of observation and a privileged locus of enunciation."[27] As a confrontational, contestatory posture it suggests fully engaged and self-aware senses of agency which reject the self-proclaimed and superior "rational" epistemology of Europe in favour of other (and otherized) nonrational and deeply contextual epistemologies exterior to

---

[24] Walter Mignolo, "Geopolitics of Sensing and Knowing: On (de)Coloniality, Border Thinking, and Epistemic Disobedience" (2011), 5, accessed July 25, 2018, http://eipcp. net/transversal/0112/mignolo/en

[25] Ibid., 7.

[26] Mark MacDonald, personal conversation with the author (Friday, June 10, 2016). Along with insights already noted by Indigenous scholars in Chap. 3, McDonald's insights about culture and other ways of knowing illustrate that "decolonial" discourses are certainly not limited to Latin American decolonial scholars. See also Martin Karen and Boora Mirraboopa, "Ways of Knowing, Being and Doing: A Theoretical Framework and Methods for Indigenous and Indigenist Re-Search," *Journal of Australian Studies* 27, no. 76 (2003): 203–14, accessed May 8, 2018, https://doi.org/10.1080/14443050309387838

[27] Walter D. Mignolo, *Local Histories*, 122.

the modern-colonial capitalist world-system.[28] The style of singing MacDonald refers to is this kind of exterior epistemology; it resists its own subalternization and affirms dignity and beauty on its own terms in the ways Indigenous communities sing. They make the hymn their own. It also epitomizes what some decolonial scholars have begun to describe as another way of feeling.[29]

Theologically speaking, MacDonald says that "underneath what we see and hear is a dynamic of life which is unveiled and released in singing."[30] He says that hymn singing enables a different cosmovision, including an eschatology which is defiant because it is present in the here and now through singing. The third verse actually emphasizes this alternative cosmovision in the text. In English, the focus is on bringing the light of the gospel, bringing salvation, to men who are "benighted"—or intellectually and morally ignorant. In contrast, the Ojibwe version encourages all who are wise to help people. There is no distinction here between some who are enlightened and "others" who are not. Rather, there is a sense that all people can be wise. Salvation is translated as *bimaadiziwin,* a term which can be understood to refer to heavenly life. But it also refers to the here and now, to "the good life, lived well in proper relationship to human and nonhuman persons."[31]

"From Greenland's Icy Mountains" is certainly an emblematic example of coloniality in hymns in its original English. Sung in its Ojibwe version by Indigenous communities, however, it expresses an epistemically disobedient stance which goes far beyond the ambivalence and "not quite-ness" of Bhabha's mimicry. It moves outside the colonial gaze and allows for the possibility of reconfiguring the way things are. It is also a song of resistance, subversive not only in the theology expressed but in the ways it is sung, with the emphasis placed on heart-felt passionate expressions. What I find most promising is that communities that sing this song (and other songs, for that matter) in Ojibwe (or in their native languages) are enacting their agency *outside* the strictures of Western European hymn singing. In doing so, they reject the dehumanizing legacy of colonization and model different avenues for existence.

---

[28] Ibid., 17.
[29] See, for example, Escobar, *Sentipensar con la Tierra.*
[30] MacDonald, personal conversation with the author.
[31] McNally, *Ojibwe Singers,* 61.

Beyond Hybridity

As we have just seen in the examination of "From Greenland's Icy Mountains," our texts, contexts, pretexts, and performance practices intermingle when we open up our voices and bodies to worship/pray together in song, just as our complex ethno/cultural, racialized, relational, and community/institutional/ecclesial identities also intermix. The stories and genealogies of songs, like those of people, shift in response and relation to their contexts. Like people's stories, the stories of songs can also be forgotten or misremembered. Also, the meanings of songs can change by being manipulated, in translation for instance, as we've just seen. One of the challenges is how to describe these complex processes of intermixing when songs—just like people's identities—change, coalesce, or even clash over time.

Hybridity is the ubiquitous English-language term generally used to describe the phenomenon of intermixture—whether between people, cultures, technology, or in the arts. Particularly pervasive in postcolonial discourses, and also common in discourses about music, hybridity debates have rich genealogies which, to put it very briefly, move between the history of the use of hybridity (originating in agriculture and used predominantly to describe physiological or biological intermixture), to cultural hybridity, to hybridity in language.[32] These discourses have enriched and problematized ways of understanding the complexity of human interaction, especially as proposed by postcolonial scholars, and particularly in the work of Homi Bhabha. They offer a rich critique of the ongoing cultural influence of colonial dynamics. Nevertheless, and despite its great insights, hybridity talk, as often as not, actually confounds and obscures the messy, extremely diverse, and specifically located reality of human intermixture, including in the songs we sing. Let us consider why in more detail.

For Bhabha, the term hybridity helps to chronicle the potentially subversive process of cultural interchange between colonized and colonizer,

---

[32] The enormous breadth of discussion on hybridity is beyond the scope of this study. Robert Young reminds us of the history of hybridity discourses in relation to human bodies and their racialization, colonization, and dehumanization. He also makes use of the work of semiotician Mikhail Bakhtin to articulate linguistic doublenesses inherent in concepts of hybridity (where something is simultaneously the same and different). Robert J.C. Young, "Hybridity and Diaspora" in *Colonial Desire: Hybridity in Theory, Culture and Race*, 1–26, (London, New York: Routledge, 1995).

across what he calls the cultural difference. It describes the double articulation of mimicry which we just explored. Mimicry—being the same and different, or "almost the same, but not quite"—is the affect, or expression, of hybridity for Bhabha.[33] "The difference that is almost nothing but not quite" quickly turns into the menace of "a difference that is almost total but not quite," he writes.[34] It thus articulates the complexity and menace of doubleness in colonial discourse and reverses the disavowal of the colonized by the colonizer "so that the violent dislocation of the act of colonization becomes the conditionality of colonial discourse."[35] It is, he argues, "not simply the violence of one powerful nation writing out the history of another (but a) contradictory utterance that ambivalently reinscribes, across differential power relations, both colonizer and colonized."[36] In other words, as much as the colonizer tried/tries to contain/control/dominate/circumscribe the colonized, the actual "colonial construction of the cultural (the site of the civilizing mission)" has embedded in its construction its own undoing, what Bhabha eventually claims as "an enunciatory present as a liberatory discursive strategy."[37]

Bhabha's insistence that this liberatory potential of the cultural difference, in which hybridity "enables a form of subversion, founded on the undecidability that turns the discursive conditions of dominance into the grounds of intervention," invites us to consider hybridity's efficacy as a descriptor for the project of liberating congregational singing.[38] We saw that the singing of "From Greenland's Icy Mountains" can be read in this way, as a mimetic utterance, as a kind of "hybrid" expression. Bhabha calls this possibility "a contingent, borderline experience [which] opens up *in-between* colonizer and colonized."[39] This borderline experience, this "metonymy of presence" is a "space of cultural and interpretive undecidability produced in the 'present' of the colonial moment," what he also articulates elsewhere as the Third Space.[40]

---

[33] Bhabha, *The Location of Culture*, 172.
[34] Ibid., 131.
[35] Ibid., 163.
[36] Ibid., 136.
[37] Ibid., 163, 256.
[38] Ibid., 160.
[39] Ibid., 295.
[40] Ibid., 164, 296. Bhabha writes that "the non-synchronous temporality of global and national cultures opens up a cultural space—a third space—where the negotiation of incommensurable differences creates a tension peculiar to borderline existences," 312.

However, we also saw that mimicry has its limits because it remains within the framework of European epistemologies and discourses. It does have a palpable connection to the reality of the interracial and intercultural mixing between human beings and its roots in violent practices of miscegenation by colonizers, embodying "the violent dislocation of the act of colonization."[41] Yet it also remains already and always circumscribed by the colonizing act and under the binary lens of the colonial gaze, wrought by the circumstances of the colonial encounter which it simultaneously resists. There is little room for what decolonial scholars articulate as another way of knowing, doing, being, or feeling. The *multiple* constitutive parts of intermixture do not necessarily fit neatly into the colonizer/colonized binary associated with articulations of hybridity. To put it concretely, the singing of "From Greenland's Icy Mountains" read through a hybrid lens is always understood in relation to the colonizing purpose of the original hymn, even in cases of resistant translation and defiant singing.

What is more, uses of the term hybridity, being the result of a complex series of intellectual analyses, have tended to remove it from the kind of specific and particular locations which it seeks to describe. As a result, especially in contemporary usage in which it has become increasingly popular and also hard to pin down, it tends to be ahistorical and overly abstract. I would argue that this increasingly amorphous and imprecise quality of hybridity-talk is also actually a symptom of its growing whiteness. Rooted in intellectual European structures and wrought under the colonial gaze, it has ironically become hemmed in by dominant Anglo Euro-North Atlantic forces because it relies on the epistemological language of modern enlightenment rationalism even though it hopes to unmask and interrogate these same forces. The use of hybridity-talk can thus become an example of bleaching and forgetting when the particularity of its constitutive parts is sanitized/white-washed. The violence of its origins is forgotten, rendering it less effective for the articulation of the complexity, messiness, violence, and multiplicity of the dynamics of human intermixture, including in singing.

In contrast, the countless other terms in languages other than English that are used to describe human intermixture, like Métis, *mestizaje, mestiçagem,* and *créolité,* for example, are historically rooted (and routed) in moments of colonization. As such, these terms reflect the concrete reality of their particular local contexts, which includes the violence of first

[41] Ibid., 163.

encounters between Europeans and those they sought to conquer/dominate as well as the subsequent multiple, and often violent, interchanges between various people groups and cultures.

Speaking about *mestizaje*, Néstor Medina notes that the term describes the joining of peoples and "subpeoples" with an emphasis placed on the "infection" by "inferior" others. As such he says that the term *mestizo* carries the stigma of inferiority, an internal schizophrenia, as well as a memory of empire and of the colonization of empire's "other."[42] The specific meanings of *mestizaje*, rising out of diverse intercultural continental American experiences of intermixture and interchange between Spanish, Indigenous, and African peoples, embody these particular histories. In other words, at its best it is not sanitized, abstract, or necessarily overly intellectual, but reflects the complex concrete reality and experience of the people groups involved.[43] The other terms listed above similarly describe particular peoples and histories. For instance, in the Canadian context, Métis refers to the intermixing between European (French) settlers and Indigenous peoples.[44]

Terms that emerge from the experience of particular people groups in relation to intermixing can certainly help unmask coloniality in song because they invite a range of perspectives between the colonized and the colonizer and contribute to multiple understandings of responses to colonization. As we saw in the example of "From Greenland's Icy Mountains," the song itself became unhinged from its intellectual and cultural tradition and reconfigured according to Indigenous knowledge and cultural ways which can in turn transform it into a locus of decolonial contestation. This shift could be described along the lines of intermixture. But, there is also

---

[42] Néstor Medina, Email correspondence with the author (28 May 2017).

[43] I do not mean to over-romanticize the term. As noted in Chap. 3, the use of *mestizaje* is not without problems. For instance, it has been coopted to describe national identity as *mestizo*—in México and Brazil, for instance. Moreover, it is not limited to use in the Americas. It has also been used in Indonesia and Africa, for example. (Néstor Medina, *Mestizaje: (Re) Mapping Race, Culture and Faith in Latina/o Catholicism* (Maryknoll, NY: Orbis Books, 2009), 112 and 113).

[44] In Canada, the term Métis is contested. While many claim to have some Indigenous ancestry, in Western Canada, the Métis Nation is understood to be the descendants of voyageurs (early explorers) and Indigenous women who settled in Manitoba and Saskatchewan and became a political force under the leadership of Louis Riel and others. Louis Riel was hanged for leading a rebellion against the government after numerous failed negotiations in 1885. Jean Teillet, *The North-West is Our Mother: The Story of Louis Riel's People, the Métis Nation* (Toronto: HarperCollins, 2019).

a risk inherent in borrowing the specific language from particular historically situated experiences (like *mestizaje* or Métis) to describe intermixture
in congregational singing, however insightful this language might be in
some cases. Its very specificity negates its effectiveness as a descriptor for
more general processes since the realities in each context involve different
dynamics and require different language.

In fact, the dynamics of intermixture between people(s), cultures, and
in song itself are always changing. There is a fluidity of boundaries between
cultures and between identities. This fluidity is always at play in congregational singing, both as the real bodies of our communities, marked as they
are by differences of race, gender, age, ability, and so on, intermingle, as
well as in the songs themselves since they also often represent cultural
multiplicity. In fact, songs and singing resist fixity, fluidly moving between
contexts with multiple meanings being experienced each time a particular
song is sung, even by the same person. Text, music, performance style, and
context coalesce in each iteration to make meaning for the singers at that
moment, inviting them into an experience of the Divine. By focusing on
process rather than product, on verb, rather than noun, and resonating
with the notion of syncopated movements between cultural spaces, the
complex dynamics of congregational singing can be more accurately articulated beyond the strictures of Western Europe. Rather than seeking fixed
descriptors of what is going on, fluid approaches allow us to articulate the
undeniable shifting that occurs, as we shall see by looking at the journey
of the hymn in the next section.

"*O STORE GUD*": THE MODULATIONS OF "HOW GREAT THOU ART"

*I am at the rehearsal of the H.E.R.E. (Hotel Employees and Restaurant
Employees) Local 75 Choir in Toronto, sometime in the year 2000. "How
Great Thou Art" is a favourite song choice, sung full-voiced and reveren-
tially, when members of the choir feel they need to "raise up a song" and lift
their spirits. In my mind's eye I can see choir members with their eyes closed,
hands beating out the rhythm of their hearts, as they belt out the chorus: "Then
sings my soul, my saviour God to Thee, how great Thou Art."*

*It is March 22, 2012. I am a student at the Seminario Evangélico de
Teología de Matanzas in Cuba. A beloved Cuban theologian and professor
from the seminary, Maestro René Castellanos Morente has just died at the*

age of 97. In the morning, the students gather around his body, which is adorned with flowers, to pray, sing, and comfort each other. At lunch I am asked to play for the funeral in the afternoon. Funerals in Cuba happen within twenty-four hours because they do not embalm the bodies. The chapel is packed. I am surprised by the three hymns we sing: Spanish translations of "Lord of the Dance," "What a Friend We Have in Jesus," and "How Great Thou Art." The latter is the Maestro's translation—"Cuán Grande Tú." The triumphant musical cadence becomes not only a celebration of the grandeur of creation but also a tribute to the Maestro and an expression of solidarity with each other.

"*O store Gud*" (O Great God), or as it is most commonly known in English, "How Great Thou Art," was written in 1885 by the Swedish poet Carl Gustav Boberg, and set, after the fact, to a Swedish folk tune.[45] The hymn text had two migration paths to the USA and into English. The first was with Swedish immigrants when, in 1925, it was translated by E. Gustav Johnson into English and published in the *Covenant Hymnal* in 1931. The other more circuitous path involved first a journey into German in 1907, translated by Manfred von Glehn in the hymnal *Blankenburger Lieder* as "*Wie gross bis Du*" (How Great You Are), and then into Russian in 1912 by I. S. Prokhanoff in the hymnal *Kimvali*. This version was discovered by English Salvation Army missionary Stuart Hine in the early 1930s, who encountered it in the Ukraine, memorized it, and sang it with his wife as they evangelized in the region. Hine was moved, like Boberg before him, by his own experiences of the awesomeness of God's creation and was inspired to pen his own English version, based on the Russian translation of the German version of Boberg's text. This English version was published in his Russian gospel magazine, *Grace and Peace* in 1949.[46] What follows is a textual analysis of various versions of this hymn.

Hine's version itself arrived via different pathways to Anglo North America in the mid-twentieth century. According to Tim Dowley, "Dr. J. Edwin Orr of Fuller Theological Seminary, California, heard a choir of

[45] See the appendix for full texts all of the versions referred to in this section. Kenneth Osbeck writes that Boberg "was surprised to hear the congregation sing his poem to the tune of an old Swedish melody." Kenneth W. Osbeck, *101 Hymn Stories: The Inspiring True Stories Behind 101 Favorite Hymns* (Grand Rapids: Kregal Publications, 1982), 99.

[46] This history can be found at Joy Bringer Ministries, "How Great Thou Art," accessed July 28, 2018, http://www.joy-bringer-ministries.org/hymns/hgta.pdf. See also Michael Hawn, "How Great Thou Art," accessed July 28, 2018, https://www.umcdiscipleship.org/resources/history-of-hymns-how-great-thou-art

Naga people [in Deolali, India] sing "How Great Thou Art" and took the
hymn back to America, where James Caldwell performed it at Stony Brook
Bible Conference, Long Island, in 1951."[47] Orr negotiated to have it pub-
lished through Manna Music.[48] Then in 1954, "Canadian bass-baritone
George Beverly Shea memorably sang "How Great Thou Art" at Billy
Graham's 1954 London Crusade."[49] It was also sung at the Toronto
Crusade of 1955 and was published when Graham collaborated with
Manna Music to make it widely available, free of charge.[50] From there, the
song continued to travel the world, translated into many languages.
Dowley notes that "Elvis Presley's second gospel album, recorded in
1966, was entitled *How Great Thou Art* and marked a milestone in his
career. Winning him the first of three Grammys, for the 'Best Sacred
Performance' … 'How Great Thou Art' was voted favourite hymn by
viewers of BBC television's perennially popular *Songs of Praise,* and a survey in the magazine *Christianity Today* in 2001 ranked it second only to
'Amazing Grace' as the all-time favourite hymn."[51]

This genealogy of "How Great Thou Art" illustrates again that a song,
like people, is susceptible to processes of migration and de-territorialization,
to what Homi Bhabha might call a kind of "unhomeliness."[52] When it
moved out of its context of origin, it was literally transformed in translation and interpretation and eventually transnationalized in its reach. Its
meaning shifted in relation to each new context which claimed it as its
own. This metamorphosis could be described along the lines of Bhabha's
mimicry as a hybrid expression, each iteration linguistically and culturally
transformed across the cultural difference. In what follows, we will touch
on this perspective, bearing in mind the limits of this approach insofar as
it tempts one to view these changes as abstract rather than localized, and

[47] Tim Dowley, "How Great Thou Art," in *Christian Music: A Global History* (Minneapolis:
Fortress Press, 2011), 218.
[48] Joy Bringer Ministries, "How Great Thou Art."
[49] Dowley, "How Great Thou Art," 218.
[50] Joy Bringer Ministries, "How Great Thou Art." The copyright of Hine's text is now
held by the Stuart Hine Trust CIO. USA print rights and all Canadian rights are administered by Hope Publishing Company. Proceeds are distributed to various organizations
throughout the world, especially those dedicated to Bible translations as well as mission
organizations supported by Stuart Hine during his lifetime. Scott Shorney, Vice President,
Hope Publishing Company, personal conversation with the author (Thursday, June
11, 2020).
[51] Dowley, "How Great Thou Art," 218.
[52] Bhabha, *The Location of Culture,* 16.

fixed rather than constantly changing. A detailed description of its pathways is also somewhat akin to the process of autobiographical narrative suggested in Chap. 3 and can therefore be unmasked and articulated drawing on notions like unbleaching and unforgetting to which we return shortly in this analysis. Finally, the song is implicated in the dynamics of a coloniality of music to which we now turn.

On one hand, it is very unlikely that an imperial agenda was part of Boberg's original intention in writing "O Great God"; the original nine-verse text celebrates the grandeur and beauty of creation and appreciates God's saving grace and accompaniment through life's struggles. Verse one of the original Swedish begins by praising the God of creation, evoking the image of feminine wisdom weaving the threads of life together: "How there [in the world], your wisdom weaves the threads of life," concluding with "and all creatures are fed at your table," an inclusive and creation-centered Eucharistic image.

On the other hand, the hymn was used as a mechanism for Christian proselytization, especially Hines's version, and it thus became associated with European and Anglo North American expansionism. His version uses arcane and triumphalist language which both distances the singer from the Divine and reinforces a hierarchical framework. Note the shift to the all-powerful, universal God in the last line of Hines's version: "Thy power throughout the universe displayed." The chorus of the original—"then the soul bursts out in sound of praising: O great God, O great God," following as it does on the Eucharistic imagery of all creatures being fed at God's table—has quite a different tone in Hine's voice, with his use of imperial English: "Then sings my soul, my Saviour God to thee: how great thou art, how great thou art."[53] The latter focuses more on the kind of distanced, superior God associated with European colonialism, through whom Christians become subjects invited into the imperial throne-room of the divine Emperor. As we have seen, this kind of "messianic and imperialistic universalism," which is evident in the Hine version throughout, has often included a notion of cultural and racial superiority.[54]

---

[53] See the appendix for the full text. © 1949, 1953 The Stuart Hine Trust CIO. USA print rights and all Canadian rights administered by Hope Publishing Company. All rights reserved. Used by permission. See also: Hope Publishing Company, "How Great Thou Art," accessed June 19, 2020, https://www.hopepublishing.com/find-hymns-hw/hw4894.aspx

[54] Letty M. Russell, J. Shannon Clarkson, and Kate M. Ott, eds., *Just Hospitality: God's Welcome in a World of Difference* (Louisville, KY: Westminster John Knox Press, 2009), 42.

Moreover, Boberg's extensively creation-oriented text is de-emphasized in the Hine version. In Boberg's original, verse two is a cosmic vision of the heavens, the sun, and the moon; verse three focuses on the elements of thunder, lightning, and rain; and verse four on the summer breezes, flowers, birds, and pine trees. While the first two verses of Hine's four-verse version do celebrate creation, the language is more triumphalist and arcane.[55] Furthermore, Hine's verse three emphasizes a strong theology of atonement that reduces human nature to its essential sinfulness. The singing subject, the "I" in the song, marvels that God sacrifices his Son by sending him to the cross to bleed and die to redeem the sinner/singer, ending with an emphasis on submission and meekness: "then I shall bow in humble adoration."

In sum, "How Great Thou Art" in Hine's version evinces a coloniality by reinforcing notions of divine superiority and human depravity, so often used as an ideological tool by colonizers to oppress those they sought to conquer and "civilize." It essentializes the singing subject as an unworthy sinful being, dependent on the superior salvific nature of the Christian God. This kind of atonement-oriented theological approach limits understandings of Christian theologies to hegemonic colonizing perspectives which emphasize sin above all else, leaving little room for those who would instead celebrate the *imago dei* visible in God's wonderfully diverse creation.[56]

Moreover, the process of multiple translations and interpretations can be a kind of betrayal of the original version. In this case, it occludes the original, which is much more of a celebration of creation and an inclusive generous God, who "helped His people out of their sin and battle/struggle of life."[57] In fact, any textual analysis is enormously complicated by issues of translation which can only briefly be addressed here. The articulation of a connection between translation and the transmission of empire

---

[55] Hine wrote two other verses which correspond roughly to Boberg's original verses 6 and 8. See appendix.

[56] Boberg's verse eight also wrestles with the weight of sin and guilt ("when pressed down by sin and guilt") and is humble in response ("I fall down at the feet of the Lord and beg grace and peace"), but the emphasis on atonement theology in the Hine version is much stronger. The colonial implications of theologies of atonement are worth exploring further, but are beyond the scope of this analysis.

[57] A reclaiming of this original meaning is akin to the process of "unforgetting," as discussed in Chap. 3. I note that the adapted version from the *New Century Hymnal* goes a long way toward this end. See the appendix for this version.

and culture goes back at least to the Middle Ages.[58] The phrase *translatio studii et imperii* describes this process, literally as the transfer or movement of political power and legitimacy (empire) through knowledge and culture. For good or ill, any translation as a transfer of culture therefore implies a betrayal of the original language as the Italian adage, "*traduttore, traditore,*" (translator, traitor) attests.[59] It is significant that the Hine interpretation which embodied a much more triumphalist, imperially oriented vision, was the version that spread throughout the world, a version which embodies musicoloniality.

While the Hine version betrays Boberg's original with its shifts away from the language of an inclusive creation and toward a more distanced, top-down God and a stronger atonement theology, processes of relocation and retranslation do not always function in this way. In fact, the Hine version itself has been translated into countless other languages, each one reinterpreting the text to make meaning in a different context and language. The most common Spanish version, for instance, "*Cuán grande es Él,*" translates the Hine text and ironically moves it back closer to its original meaning. The title, for instance, "How great is he" is in the third person, which is deferential and creates some distance, but is not totally imperial either. Moreover, in verse three, though the text states that Jesus "suffered on a cross and died for me," its emphasis rests on Jesus being sent to save, out of God's "divine love": "*Cuando recuerdo del amor divino,/Que desde el cielo al Salvador envió./Aquel Jesús que por salvarme vino,/Y en una cruz sufrió y por mi murió.*"[60] This Spanish version is in stark contrast to Hine's version which entirely and graphically focuses on the atonement oriented sacrifice of God/Jesus: "And when I think that God, His Son not sparing,/Sent Him to die, I scarce can take it in;/That

---

[58] Thomas Cooper, "Blog Post 1: Translatio Studii et Imperii," in *Thomas Cooper Individual Blog* (3 February 2010), accessed July 25, 2018, http://cantst1.blogspot.ca/2010/02/blog-post-1-translatio-studii-et.html

[59] Maria Khodorkovsky, "Traduttore, Traditore," in *Beyond Words—Language Blog*, October 9, 2008, accessed July 25, 2018, http://www.altalang.com/beyondwords/2008/10/09/traduttore-traditore/

[60] This Spanish version was translated by Argentine Pastor Arturo Hotton in 1958. The English would be "When I recall the divine love/which from heaven sent the Saviour,/That Jesus came to save me/and in a cross suffered and died." Translation mine. See the appendix for the full text.

on the cross, my burden gladly bearing,/He bled and died to take away my sin."[61]

In verse four, the language is much more intimate and gentle in this Spanish version, as the singer imagines being called into God's presence at the sweet home where they will adore the Lord in all his power and infinite love. As we have already seen, Hine's version of verse four includes bowing in humble adoration and a reaffirmation of the more distanced "Thou" language. Also, the chorus in Spanish—"My heart sings this song: How great He is! How great He is!"—is much less distanced. Another Spanish version, the one I referred to in the opening narrative by Maestro Castellanos, is even less distanced, using the more informal "*Tú*" in the chorus to address God directly: "*Cuán grande Tú*"—"How great you."[62] The informality is intensified by the choice of translation, which forgoes the use of a verb in the sentence, suggesting the affectionate and colloquial style of Cuban cultural expressions.

One could argue that other perspectives, other ways of knowing and theologizing, emerge in the more intimate language of these translations which emphasize divine love and God's saving act on behalf of the poor and marginalized—"he suffered and died for me." Though liberating language is not explicit here, in certain contexts in Latin America, in LatinaXo contexts in Canada and the USA, or in other Canadian and USA contexts for that matter, a congregation of singers could include many who are marginalized. Reading the hymn from their perspective affirms practices of accountability and contextuality by drawing on the lived experience of those assembled, particularly their experiences of exclusion and marginalization, as a hermeneutical lens with which to interpret the hymn.

Along the lines of what Medina proposes as a lived hermeneutics for interpreting the biblical narrative, such a liberating optic for singing goes beyond a simple consideration of textual or musical matters in hymns and takes into account performance practices and the context, especially the lived daily reality of the people singing.[63] In other words, it foregrounds

---

[61] See the appendix for the full text. © 1949, 1953 The Stuart Hine Trust CIO. USA print rights and all Canadian rights administered by Hope Publishing Company. All rights reserved. Used by permission.

[62] See the appendix for full text and translation.

[63] Medina proposes a lived LatinaXo Canadian hermeneutics that interprets the biblical narrative with the lens of everyday life through which "Latinas/os find in their lived-faith and lived-experiences the hermeneutical rubric for 'reading' and 'interpreting' their own story in the biblical narrative." Néstor Medina, "Latinaos, Culture and the Bible," in

lived experience as a means to interpret hymns. Singing, as an embodied activity, is conducive to this kind of approach which recognizes that singers experience the singing of a hymn/song on multiple levels, not the least of which are cultural and contextual. For example, the singing of Hine's version by the members of the H.E.R.E. Local 75 Choir can be read along these lines—the lived experience of violence and marginalization of the Caribbean-Canadian women of the choir is uplifted by a God who is willing to sacrifice everything on their behalf.

Along similar lines, former United Church Moderator Stan McKay recognizes the power of translating hymns into Indigenous languages. Writing about Cree, he affirms, with Mark MacDonald, that "our language continues to carry the culture."[64] He notes that "because 'Kitsay Manitou,' the word we use for God, Great Mystery, Great Spirit, is of our language, the name carries some of the flavour of our culture."[65] McKay also notes that it is a challenge to reconcile the "descriptions of the caring, loving God [which] come through in the Cree language in a very helpful way … [with the] imposed concepts of a fearful relationship to a judgmental God," much like the distanced God in Hine's English-language version of "How Great Thou Art."[66]

Drawing the Threads Together

While it cannot be denied that "How Great Thou Art" has been embraced as an emblematic expression of Christian identity in communities throughout the world, it must also be acknowledged that its widespread acceptance is the result of the impact of missionaries from the North. Still, it has been concretely localized when sung in each community, as people take it into their bodies and make meaning for their particular time and place.[67]

Reading In-Between: Biblical Interpretation in Canada, ed. Néstor Medina, Alison Hari-Singh, and HeyRan Kim-Cragg (Eugene, OR: Pickwick, 2019).

[64] Stan McKay and Janet Silman, *The First Nations: Canadian Experience of the Gospel-Culture Encounter* (Geneva: WCC Publications, World Council of Churches, 1995), 43.

[65] Ibid., 42.

[66] Ibid.

[67] The version in *Voices United* is translated into French, Cree, Ojibwe, and Mohawk. United Church of Canada, *Voices United: The Hymn and Worship Book of the United Church of Canada* (Etobicoke, ON: United Church Publishing House, 1996), #238.

It has crossed boundaries of gender, race, ethnicity, class, nation, and generation and is beloved the world over in multiple translations.[68]

It is, on one hand, moveable and unfixed and, on the other, rooted in and intertwined with people's practices and Christian identities. It is both embraced as a Christian anthem around the globe and celebrated in each local expression. Like "From Greenland's Icy Mountains," the singing of "How Great Thou Art" demonstrates a paradoxical flipping of meaning-making. It was once used as a tool to further expansionist agendas, however noble missionary intentions may have been. But it has also provided "one of the most powerful records of resistance to the colonial experience," since, in the moment of performing missionary hymns, ownership passes "from the colonizer to the colonized, who transform music into a means of responding to domination."[69] The consequent potential for hymnody to become a contested site could be understood along the lines of Homi Bhabha's concept of hybridity or, more concretely, in the language of specific contextually located experiences, like *mestizaje*. Such perspectives offer ways to conceptualize the repetition of colonial hymns as potentially subversive acts.

But the dynamics involved are always fluid and shifting. Even language borrowed from experiences of intermixture, like *mestizaje*, risks fixing these processes however much the crucial insights these categories offer help to describe the processes involved.[70] To help with liberating congregational singing, such descriptions need to take into account the fluidity of these processes along with the other factors we have been exploring. These include: the potential violence of cultural imposition; the interculturality of the dynamics; the multiple and complex identities of the singers; the multiple versions of songs, including issues of translation; the historical contexts of the hymn/song's creators; and the contexts of the singers. Congregational singing also needs to be interrogated for the internal dynamics of musicoloniality which include not only colonial

---

[68] The Spanish Wikipedia site for *Cuan grande es Él* claims the hymn has been translated into 100 languages. Wikipedia, "Cuan Grande es Él," accessed July 25, 2018, https://es.wikipedia.org/wiki/Cu%C3%A1n_grande_es_%C3%89l

[69] Philip V. Bohlman, "World Musics and World Religions: Whose World?" in *Enchanting Powers: Music in the World's Religions,* ed. Lawrence E. Sullivan (Cambridge, MA: distributed by Harvard University Press for the Harvard University Center for the Study of World Religions, 1997), 71, 72.

[70] Moreover, *mestizaje* used to describe intermixture beyond the mostly Latin American and LatinaXo contexts of its origin, could be read as misappropriation.

violence but also people's resistance to coloniality, as well as the ways in which they (dis/re)-locate themselves outside the scope of the colonial gaze. This is the colonial difference where both the coloniality of power is enacted, and where other ways of knowing begin to become visible, where "border-thinking" emerges.[71]

As we have seen this movement between cultural spaces can be described as syncopated. Such a movement opens us to an interruption of the "normative" beat and responds to the dislocating rhythm of the experience of marginalization of the people with whom we are in relationship. Such a syncopated movement between spaces is crucial in a liberating praxis, including liberating congregational singing. As we have seen, Christopher Small goes a long way toward unfixing musical processes by insisting that music(king) is a verb. It is a participatory process to which people contribute in a variety of ways "by performing, by listening, by rehearsing or practicing, by providing material for performance (what is called composing), or by dancing"[72] However, his inclusive, relational, and participatory vision does not account for the complex processes of identification among the people singing, or in the song itself as its own identity/meaning shifts in relation to the people who sing it. Neither does it necessarily allow us to fully come to terms with musicoloniality.

We can deepen our engagement with the stories and meanings of "*O store Gud*"/"How Great Thou Art"/"*Cuán Grande es Él*" along these lines by thinking in terms of unbleaching and unforgetting.[73] Unbleaching allows us to reclaim the original "colours" of meaning in Swedish with its focus on creation and a loving God who accompanies us in times of struggle. Unforgetting helps us confront the fact that the language of Hine's interpretation is problematic because of its reinforcement of the triumphalist, hierarchical God of the civilizing mission/imperial-colonial project; we can thus confront the epistemic violence of this version. It also draws our attention to the fact that it was part of evangelizing processes, particularly for missionaries from the USA.

At the same time, both unbleaching and unforgetting invite us to consider the ways in which communities around the world have embraced this hymn. In a variety of forms, and localized it to their particular contexts,

---

[71] Mignolo, *Local Histories/Global Designs*.

[72] Christopher Small, *Musicking: The Meanings of Performing and Listening* (Hanover, NH: Wesleyan University Press, 1998), 9.

[73] The notions of unbleaching and unforgetting were explored in Chap. 3.

people continue to sing it to help them make meaning of their lived experience, even to the point of resisting the colonial structures and powers with which the hymn, at least in Hine's version, is associated. But those same people also sing songs that rise up out of their culture and experience. Embracing their own cultural expressions, they sing outside of the strictures of the Europe, embodying other ways of worshipping beyond the colonial gaze.

ANOTHER WAY OF KNOWING/SINGING: EL ESPÍRITU DE DIOS[74]

It is the end of the Easter morning service at the Anglican community of Holy Trinity in downtown Toronto where I am the music director. A man named Guillermo from the community of San Esteban, our sister Anglican LatinaXo congregation, approaches me with a glint in his eye. He tells me he has a song he thinks I might like and sings "El Espíritu de Dios." I am immediately captivated by the melody, rhythm, and joy. Guillermo teaches me the song and I teach it to both communities for our shared worship. We sing it often when the two communities come together. … Everyone loves singing and moving to it—young and old, Spanish and English speaking.

This *corito* has been sung all over Latin America for many years, by all accounts originating from the "oral tradition of poor and marginalized community contexts."[75] The obsession with the question of who composed or who "owns" the music, to which we return shortly, is largely a Western (Euro-North Atlantic) preoccupation which insists on considering music primarily a written and/or recorded artifact. In contrast, many

---

[74] Portions of the material in this section have been revised from a presentation at the Canadian Theological Society, Toronto, June 2017 which was subsequently published as Becca Whitla, "Singing as *un Saber del Sur*, or Another Way of Knowing," *Toronto Journal of Theology* 33, no. 2 (2017 Fall 2017): 289–94.

[75] Oral versions of this song go back as much as forty years and were confirmed in conversation with colleagues in 2014: Gerardo Oberman (Argentina), Leonel Abaroa-Boloña (Cuba), Néstor Medina (Guatemala). A YouTube search reveals that it is claimed as both a Pentecostal and Roman Catholic chorus. See, for example: Diocese of Gauleguaychú, "El Espíritu de Dios," accessed July 25, 2018, http://www.obispadogchu.org.ar/cancionero/09pentecost es/220ElEspiritudeDios.htm. For other print versions, see also: Helen Kalssen, ed., *International Songbook* (Carol Stream, IL: Mennonite World Conference, 1990), 64; Presbyterian Church of Canada, *The Book of Praise* (Toronto: Presbyterian Church of Canada, 1997), 398. These versions date from an earlier iteration of the *International Songbook* of the Mennonite World Conference from 1978.

of the Latin American communities that sing *coritos* like this reject notions of individual ownership; for them it rises out of and belongs to the community.[76] Pablo Sosa observes that such songs "were usually not annotated, but transmitted orally and spontaneously in a worship context, and their authors not identified—either out of respect for the biblical text ... or because the song was a collective creation or a melody already familiar to the communities" (Fig. 5.2).[77]

This *corito* displays an intensely physical, sensual, emotive, relational, and communal liturgical activity which has great potential to usher in a bodily experience of the Divine, especially by involving actions in the singing—praising (hands in the air), praying (hands held together), jumping, dancing, and laughing. Its textual simplicity also allows the critical focus to shift from traditional approaches which analyze text, to an approach that affirms the holistic inclusion of one's entire being. Our voices vibrate in our bodies and our bodies reverberate with the shared task of sounding the Body of Christ, explicitly animated in this song by the Spirit of God which moves in us, *el espíritu de Dios (que) se mueve en mí.*

These qualities embody an epistemological break from dominant Enlightenment values which privilege Eurocentric emphases on the written, individual, rational, and intellectual as the superior and universal modes of thinking, being, and doing. The song thus affirms what decolonial scholars call another way of knowing, which is instead embodied, emotive, and communal, rising up from an oral tradition on the underside of modernity. It is locally rooted in a particular place and comes out of a particular experience. As such it could be called a *sentipensar*, a thinking that is felt.[78] When singers move, feel, and know together, the very act of singing is resignified; it becomes a *locus theologicus.*

---

[76] In LatinaXo theological contexts, this process of community creation is described as *teología en y de conjunto* (theology in and from community). Neomi DeAnda and Néstor Medina, "Convivencias: What Have We Learned? Toward a Latino/a Ecumenical Theology," in *Building Bridges, Doing Justice: Constructing a Latino/a Ecumenical Theology*, ed. Orland Espín (New York: Orbis, 2009).

[77] Pablo Sosa, "Christian Music in Latin America since 1800," in Dowley, *Christian Music*, 208. Sosa also notes that "hundreds of these anonymous psalms and other biblical songs are sung today all over Latin America." Ibid.

[78] Arturo Escobar, "Desde Abajo, por la Izquierda, y con la Tierra: La Diferencia de Abya Yala/Afro/Latino-América," *Intervenciones en Estudios Culturales* 3 (2016): 123. See also Escobar, *Sentipensar con la Tierra* in which he is clear that the idea of *sentipensar* rises out of the experience of Afro-descendent communities and their relationship with their local natural environment in Northern Colombia.

1. // Si el Espíritu de Dios se mueve en mí, yo canto como David //
// Yo canto, yo canto, yo canto como David //

2. Yo alabo......(praise)
3. Yo oro.........(pray)
4. Yo salto.......(jump)
5. Yo danzo.....(dance)
6. Yo río..........(laugh)

If the Spirit of God moves in me,
I will sing like David!

Words and Music: Anonymous, Latin America
Transcription: Becca Whitla (2008)

Fig. 5.2 "El Espíritu de Dios," traditional Latin American *corito*

In examining "From Greenland's Icy Mountains," we have already seen that epistemic disobedience can be a component of thinking, being, doing, and feeling decolonially. Walter Mignolo argues that epistemic disobedience takes place in what he calls the space of the colonial difference "where the coloniality of power is enacted [but also] where the restitution of subaltern knowledges is taking place and where border thinking is emerging."[79] In this space of the colonial difference (where border thinking emerges), subaltern reason, and its expression in subaltern knowledges, becomes apparent as other ways of knowing. Mignolo describes subaltern reason as an alternative to the unreasonable violent supremacy of "modern" rational reason, or "a diverse set of theoretical practices emerging *from* and responding *to* colonial legacies at the intersection of Euro/American modern history."[80] Subaltern reason resists being "restricted and privileged by Western epistemology" by inhabiting different bodies, drawing on different sensibilities and memories, being intersubjective rather than individualistic, and having what Mignolo calls an "overall different world-sensing" which draws on the "realms of the senses beyond the eyes."[81] The resulting other ways of knowing (doing, being, and feeling) are expressed in songs like "*El Espíritu de Dios*" and can also be experienced, as we have seen, in the flipping of songs like "From Greenland's Icy Mountains" and "How Great Thou Art."

Other ways of knowing are present in many places. Congregational singing marks such a space where these other ways of knowing can manifest as acts of epistemic disobedience amidst the power dynamics and negotiations of human relations and the messiness of life in its range from pain and suffering to happiness and hope. Our complex ethno/cultural, racialized, gendered, and relational identities intermingle in-between each other, in the in-between space-and-time of our congregational singing. The embodied, collective, relational activity of congregational singing can thus embody a kind of resistance to oppressive systems through these other ways of knowing. This liminal activity can be described as border singing, along the lines of the decolonial notion of "border thinking."

It bears recalling briefly here that many in our churches live in the dangerous reality of a borderland existence. This messiness of life reflects the fact that many in our churches and communities live in contexts of dehumanization and discrimination, of violence and, at times, even death. These borders of our lives are present when we sing. They are present yet

---

[79] Mignolo, *Local Histories*, xxv. Mignolo uses the language of "subaltern," common among postcolonial scholars, but less so among decolonial thinkers. I use it here in my summaries of his thinking.

[80] Ibid., 95.

[81] Ibid., 3, 60.

porous; at any given moment they can be permeable, fluid, or shifting. They depend on the terms of present geopolitical, social, national, and political configurations which leave many people outside the centres of power. Some of us can easily cross back and forth and others cannot. Guillermo invited me into a border space when he shared the song with me. Yet, the border between Canada and El Salvador was closed to him when his refugee claim was denied and he was deported.

The rising up of this particular song, this "other" way of singing as an act of epistemic disobedience, as border thinking, has also been complicated by the ongoing global interplay of the dynamics of musicoloniality. In 1996, this *corito* was recorded and copyrighted by gospel musician Fred Hammond as "The Spirit of the Lord," inspiring the title of the album on which it appeared, *The Spirit of David*.[82] Aided by its commodification through the engines of the music industry of the USA, it was deterritorialized and has proliferated throughout the world and can now be heard on YouTube in a variety of versions. These versions include a call and response arrangement by Anil Kant of India, a light pop version by the GKPB Fajar Pengharapang group in Indonesia, a country western version by a small USA Pentecostal Holiness congregation, as well as a Scandinavian metal rock version, among others.[83] It continues to move around the globe and be made available in multiple versions, identifiable as a "transnationalized" or "globalized" song, yet adapted distinctly in each local embodied expression.[84]

---

[82] Fred Hammond, "The Spirit of the Lord," in *The Spirit of David*, accessed July 25, 2018, http://www.allmusic.com/album/the-spirit-of-david-mw0000073417

[83] The GKPB church is a member of the Huria Kristen Batak Protestan (HKBP) or Batak Christian Protestant Church. It is the largest Protestant denomination in *Indonesia*, with a baptized membership of 4,500,000. Lim Swee Hong, personal conversation with the author, March 20, 2018. See also Wikipedia, "Batak Christian Protestant Church," accessed June 26, 2018, https://en.wikipedia.org/wiki/Batak_Christian_Protestant_Church. See also the following YouTube links (all accessed July 25, 2018): Anil Kant of India: https://www.youtube.com/watch?v=whIez4iQPiM&feature=share&list=UUY5d9fqvDTohI7lyhd1Gqt QGKPB; Fajar Pengharapang group in Indonesia: https://www.youtube.com/watch?v=RUFgf1CPs28; U.S. Pentecostal Holiness congregation: https://www.youtube.com/watch?v=Je99T_7kScA; Scandinavian Metal version: https://www.youtube.com/watch?v=pFCNRMv77Q4

[84] Ethnomusicologist Philip Bohlman argues for an emphasis on the local, rather than the "ineluctable transnationalism imposed by many cultural-studies scholars on global culture." He continues that "it is a contestation between everyday religious practices, performed through song and bodily practices that themselves constitute the cultures of contested

Troubling questions about power emerge like "Who represents whom?" and "Who owns the music?" When the song moved from being an "anonymous" oral artifact to a recorded commodity, its ownership—at least in terms of copyright and the resulting financial gains—was effectively coopted from its communities of origin by a successful North American gospel singer. Issues of identity and misappropriation are further complicated in this narrative because of Fred Hammond's racialization as an African American with all the attendant complexity and potential (dis) location in the social margins of USA society.[85] The song's appropriation is but a sampling of a large complex of ongoing colonization in music, another facet of musicoloniality which here can also be understood to include the wanton appropriation of all "other" musical traditions without regard for the contexts of their origin, along with systems which entrench European-North-Atlantic superiority in music making. Musicoloniality is a symptom of the ways in which the coloniality of power is still at play.[86] On display are consumer-capitalist extractivist methods and approaches adapted to the reproduction of musical pieces from the Global South.[87] The musical gifts of people, these other ways of singing and being in the world, are no longer secure.

The movement around the globe of "*El Espíritu de Dios*," including its appropriation in a variety of contexts raises significant ethical issues.[88]

---

sites … where exchange and musical performance are not simply the products of transnational forces." Bohlman, "Whose World?" 83.

[85] For ethnomusicologist Melvin Butler, the "Spirit of the Lord" epitomizes black gospel music and accentuates black masculinity. In an article exploring queerness and masculinity in black gospel music, he asserts that "this [sonic phenomenon] is to be understood as the musical praise of a muscular man—a fully *masculine* man, trained and equipped, as it were, for musical battle—a man, who like King David, is not the least bit ashamed to praise God with everything he has." The song is, according to Butler, an emblematic and particular representation of black male identity. Melvin L Butler, "Singing Like David Sang: Queerness and Masculinity in Black Gospel Performance," in *Readings in African American Church Music and Worship: Volume 2*, comp. and ed. James Abbington (Chicago: GIA Publications Inc., 2014), 718.

[86] See Aníbal Quijano, "Coloniality of Power, Eurocentrism, and Latin America," *Nepantla: Views from the South* 1.3 (2000): 533–80, accessed July 25, 2018, http://www.unc.edu/~aescobar/wan/wanquijano.pdf

[87] For a detailed conversation about intellectual and cultural extractivism see Ramón Grosfoguel, "Del 'Extractivismo Económico' al 'Extractivismo Epistémico' y al 'Extractivismo Ontológico:' Una Forma Destructiva de Conocer, Ser y Estar en el Mundo," *Tabula Rasa. Bogotá – Colombia* 24 (enero-junio 2016): 123–43.

[88] I remind the reader of my own mis-use of the song as recounted in Chap. 2.

Moreover, unless and until there is a relationship between song practitioners, their communities, and the marginalized communities to whom the
song originally belonged, practices of accountability remain theoretical
and abstract. Michael Hawn writes that singing songs from around the
world can help us sing and pray "for the sake of the world."[89] However,
the fact that we are often disconnected from the lived reality and the people of those contexts can suggest a lack of integrity in our engagement.
This is especially the case when a person or institution benefits from the
reproduction of the knowledges—here in the form of (uncopyrighted)
songs from the Global South—like "*El Espíritu de Dios.*" S.T. Kimbrough
is unequivocal about these ethical implications: "You honor another culture and its song when you take great care with copyright registrations. ...
Honor the origins of songs. Do not violate copyrights."[90]

SINGING IN A DECOLONIAL KEY

What remains clear is that when "*El Espíritu de Dios*" is sung from below,
understood as belonging to the community, it offers an alternative to the
Eurocentric norm which emphasizes individual ownership and epistemologies based on things which are written down rather than those which
emerge from the oral tradition from the heart of a community's life and
experience. "*El espíritu de Dios,*" like "How Great Thou Art," and "From
Greenland's Icy Mountains" is not evaluated by these communities
through an analysis of text and tune, but by what meaning is made through
the singing of the song. Particular communities have taken on ownership
of the song, shaping their own identities as Christians, making meaning in
their own local contexts.

When people sing their faith as performative and embodied practices,
they can thus be empowered "to challenge, to resist, or otherwise to

---

[89] C. Michael Hawn, *Gather Into One: Praying and Singing Globally* (Grand Rapids, MI:
Eerdmans Publishing, 2003), 4. Christian practitioners from dominant culture settings
might consider ways of financially compensating the communities who birthed the songs, as
outlined in Chap. 2.

[90] S. T. Kimbrough, "Global Song and Cultures," in *Music and Mission: Toward a Theology
and Practice of Global Song* (New York: GBG Musik, 2007), 107. As already noted, concerns
about copyright vary significantly. Many in the Global South are not too concerned about
ownership per se. As we saw in Chap. 4, ideas of intellectual ownership developed in music
along with classical music ideology. Still, when profits accrue, it is ethically imperative that
they be shared with the songs' creators.

'respond' to the worlds in which they live and believe."[91] Singing can confront the reality of the world in an eschatological mode; we sing the "not yet"—what is to come—of God's future while living in the "already"—what is—of our present reality. Or to flip it, we sing the already of God's future while living the "not yet" of our present reality. This is not an escapist eschatology, however. It acknowledges the pain and suffering of present reality, of the "already," especially for the disenfranchised, and it affirms their crucial role in partnering with God to bring about the "not yet." Don Saliers asserts this perspective, writing that "whenever and wherever we sing of God's future there remains the possibility of our singing being intrinsically a political act. In this sense all faithful praise and lament carries the seeds of recognizing the huge gap between the IS and the OUGHT TO BE, [or the "already" and the "not yet"] of this world."[92] As such, these three examples can embody acts of hope, other ways of knowing, and the celebration of peoples' cultural traditions, all of which defy forces that oppress and the ongoing pervasiveness of (music)coloniality.

Singing "*El Espíritu de Dios*," drew me into relationship with the people who sang the song from San Esteban and contributed to my own conversion through a reorientation to another way of being. It invited me to wrestle with deeply troubling ethical issues, by singing with people in a "decolonial key."[93] In this space, singing is a way to do theology. Our singing is about who we are and who we want to become as active agents of a liberating praxis, proclaiming what is and what ought to be, the already and not yet of the kin-dom of God. When *el espíritu de Dios se movió en mí*, I experienced the Trinitarian perichoretic dance, as my body joined others in reconfiguring worship in a decolonial key as we sang the body of Christ.

The singing of these songs, however, does not in itself create relationships. It is but one action in an ongoing dynamic of relationship-building through worship. In the next chapter, intercultural relationships are examined for their potential to contribute to liberating congregational singing. Such interculturality is explored through the shared musical and liturgical practices in the two communities which sang *El Espíritu de Dios*, namely San Esteban and Holy Trinity.

[91] Bohlman, "Whose World?" 84.
[92] Don E. Saliers, *Music and Theology* (Nashville: Abington, 2007), 53.
[93] Medina, Email correspondence with the author (28 May, 2017).

BIBLIOGRAPHY

Bhabha, Homi K. 1994. *The Location of Culture*. New York: Routledge.

Bohlman, Philip V. 1997. World Musics and World Religions: Whose World? In *Enchanting Powers: Music in the World's Religions*, ed. Lawrence E. Sullivan, 61–90. Cambridge, MA: Distributed by Harvard University Press for the Harvard University Center for the Study of World Religions.

Butler, Melvin L. 2014. Singing Like David Sang: Queerness and Masculinity in Black Gospel Performance. In *Readings in African American Church Music and Worship: Volume 2*, compiled and edited by James Abbington, 715–725. Chicago: GIA Publications Inc.

DeAnda, Neomi, and Néstor Medina. 2009. Convivencias: What Have We Learned? Toward a Latino/a Ecumenical Theology. In *Building Bridges, Doing Justice: Constructing a Latino/a Ecumenical Theology*, ed. Orland Espín, 185–196. New York: Orbis.

Diocese of Gauleguaychú. El Espíritu de Dios. http://www.obispadogchu.org.ar/cancionero/09pentecostes/220ElEspiritudeDios.htm. Accessed 25 July 2018.

Dowley, Tim. 2011. How Great Thou Art. In *Christian Music: A Global History*, 218. Minneapolis: Fortress Press.

Dussel, Enrique. 1995. *The Invention of the Americas: Eclipse of "the Other" and the Myth of Modernity*. New York: The Continuum Publishing Company.

Escobar, Arturo. 2014. *Sentipensar con la Tierra: Nuevas Lecturas Sobre Desarrollo, Territorio y Diferencia*. Medellín: Ediciones UNAULA.

———. 2016. Desde Abajo, por la Izquierda, y con la Tierra: La Diferencia de Abya Yala/Afro/Latino-América. *Intervenciones en Estudios Culturales* 3: 117–136.

Grosfoguel, Ramón. 2016. Del 'Extractivismo Económico' al 'Extractivismo Epistémico' y al 'Extractivismo Ontológico:' Una Forma Destructiva de Conocer, Ser y Estar en el Mundo. *Tabula Rasa*. Bogotá – Colombia 24 (enero–junio): 123–143.

Hammond, Fred. The Spirit of the Lord. *The Spirit of David*. http://www.allmusic.com/album/the-spirit-of-david-mw0000073417. Accessed 25 July 2018.

Hawn, C. Michael. 2003. *Gather into One: Praying and Singing Globally*. Grand Rapids: Eerdmans Publishing.

———. How Great Thou Art. https://www.umcdiscipleship.org/resources/history-of-hymns-how-great-thou-art. Accessed 28 July 2018.

Hope Publishing Company. How Great Thou Art. *hopepublishing.com*. https://www.hopepublishing.com/find-hymns-hw/hw4894.aspx. Accessed 19 June 2020.

Hughes, Derrick. 1986. *Bishop Sahib: A Life of Reginald Heber*. West Sussex: Churchman Publishing Ltd.

Joy Bringer Ministries. How Great Thou Art. http://www.joy-bringer-ministries. org/hymns/hgta.pdf. Accessed 28 July 2018.

Kalssen, Helen, ed. 1990. *International Songbook*. Carol Stream: Mennonite World Conference.

Khodorkovsky, Maria. 2008. Traduttore, Traditore. *Beyond Words—Language Blog*, October 9. http://www.altalang.com/beyond-words/2008/10/09/ traduttore-traditore/. Accessed 25 July 2018.

Kimbrough, S.T., ed. 2007. *Music and Mission: Toward a Theology and Practice of Global Song*. New York: GBGMusik.

Martin, Karen, and Boora Mirraboopa. 2003. Ways of Knowing, Being and Doing: A Theoretical Framework and Methods for Indigenous and Indigenist Research. *Journal of Australian Studies* 27 (76): 203–214. https://doi. org/10.1080/14443050309387838. Accessed 8 May 2018.

McKay, Stan, and Janet Silman. 1995. *The First Nations: Canadian Experience of the Gospel-Culture Encounter*. Geneva: WCC Publications, World Council of Churches.

McNally, Michael. 2009. *Ojibwe Singers: Hymns, Grief, and a Native Culture in Motion*. St. Paul: Minnesota Historical Society Press.

Medina, Néstor. 2009. *Mestizaje: (Re)Mapping Race, Culture and Faith in Latina/o Catholicism*. Maryknoll: Orbis Books.

———. 2019. Latinaos, Culture and the Bible. In *Reading In-Between: Biblical Interpretation in Canada*, ed. Néstor Medina, Alison Hari-Singh, and HeyRan Kim-Cragg. Eugene: Pickwick.

Mignolo, Walter D. 2000. *Local Histories/Global Designs: Coloniality, Subaltern Knowledges, and Border Thinking*. Princeton: Princeton University Press.

———. 2011. Geopolitics of Sensing and Knowing: On (de)Coloniality, Border Thinking, and Epistemic Disobedience. http://eipcp.net/transversal/0112/ mignolo/en. Accessed 25 July 2018.

Osbeck, Kenneth W. 1982. *101 Hymn Stories: The Inspiring True Stories Behind 101 Favorite Hymns*. Grand Rapids: Kregal Publications.

Presbyterian Church of Canada. 1997. *The Book of Praise*. Toronto: Presbyterian Church of Canada.

Quijano, Aníbal. 2000. Coloniality of Power, Eurocentrism, and Latin America. *Nepantla: Views from the South* 1 (3): 533–580. http://www.unc. edu/~aescobar/wan/wanquijano.pdf. Accessed 25 July 2018.

Richards, Jeffrey. 2002. *Imperialism and Music: Britain, 1876–1953*. Manchester: Manchester University Press.

Russell, Letty M., J. Shannon Clarkson, and Kate M. Ott, eds. 2009. *Just Hospitality: God's Welcome in a World of Difference*. Louisville: Westminster John Knox Press.

Said, Edward. 2003. *Orientalism*. New York/London: Penguin Classics.

Saliers, Don E. 2007. *Music and Theology*. Nashville: Abington Press.

Scheer, Greg. From Greenland's Icy Mountains. *Hymnary.Org*. http://hymnary. org/text/from_greenlands_icy_mountains. Accessed 4 Feb 2017.

Small, Christopher. 1998. *Musicking: The Meanings of Performing and Listening*. Hanover: Wesleyan University Press.

Sosa, Pablo. 2011. Christian Music in Latin America since 1800. In *Christian Music: A Global History*, ed. Tim Dowley, 206–209. Minneapolis: Fortress Press.

Spivak, Gayatri Chakravorty. 1988. Can the Subaltern Speak? In *Marxism and the Interpretation of Cultures*, ed. Cary Nelson and Lawrence Grossberg, 271–313. Urbana: University of Illinois Press.

Teillet, Jean. 2019. *The North-West Is Our Mother: The Story of Louis Riel's People, the Métis Nation*. Toronto: HarperCollins.

United Church of Canada. 1996. *Voices United: The Hymn and Worship Book of The United Church of Canada*. Etobicoke: United Church Publishing House.

Whitla, Becca. 2017. Singing as *un Saber del Sur*, or Another Way of Knowing. *Toronto Journal of Theology* 33 (2, Fall): 289–294.

———. 2018. The Colonizing Power of Song. In *Decoloniality and Justice: Theological Perspectives*, ed. Jean-François Roussel, 43–50. Saõ Leopoldo: Oikos: World Forum on Theology and Liberation.

Wikipedia. Batak Christian Protestant Church. https://en.wikipedia.org/wiki/ Batak_Christian_Protestant_Church. Accessed 26 June 2018.

———. Cuan Grande es Él. https://es.wikipedia.org/wiki/Cu%C3%A1n_ grande_es_%C3%89l. Accessed 25 July 2018.

———. Grand River (Ontario). https://en.wikipedia.org/wiki/Grand_River_ (Ontario). Accessed 3 May 2018.

Young, Robert J.C. 1995. *Colonial Desire: Hybridity in Theory, Culture and Race*. London/New York: Routledge.

CHAPTER 6

Border Singing

Introduction

In this chapter the focus will shift from a consideration of particular songs to an analysis of the musical and liturgical practices in one context, at the Anglican Church of the Holy Trinity in downtown Toronto. Specifically, two Christmas practices will be examined: the church's Christmas production, "The Christmas Story," and a bilingual Christmas Eve service hosted by the church's two Anglican congregations—one Spanish-speaking and the other English-speaking. In the first example, we explore the tension between perpetuating coloniality and resisting it through a kind of mimicry. In the second, the liminal space where the two communities intermix invites a consideration of what it means to worship interculturally and suggests constructive liberating examples for our examination. Specifically, their border(ed) liturgy—experienced through the LatinaXo ritual of *Las Posadas* and in a Christmas carol written by a community member—helps to prepare a fertile ground for concrete and constructive—more praxical—lenses.

The Christmas Story

When I was a teenager, I played the trumpet as an angel in "The Christmas Story" for the final carol, "O Come All Ye Faithful." Both of my children played the baby Jesus. Emma was eleven months old and David, only three

© The Author(s) 2020
B. Whitla, *Liberation, (De)Coloniality, and Liturgical Practices,*
New Approaches to Religion and Power,
https://doi.org/10.1007/978-3-030-52636-8_6

weeks. When David was baby Jesus, on Christmas Eve, 2005, his Ohio family came east to see him, celebrating with joy the new baby in our family. We were delighted that our real live baby could represent the symbol of hope at the heart of the Christian story. Emma was a king's page that year. When she knelt to kiss the baby Jesus, her brother reached out his hand to touch her.

Holy Trinity's large-scale Christmas pageant, "The Christmas Story" has been running for 80 years.[1] Over three weekends each December, the production requires two volunteer casts of 30 actors (one of which is associated with the church's congregation), a paid vocal quartet, a professional organist, a stage director and a lighting director, wardrobe and make-up volunteers, a technical crew, ushers, and others. Together they reproduce and mount the hour-long mimed presentation, using a narrated synthesized biblical text of the gospel accounts of the birth story. Since its founding in 1938, The Christmas Story participants and audience alike have celebrated the authenticity of the production which reproduces a performance originally staged at St. Martin-in-the-Fields in Trafalgar Square, London—at the heart of the British Empire in the 1930s—with its King James language, its austere costuming, and its English-style church music.

The Christmas Story was brought to Holy Trinity by Patricia Frank when she moved to Toronto with her husband, the Reverend John Frank. Begun by her father, Reverend Pat McCormick, at St. Martin-in-the-Fields in 1928, it was stopped due to London blackouts during the Second World War. She imported this version with "cobbled together Gospel passages from the King James Version of the Bible and set it to what they regarded as the most beautiful seasonal music."[2] Reportedly, Queen Elizabeth herself and "her sister Margaret were taken to see this production when they were little girls."[3] In the eighty intervening years, the production has prided itself on maintaining this heritage, combining "tradition, community, innocence, trembling nerves, miracles and soaring choral music."[4] The congregation has supported the venture by participating in the production, by underwriting the up-front financial costs, and by making the space available for the twelve performances and many rehearsals. Many in the congregation are proud of the legacy, are fiercely loyal, see

---

[1] For ease of reading, I'll refer to "The Christmas Story" without quotation marks for the rest of the chapter, thus: The Christmas Story.

[2] The Christmas Story, "History of the Pageant," accessed June 6, 2017, https://www.thechristmasstory.ca/history-of-the-pageant

[3] Ibid.

[4] Ibid.

"The Story" as part of the ministry of the church, and look forward to their involvement with The Christmas Story community every year. Others feel it places an undue burden on the congregation by taking over the life of the community with a production that is outdated, conservative, costly, and antithetical to the justice-seeking, inclusive values of the church. They wish it reflected a more contemporary and progressive outlook and theology.

With the exception of the three carols which bookend the show, the music of The Christmas Story is entirely professionally performed. Little has changed since 1938. The narrative is interspersed with organ music and music sung from the west gallery by an unseen quartet who offer "well-loved Christmas favourites, as well as beautiful English carols not normally heard in the shopping malls"—in other words, English choral music, mostly Victorian, popular in the era when the pageant first crossed the Atlantic with the Franks.[5] This music—which is described as showcasing "outstanding voices" and featuring the organ which is "heard in its full glory"—leaves little room for congregational or community participation.[6] The audience is sung to so that they might enjoy the gift of this lavish cultural presentation, a cherished, pristine, unaltered, and unalterable tradition that has been passed down through the years.

The community is invited to join in musically by singing three carols: two at the beginning, "Hark the Herald Angels Sing," by Charles Wesley (1707–1788) and "Once in Royal David's City," written by Cecil Francis Alexander (1818–1895) in 1848; and one at the end, "O Come, All Ye Faithful," attributed to John Francis Wade (1711–1786) and translated by Frederick Oakeley (1802–1880) in 1841. They are all strongly associated with English culture and hymn-writing, particularly of the Victorian era at the height of the British Empire.[7] The language of triumph and kingship

---

[5] The Christmas Story, "Music," Accessed June 6, 2017, https://www.thechristmasstory.ca/music. The English style of choral music can be heard in the excerpt of "Angels from the Realms of Glory" on the same webpage. See page six of the commemorative program for the list of music included. Page seven includes the texts of the carols sung. The Christmas Story, "75th Anniversary Programme," accessed June 6, 2017, https://www.thechristmasstory.ca/commemorative-program

[6] The Christmas Story, "Music."

[7] Interestingly, all three carols are regularly featured in the famous and quintessentially British lessons and carols service at King's College in Cambridge, UK. See the service booklet for 2015, King's College Cambridge, "A Festival of Nine Lessons and Carols: Service Booklets from Previous Years," accessed June 6, 2017, http://www.kings.cam.ac.uk/files/services/festival-nine-lessons-2015.pdf

abounds in the first and third hymns, and the language of servanthood and obedience proliferates in the second in the sentimental poetic style common in many Christmas carols.

In order to focus on the broader implications of The Christmas Story, I will not engage in a detailed textual analysis of these hymns, per se. However, it is worth noting that the first verse of "Once in Royal David's City" evokes a sentimental sanitized version of the Christmas story: "Once in royal David's city,/Stood a lowly cattle shed,/Where a mother laid her Baby,/In a manger for His bed:/Mary was that mother mild,/Jesus Christ, her little Child."[8] The effect of these hymns along with the other music in the production is to culturally reinforce the sentimental Christmas myth of the Victorian middle-class family, epitomizing Victorian domesticity and represented in Charles Dickens' *A Christmas Carol* and the Christmas scene at Dingle Dell in his *Pickwick Papers*.

Given this imperial overlay in The Christmas Story, are there any fissures through which we can glimpse an alternative vision? Can the production itself or the congregational singing before and after the presentation be considered in any way subversive or liberating, or does The Christmas Story simply "reproduce" and "re-present" empire, or are both things happening simultaneously, or is something else happening?

Once again, we can draw on Homi Bhabha for his insights into human interactions in the wake of colonialism. His articulation of the dynamics of mimicry and his notion of the Third Space offer the possibility of reading The Christmas Story with a postcolonial optic. Such an optic, while limited in some of the ways previously described—particularly because it remains circumscribed by the Western European colonial gaze—nevertheless suggests ways of retrieving elements of The Christmas Story to be reconfigured or reimagined in the future.

Bhabha challenges us to understand that all "cultural statements and systems are constructed in a contradictory and ambivalent space of enunciation."[9] In other words, claims to cultural purity are untenable. He articulates the location in which cultural differences are negotiated as the

---

[8] The third verse, not sung during The Christmas Story intensifies the "mild," "lowly," and "gentle" gendered and domesticated nature of Mary, and holds up the obedience of Jesus (which is not born out biblically), as the appropriate model of servanthood or servitude for Christian children: "And through all his wondrous childhood/He would honour and obey,/Love and watch the lowly maiden/In whose gentle arms he lay;/Christian children all must be/Mild, obedient, good as he."

[9] Homi K. Bhabha, *The Location of Culture* (New York: Routledge, 1994), 55.

Third Space. Here, (cultural) differences and identifications are always incommensurable. They are enunciated in performative gestures that are "continually, *contingently*, 'opening out', remaking the boundaries, exposing the limits of any claim to a singular or autonomous sign of difference—be it class, gender or race."[10] As such, a Third Space lens presumes that cultural discourses and cultural identities are enunciated and located ambivalently, fluidly, and performatively, resisting the reductive fixity of racial and cultural stereotypes which tend to locate the Other in a space that does not exist. Let us consider what, if any, possibilities there are to read The Christmas Story as such a Third Space.

To begin with, the biblical story itself can be read as a "flipped" narrative, as the subversive story of a revolutionary. It tells about a "king," born in utter poverty, conceived outside of wedlock, to parents who become refugees. This perspective is not lost on Christmas Story enthusiasts. Writing about it, journalist Deirdre Kelly remarks that it is "nothing short of relevant" since "at its core, the Jesus story is about the disenfranchised. It is a story of the poor and the oppressed asserting themselves within a corrupt political system—in short, a story of social revolution."[11] Read this way as a subversive biblical text, it reminds the audience of the alternative to the Christmas narrative of neo-liberal consumer capitalism which is alive and well just a few steps from the doors of the church at the adjacent mall and temple to mammon, the Toronto Eaton Centre.[12] Whether audience members and Christmas Story participants choose to hear it or not, the story of Jesus' birth can draw us back, theoretically at least, to the revolutionary impetus and heart of Jesus' life and ministry, articulated in The Christmas Story production in the voice of Mary's Magnificat (Luke 1:46–55).

Certainly, a more radical interpretation of the biblical themes of the nativity resonates with the grassroots historic commitments of the church on behalf of the excluded. The Church of the Holy Trinity was founded by virtue of an anonymous donation which sought to minimize class

---

[10] Ibid., 312–13.

[11] Deirdre Kelly, "Angels in the Dark: The Church of the Holy Trinity's A Christmas Story," in *Critics at Large* (20 December 2013), accessed June 8, 2017, http://www.critic-satlarge.ca/2013/12/angels-in-dark-church-of-holy-trinitys.html

[12] For a good discussion of the ideology of neoliberalism, see: George Monbiot, "Neoliberalism – The Ideology at the Root of All Our Problems," in *The Guardian* (15 April 2016), accessed June 16, 2020, https://www.theguardian.com/books/2016/apr/15/neoliberalism-ideology-problem-george-monbiot

distinctions by stipulating that the pews were never to be rented.[13] It was also home to a vibrant expression of the social gospel in the 1930s under the rectorship of the Reverend John Frank (husband of Patricia, the pageant director). It allowed draft dodgers to sleep on the floor in the 1960s, held one of the first public gay dances in Toronto (in 1971, hosted by the University of Toronto Community Homophile Association), and was the first home for the Metropolitan Community Church. It has also been sponsoring refugees ever since the Canadian government first allowed private sponsorship in the early 1970s and has advocated for social housing and on behalf of the homeless. In 2007, Holy Trinity was joined by the LatinaXo congregation of San Esteban, a ministry to the Hispanic community in Toronto supported by the Anglican diocese. Most recently, it made a commitment to respond to the calls of action of the Truth and Reconciliation Commission and welcomed the Toronto Urban Native Ministry into its space.[14]

Yet there can be no denying that the pageant still reproduces the culture of empire, with costumes, gestures, sounds, and carols imported from England and proudly reproduced as a repetition of tradition. Indeed, The Christmas Story, along with its accompanying theologies, ecclesiologies, and hymns, is also constitutive of coloniality. Given this reality, it can be hard to read this version of the story of Jesus as liberating at all, especially when the production reproduces biblical interpretations which sanitize the nativity in the way the production is mounted. The Christology of the story remains circumscribed by the poised middle-classness of the production while the real "flipping" of the narrative, its incarnational heart—that God actually chose to become human, and moreover among the lowliest peoples—risks being obscured. At the end of the production, the crowd is enjoined to "be of good courage" and to "strengthen the faint hearted,

---

[13] Pew renting was a common practice in mid-nineteenth-century England, the USA, and Canada. It provided a steady source of income and also allowed those with status and means to have the best seats in the house. At the St. James Anglican Cathedral in Toronto, little plaques still indicate which families rented particular pews. For a general overview of the practice see: J. C. Bennet, "How Formal Anglican Pew-Renting Worked in Practice, 1800–1950," in *The Journal of Ecclesiastical History* 68, no. 4 (Cambridge: Cambridge University Press, 2017), 766–83. See also: Wikipedia, "Pew," accessed June 21, 2017, https://en.wikipedia.org/wiki/Pew

[14] For more details about the church and its history, see the following: Church of the Holy Trinity, "Church Website," accessed June 21, 2017, http://www.holytrinitytoronto.org/wp/; Church of the Holy Trinity, "A Very Brief History," accessed June 21, 2017, http://www.holytrinitytoronto.org/wp/about/a-very-brief-history/

support the weak, help and cheer the sick, honour all people, love and serve the Lord."[15] This exhortation reinforces an attitude of charity toward the poor and needy as sources of pity and recipients of our "good deeds," rather than as agents for God's kin-dom following Jesus' liberating example, as God-among-us.

Still, the rich historical inheritance of Holy Trinity, especially the congregation's commitment to social justice, invites further scrutiny of the complexity of what The Christmas Story could signify. Is there any way it could be read as a kind of mimicry in which the (subversive) biblical narrative interweaves with English cultural interpretations/expressions in a kind of Third Space? The cultural dynamics of this engagement are certainly complexified by the participation of a richly diverse group of people in The Christmas Story. If one were to imagine the space of The Christmas Story as a kind of Third Space, could the spectrum of people who participate, both marginalized and not, be understood to be embodying a complex and inescapable process, along the lines of what Bhabha describes, one that is not limited to exclusively subaltern participation. Could The Christmas Story be read in this light for its emancipatory potential?

In 2015, Donovan Vincent documented the participation of one such person, Eileen Rojas, a 9-year-old refugee who had arrived in Toronto earlier that year. Vincent notes that when Eileen raises "her arms above her head triumphantly," as an angel in the pageant, it is a "far cry from the grinding poverty and hopelessness Eileen and her family faced before coming here."[16] The article connects the story of Eileen's family—they fled from Colombia to Ecuador where they lived on the street and "the family had to pick through rags and refuse looking for anything to salvage for money"—with the biblical story and the church's advocacy for refugees, having "sponsored 125 refugees from war-torn countries such as Afghanistan, Burundi, Cambodia, Colombia, Iran, Kosovo, Somalia and Sudan" since 1991.[17]

---

[15] This benediction first appeared in 1892 and was in a draft of the 1928 version of the *Book of Common Prayer* at the end of the confirmation service, though it was not included in the final version. "Go Forth Into the World," accessed May 9, 2018, https://johnian.wordpress.com/2012/02/05/go-forth-into-the-world/

[16] Donovan Vincent, "Three Torontonians Taking Their Turn in the Spotlight This Christmas," *The Toronto Star* (20 December 2015), accessed June 9, 2017, https://www.thestar.com/news/insight/2015/12/20/three-torontonians-taking-their-turn-in-the-spotlight-this-christmas.html

[17] Ibid.

The question is whether the participation of Eileen, and others like her, changes the meaning of the pageant. Does her presence, clothed in the white and gold costume of the original pageant, using the same gestures, accompanied by the same music, allow the production to be understood as mimicking imperial English culture, in the Bhabhian sense? Does her participation witness to the possibility of understanding The Christmas Story as a Third Space from which the subversive/revolutionary message of the biblical nativity story can emerge? Does it witness to what journalist Deirdre Kelly calls the "wildly inclusive," in the self-described inter-generational, interracial nature of the production, which includes a sign language interpreter for the deaf community?[18] Questions of representation, as well as misrepresentation, nonrepresentation, and misrecognition, lurk. Who speaks for whom? Whose voice is not heard, listened to, or even accounted for? How are people's stories and identities represented? Is their agency empowered, or how are they misrecognized or objectified through representation? Is Eileen's presence an affirmation of her as a person or is it a move to assimilate her and co-opt her involvement as part of a re-inscription of empire and coloniality? Could it be a catachresis for inclusion, allowing those in power to feel good about welcoming diverse participation, without attending to a shift in fundamental power structures? The range of potential interpretations of what is going on thus stretches from mimicry at best to mere representation and coopting at worst and is likely some combination of both at the same time.

Along the same lines, in an age of the diminishment of community singing in general, it can be argued that the very fact that people are invited to sing together at all is counter-cultural. The singing of the carols which bookend the pageant could be read as a kind of mimicry in which these English hymns confront the consumer capitalist version of Christmas expressed next door in the Eaton Centre. The singers could be understood to be subverting the neo-colonial capitalist agenda through mimicry in the very agency of their singing. Yet these Christmas carols still remain clothed in the garments of European hymnody and sentimental Victorian poetry, associated with the zenith of the British Empire. As such, they impede the possibility of telling the story of God's subversive incarnational act—the scandalous reality of God choosing a lowly place for divine disclosure as a rebuke against unjust structures. They also impede the

---

[18] Kelly, "Angels in the Dark: The Church of the Holy Trinity's A Christmas Story."

possibility of telling the story from other cultural perspectives, particularly from the underside.

The question remains whether it is possible to read the subversive biblical narrative of the nativity, the inclusive nature of volunteer participation, the community/congregational singing, as fissures in the imperial fabric of the production. Does a postcolonial optic, understood along the lines of Bhabha's mimicry, and as a glimpse of the Third Space, help us deconstruct the colonial gaze and expose, unmask, and interrogate the pervasive cultural influence of English colonialism and imperialism in the production? Does it invite us to appreciate potential glimmers of resistance to the status quo? Or, does reading The Christmas Story as a "coming together" in the Third Space actually leave structures of power and power differentials among participants unchallenged, allowing it to become a place of co-opting? Instead of "allowing" a subversion of power structures, does the power imbalance co-opt the "others" into becoming cogs in the machine of empire?

It can be argued that the liberating potential of The Christmas Story is largely nascent rather than actualized. The production still reinscribes empire, even though it could be deconstructed and read as "mimicking" empire and therefore postcolonially offering alternative visions in a kind of Third Space nativity. We are left to ask what it would mean to actually hear The Christmas Story from the underside, told from the perspective of the marginalized and excluded. How could it begin to be de-linked from Europe? How could it be reconfigured with an optic that privileges the experiences and voices of the colonized "others?"

Theoretically speaking, the Third Space certainly has the potential to be both resistant and liberating, as Bhabha has articulated it. His contribution to discourses which grapple with colonialism and articulate the complex interwoven nature of violence, liberation, oppression, and resistance—all inhabiting the same geopolitical spaces—is invaluable. Yet our use of Bhabha here also points to the limits of mimicry and Third Space thinking, despite the critical contribution these key concepts have made to broader post-colonial discourses. Specifically, the notion of the Third Space limits how we can read the dynamics of these exchanges because it occludes more than it reveals. It disallows us to challenge the power differential operative in The Christmas Story, because the power of the dominant culture is such that it ultimately obscures any other cultural expression. As long as the Third Space is circumscribed by the colonial gaze and Anglo North Atlantic discourses, the possibility of telling the story otherwise remains quiescent. Similarly, while mimicking can be read as undermining empire, it can also be understood as a sophisticated reproduction of empire because communities are still excluded and absent from this production by virtue of not being reflected in the culture that is reproduced, whether in the music or the rest of the production. Their stories are not told. Of course, the dynamics at play can also be both, or even multiple, simultaneously.

Alternatively, decolonial scholars are interested in affirming marginalized agencies and (re)claiming other (non-European) ways of knowing, being, doing, and feeling. These ways are understood on their own terms, as "de-linked" from Europe in ways that do not depend on Western European Anglo North Atlantic intellectual traditions.[19] Decolonial approaches strive to affirm the ways in which people's lived experience represents marginalized voices. Hence, a decolonial perspective would ask how the story would change should those on the underside participate by actually being agents in the story, changing the very nature of the story itself.

Along these lines, let us briefly consider a couple of concrete proposals in relation to the music of The Christmas Story as ways to encourage an opening up of liberating potential. First, what if the choir were to sing music that better reflected Toronto's diversity? How would a change in the sonic landscape challenge the audience and Christmas Story participants to reimagine the nativity story in a different cultural setting, as coming from below and not being told in the sanitized garb of 1930s imperial England? Second, the professionally produced music could also include instrumentation other than the organ—perhaps percussion, guitar, or flute could be used. Many in the audience come to see The Christmas Story in order to satisfy a sentimental Christmas itch to hear and see a "traditional" English-style presentation of the story. The carols that are sung with organ accompaniment at the beginning and the end reinforce this version. Thus, a third proposal: what if a different or additional carol was (also) chosen, or more community singing was included at the beginning? Perhaps a volunteer group of singers could be added to bolster the singing of some carols, supporting diversity in the carols, as well as in the carollers themselves.

---

[19] Walter D. Mignolo, "Epistemic Disobedience, Independent Thought and Decolonial Freedom," *Theory, Culture & Society* 26, no. 7–8 (2009), 178.

No doubt, a community consultation/collaboration would yield other ideas and such changes would also need to be undertaken with pastoral sensitivity, a commitment to long-term engagement, and belief in the value of intercultural and community engagement and transformation. Even these small suggestions disrupt power at the centre. The "tradition" would be challenged and things would not be the same. Such shifts would be threatening for some. But no change is threatening for some others as well. The pull toward the-way-things-were remains strong and empire at the heart of liturgy too easily reasserts itself.

Christmas Eve: *Las Posadas*

I am at a planning meeting for the Holy Trinity Christmas Eve service in November of 2007. There are about twelve of us, half from the English-speaking congregation of Holy Trinity and the other half from the Spanish-speaking congregation of San Esteban. For an ice-breaker, we are asked to describe how we understand Christmas. Someone from Holy Trinity begins by describing their childhood family celebration of Christmas. I am transported into their vision of a perfect family gathering where all expectations are met in a reproduction of a Victorian Christmas: turkey is on the table, children's eyes glisten with expectation as they anticipate opening presents which are under the tree, and all the family has gathered. Then someone from San Esteban speaks: "The most important thing to remember about Christmas is that Jesus came in poverty." I am dumbstruck and ashamed to have been so caught up in the traditional sentimental vision of an ideal middle-class Anglo Christmas. How could I have forgotten the messy, dirty, poor, scary, painful reality of God's coming among us as a vulnerable baby?

It is Christmas Eve. We are gathered for a rehearsal. There are two guitar-ists—one from each community—and a group of people who will play the parts of Maria, José, and Jesús, in our version of the Mexican tradition of Posadas. The peregrinos or pilgrims will knock twice at the doors of the church and will be denied entry. Finally, we will let them in, in a celebratory entrance that will begin our bicultural and bilingual service.

Las Posadas, meaning lodging in English, is a nativity tradition that goes back 400 years in Mexico (including what is now part of the Southern USA) and Guatemala, with similar traditions being practiced in other parts of Central America. The celebration begins nine days before Christmas (each day representing a month of Mary's pregnancy) and involves a re-enactment of the journey to Bethlehem. Mary and Joseph, either as puppets or as children or as adults dressed up, are accompanied by a group of pilgrims (*peregrinos*) who visit houses in the community to seek "lodging." They are rejected at first by the hosts (*posaderos*), but are eventually warmly welcomed in. The traditional ritual is accompanied by costumes, prayers, food, and a traditional song. A mixed (or *mestizo*) rite, it has some roots in popular medieval Spanish Catholicism and also corresponds with the Aztec winter festival celebrating the sun god Huitzilopochtli. Though associated with popular Catholicism, it is celebrated by LatinaXo Protestants as well.[20]

At Holy Trinity, as in other LatinaXo-Anglo contexts in the USA and Canada, the two communities decided to adapt the ritual for liturgical purposes on Christmas and sing it bilingually.[21] After a time of socializing, singing, and eating, the community gathered at the east door of the church in candlelight. Led by our group of singers and two guitarists, they received the *peregrinos* who sang to be invited in: "In the name of heaven, I ask you for a place to stay, because my beloved wife cannot walk."[22] Refused with "This is not an inn, keep looking, I can't open, you might be a rogue!" the group walked around outside to the south door while the rest of the community moved inside (Fig. 6.1).

But at the second door, they were still not granted entrance:

Peregrinos: Don't be inhuman, have pity on us, and the God of heaven will reward you.

Posaderos: You can go already and not bother us because if I become angry I am going to beat you with a stick.

---

[20] Franciscan Media, "Las Posadas: A Mexican Christmas Tradition," accessed June 11, 2017, https://www.franciscanmedia.org/las-posadas-a-mexican-christmas-tradition/. See also: Wikipedia, "Las Posadas," accessed June 13, 2017, https://en.wikipedia.org/wiki/Las_Posadas

[21] For another example of the liturgical use of *Las Posadas*, see Hugo Olaiz, "How to Celebrate a Mexican Posada: A Packet for Lay Leaders, Musicians, and Clergy," *Chartered Committee on Hispanic Ministry, Episcopal Diocese of North Carolina*, accessed June 11, 2017, http://www.tens.org/download_file/view/221/

[22] This and the following translations are from the version sung at Holy Trinity (see Figs. 6.1 and 6.2), translation, Leonel Abaroa Boloña. For other verses and further descriptions, see Timothy M. Matovina, "Liturgy, Popular Rites, and Popular Spirituality," in *Mestizo Worship: A Pastoral Approach to Liturgical Ministry*, ed. Virgilio P Elizondo and Timothy M. Matovina (Collegeville, MN: The Liturgical Press, 1998), 83–84; Virgilio Elizondo, "Living Faith: Resistance and Survival," in *Galilean Journey: The Mexican-American Promise* (Maryknoll, NY: Orbis Books, 2007), 34–37.

Door One: East Door

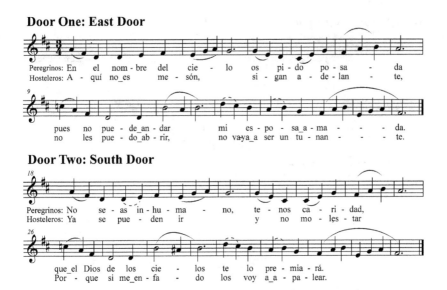

Door Two: South Door

Fig. 6.1   Music for *Las Posadas* as sung at Holy Trinity, first two doors

Eventually, at the third and final west door, the *peregrinos* were welcomed in:

Peregrinos: My wife is Mary, she is the Queen of Heaven, and she is going to be the mother of the Divine Word.

Posaderos: Are you Joseph? And your wife is Mary? Come in, pilgrims. I didn't recognize you.

Final chorus (with different music and sung in English):

> Enter Holy Pilgrims into this little corner.
> Even though it is poor, we offer it with all our heart
> Let us sing with joy, as we consider
> that Jesus, Joseph and Mary came to honour us today.

The lively music of the final chorus lifted the community celebration and people settled in for the rest of the worship service (Fig. 6.2).

Door Three: West Door

Final Chorus: Everyone, Todos

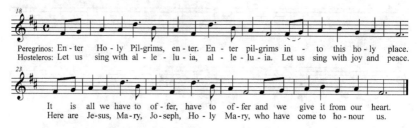

Fig. 6.2   Music for *Las Posadas* as sung at Holy Trinity, last door and final chorus

The celebration of the *Posadas* created a space of rich encounter, a liminal space, in which both communities metaphorically journeyed together, physically moving around the church, both inside and outside. People played with the borders between the "church" and the "world," between popular expressions and more formal liturgical traditions, and between the very different lived experiences of the two communities.[23] Children played the roles of Mary and Joseph. Some English-speaking members of the congregation learned how to sing the song in Spanish. And all were able to participate in some way, whether by singing, moving, or simply by

---

[23] Because of differences of language and culture (Spanish/LatinaXo and English/Anglo), people from the two communities have vastly different life experiences. San Esteban's members are mostly new immigrants to Canada, many of whom struggle with poverty, racism, lack of employment, homesickness, and other issues. Members from Holy Trinity are predominantly "white," educated, middle class folks who were born in Canada. Of course, the lines between these various identity makers are blurry. There are, for instance, poor and racialized members from Holy Trinity, and well-educated, well-employed, "white" members from San Esteban.

witnessing the re-enactment of the biblical nativity story in the form of this adapted North/Central American tradition. The rite was led by lay people from San Esteban rather than dominant-culture members from Holy Trinity and was made all the more poignant because "Mary" came from a Guatemalan family who were struggling to stay in Canada.[24]

The possibility of telling the Christmas story otherwise emerged through the *Posadas* celebration, highlighting the fundamentally liberating and incarnational theme at its centre, namely that God chose to become human as a poor, vulnerable refugee child. Latino theologian Virigilio Elizondo affirms this perspective, noting that the "rite is centered on two experiences that bring out key themes of the gospel proclamation: the *rejection* of the poor, nameless couple from the 'inferior' region of Galilee, and the *joy* that comes to those who open the door of their home and heart to shelter and welcome the rejects, because they recognize them for what they truly are: God's chosen ones."[25]

Border thinking, as articulated by Walter Mignolo, offers a lens which enriches this reading of the *Posadas,* as just such a liminal liturgical activity that has the potential to be resistant and liberating. Or, to flip it and be praxiological about it, *Las Posadas* offer a way to understand border thinking. As we saw in the last chapter, border thinking emerges from the space of the colonial difference where both the "coloniality of power" is enacted—and colonial violence is experienced—and where other ways of knowing begin to become visible. It thus rises up from the experience of the people of the Global South, especially those who were vanquished in the colonial project. In other words, it accounts for how the "coloniality of power" is expressed in the cracks of the modern-colonial capitalist world-system but looks beyond these paradigms as well.[26] Of course, it is impossible to return to a time before the modern-colonial capitalist world-system, but decolonial scholars choose to affirm knowledges and histories that pre-date it or exist outside it, as much as possible, while also affirming discourses of resistance that engage it.

[24] A group of members from both churches was working hard on behalf of the Guatemalan family, with lawyers and advisors, to ensure the best possible outcome. Eventually the family was given refugee status which allowed them to stay in Canada and pursue Canadian citizenship.

[25] Elizondo, *Galilean Journey,* 37–38.

[26] Aníbal Quijano calls the co-constitutive phenomenon of colonialism, modernity, and capitalism the "coloniality of power." See Aníbal Quijano, "Coloniality of Power, Eurocentrism, and Latin America." *Nepantla: Views from the South* 1.3 (2000).

Border thinking is thus a process which calls both for (1) delinking and decolonizing knowledge from European/modern/colonial/patriarchal epistemologies and the coloniality of power, or the modern-colonial capitalist world-system of which it is a part, and also for (2) building up "local histories, restoring the dignity that the Western idea of universal history took away from millions of people."[27] As such, it emphasizes an integration between thinking, being, and doing—and feeling—which is "from and beyond colonial legacies; from and beyond gender divide and sexual prescriptions; and from and beyond racial conflicts."[28] It is both (1) resistant, because it deconstructs forces that marginalize and (2) liberating, as it builds up marginalized (and potentially other) agencies. As a liberating force, the reality and experience of the people are understood to constitute the primary step in this reflective process. As such, border thinking is always inadequately described by the resulting theory, defying easy categorization and authoritative conclusions. It is lived and known in the concrete experience of the people in border spaces, including in border liturgies.

It is in this messy, indescribable, perhaps incomprehensible—and mysterious—space in which the Holy Spirit is most at home, preferentially present. Thus, rising up out of our community(ies), *Las Posadas* as a border(ed) liturgical act invited the subversive breath of the Holy Spirit to infuse the rest of our Christmas Eve celebration. It also offered to both communities another way of knowing, a *saber del sur* (knowledge from the south), at least partially de-linked from Europe. It was a *mestizo* ritual which blended indigenous and Spanish traditions. Finally, it was built up from local histories and practices, in this case rising up from the context of the LatinaXo community in Toronto.

Yet, questions of representation, misrepresentation, nonrepresentation, and misrecognition that we considered vis-à-vis. The Christmas Story also haunted the two communities as they wrestled with how the "I's," the "we's," and the "us's" of the liturgy were expressed. As the congregation sang the verses of the *Posadas* song, issues of agency and identity mixed together, as in the questions we previously asked: Who speaks/sings for whom? Whose song/singing is not heard, listened to, or even accounted for? How are people's stories and identities represented? Is their agency

---

[27] Walter D. Mignolo, *Local Histories/Global Designs: Coloniality, Subaltern Knowledges, and Border Thinking* (Princeton: Princeton University Press, 2000), x.

[28] Ibid., 95. See also 85.

empowered, or how are they misrecognized or objectified through representation? And to add another question, are they ignored, erased, or disposed of? The risk of the Anglo-speaking congregation misappropriating the ritual loomed as an ever-present possibility. The question: which "subject" cannot speak/sing?—as Gayatri Chakravorty Spivak might say—was made poignant by members of the Spanish congregation who were in conflict with Canadian immigration policy, under the threat of being deported. But, even in their vulnerability and utter powerlessness, the scandalous message of the gospel spoke to their condition, especially in the birth narrative. God is present among us. God chose to self-disclose through the life and witness of Jesus Christ.

By reading the Bible in a decolonial key, and re-living the nativity story through the *posadas* ritual, people lived into the hope of the narratives of power being "flipped." The communities experienced eschatological possibility as the words of Mary's song reverberated—in which God sides with the poor by bringing justice, "scattering the proud and mighty," "bringing down the powerful from their thrones," "lifting up the lowly," and "filling the hungry with good things and sending the rich away empty" (Luke 1:51–53). At its best, the *Posadas* gave voice to the disempowered, both metaphorically, in the re-enactment of the biblical story, and literally, as immigrants and refugees led the ritual. Anglo-speaking congregation members exercised their muscles of solidarity and accompaniment by participating in the rite as our border singing became a "defense and protest against the demands of the dominant culture."[29]

These themes can be illuminated through Néstor Medina's "lived hermeneutics," in which LatinaXo Canadians move "beyond a 'literalist' reading of the Bible," and "enter into a complex dialogical relation with

[29] Ricardo Ramírez, quoted in Matovina, "Liturgy, Popular Rites, and Popular Spirituality," 89. I am well aware of the risk of essentializing *Las Posadas* for the purposes of my own analysis from a White Anglo dominant culture perspective; the tension of romanticizing the rite is a danger that is held in tension with the anti-establishment, prophetic, and embodied critique that it appears to offer. From anecdotal conversations with colleagues, I am also aware that enactments of *Las Posadas* can be, among the original communities who practice the rite, sites for multiple power plays. People fight over who will have which role, by paying money to the church to secure a role for instance, or by jockeying to be a host family for community celebrations. In the future, a more detailed exploration of all of these dynamics—from the perspective of the original communities who practice the rite as well as communities in which it has been adopted—would enrich this analysis and mitigate against the risk of essentializing and romanticizing a community practice from the Global South when it moves to intercultural contexts in the Global North.

the biblical narrative" where the "impact and conditioning character of their cultural traditions as experienced in daily life induce them to find themselves in the biblical narrative."[30] He describes how a lived hermeneutics can reflect the "dynamic back-and-forth interweaving of the messy and difficult reality of daily life, individual experience, cultural traditions, and the reading of the biblical text."[31] As such, it is part of "the larger interlacing of context, community, cultural tradition, and Bible."[32] A process of lived hermeneutics does not involve abstract categories but reflects the fact that "Latina/o Canadians live their faith as Latinas/os in a context of great social inhospitality, under enormous cultural pressures by a dominant culture, and at the same time with rich, promising possibilities of having a better life than the life left behind in their birth countries."[33]

With that in mind, the *Posadas* can be understood as a liturgical embodiment of lived hermeneutics. The "struggle to make ends meet," the perils of border crossing, the reality of being "stigmatized as foreigners or illegals" is affirmed in the *Posadas* retelling of the nativity narrative.[34] The experience of migration, of being sojourners, is transferred onto the archetypal story, as they identify with the struggles of the holy family. At Holy Trinity, the LatinaXo community gained "inspiration and insights in order to understand their living situation and to find hope as they confront their new social and political context."[35] It also, to repeat, invited the Anglo-speaking congregation to walk with their sisters and brothers from San Esteban, together imaginatively constructing new meaning in the Christmas story by participating in its retelling from the underside, and sharing in the struggles of their friends and neighbours. The risk of misappropriating the *Posadas* by the Anglo-speaking community was mitigated by the fact that the ritual became a social and theological critical indictment of present social structures.

For me, as the dominant culture music leader from the Anglo-speaking congregation, this intercultural moment, this invitation into a border space, this opportunity to make space for the expressions of a *saber del sur*,

[30] Néstor Medina, "Latinaos, Culture and the Bible," in *Reading In-Between: Biblical Interpretation in Canada,* ed. Néstor Medina, Alison Hari-Singh, and HeyRan Kim-Cragg (Eugene, OR: Pickwick, 2019), 68.

[31] Ibid., 70.

[32] Ibid., 70.

[33] Ibid.

[34] Ibid.

[35] Ibid., 70–71.

was a moment of conversion. The fabric of my conversion is woven from a thousand tiny epiphanies. These moments, in which I catch but a glimpse of the Divine, are enfolded into my relationships and experiences as embodiments of the Holy Spirit, and as the *imago dei* in those I encounter. The experience of facilitating the use of the *Posadas* humbled me in processes of deep listening and learning. In the uncomfortable dislocation I experienced; in witnessing people's empowerment through song and ritual; in the testimonies from members from both communities who experienced the Holy Spirit's movement through our shared rite—I was changed.[36] These factors also contributed to a communal call to *metanoia* through which the entire community was called to live the Christian vocation of embodying a liberating praxis of life in syncopated movements between cultural spaces.

THE MIDWIFE'S CAROL

As the two communities work together to plan the Christmas Eve service, I realize that there is a Holy Trinity tradition, beloved by the community, that needs to be brought to the table: the singing of the "The Midwife's Carol." About fifteen years prior, community member Ian Sowton asked me to compose a folk tune for his words. The song tells the story of Jesus' birth from the perspective of an imagined midwife, replete with afterbirth and the tying of the umbilical cord. The people of Holy Trinity relish singing this song each Christmas; it has become a community favourite. I'm really not sure how it is going to go over with the people of San Esteban. I am worried that the feminist language and the messy description of the birth will be offensive to some. But, encouraged and aided by the priest of San Esteban, we translate the chorus ("Wash him clean, wipe him dry, hush you, shush you rock-a-bye, rock-a-bye") into Spanish: "lo bañamos, lo secamos, le cantamos al dormir, al dormir." The literal translation is: "We wash him, we dry him, we sing him to sleep."

Since the 1960s, there has been a strong emphasis at Holy Trinity on lay liturgical leadership. The community was inspired by the politics of the 1960s, including the liturgical reforms sweeping mainline churches and

[36] I do not intend to romanticize this work or its impact. For instance, I note that although all shared services (Christmas and Holy Week) had fully bilingual bulletins, the services were generally not bicultural, tending to be translations of dominant culture (Anglo) liturgical traditions.

articulated in *Sacrosanctum Concilium* of Vatican II. They experienced a fantastic creative energy for liturgical renewal in all aspects of the services, including advocating for an open communion table, the extensive use of "inclusive" and liberating language, and the creation of new Eucharistic prayers and new hymns.[37] This renewal in worship resonated with the community's historical commitment to social and economic justice (Fig. 6.3).

The community's commitment to "inclusive" and liberating language in worship was inspired respectively by feminist theology and liberationist theology, especially Latin American liberation theology.[38] Yet, the community continues to wrestle with its Anglican inheritance, a tradition which is one of those which "function in the field of liturgical studies as the norm and measure of Christian worship."[39] As Ruth Duck notes, "it is not as easy as it might seem for members of dominant groups to discern how a White Eurocentric norm continues to operate, assuming what is only contextual is transcultural."[40] In other words, the historic Anglican tradition, like other dominant denominational/liturgical traditions, is contextual, not universal, even though it imposed itself *as* universal, particularly in processes of colonization. The Holy Trinity community grapples with these issues and realities but cannot escape the privilege of its mostly "white," university educated, and middle-class members, along with its denominational tradition. Like Duck, many are self-aware and confess that their "worldview is subconsciously shaped by the canon of literature (and other life experiences) to regard the Euro-Anglo-White traditions of worship as the 'real' tradition of worship, with others being variations of lesser import."[41]

---

[37] Community members were leaders in the movement for inclusive (non-gendered) language, both in reference to humanity and to God. They also self-published a hymn book with 46 original hymn texts in 2007, a significant proportion of which have original music. "The Midwife's Carol" is one of these hymns.

[38] "Inclusive" language is the term the community used to describe this commitment. Ruth Duck suggests broadening the scope of this commitment through "expansive" language and Marjorie Proctor-Smith prefers "emancipatory" language. William S. Kervin, "Joyful is the Dark: Expansive and Emancipatory Language," 36–39, In *Gathered for Worship: A Sourcebook for Worship Committees, Leaders, and Teams* (Toronto: United Church Publishing House, 2017).

[39] Ruth C. Duck, *Worship for the Whole People of God: Vital Worship for the 21st Century* (Louisville, KY: Westminster John Knox, 2013), xvii.

[40] Ibid., xviii.

[41] Ibid., xxi.

The Midwife's Carol

Ian Sowton, 1994

Midwife's Carol
(Becca Whitla, 1994)

1. The birth it-self was not too hard, good pres-en - ta-tion, fine strong mum.

But my dear it was a cir - cus, I thought that half the town had come.

Chorus

Lo ba - ña - mos, lo se - ca - mos, le can - ta - mos al dor - mir, al dor-mir.

2. There were these shep - herds who burst in, my dear they said a talk - ing

light told them to come and pay res-pects, kneel - ing they were to that wee mite.

Chorus

Lo ba -ña-mos, lo se - ca-mos, le can - ta - mos al dor-mir, al dor-mir

3. He's breathing well, the cord's tied off,
her afterbirth's come free my dear
when three fine scholar blokes squeeze in
saying a star has brought them here.
Lo ba-ña-mos...

4. "You selling tickets then?" I said,
"Buzz off you lot and let her rest."
And they did too, leaving presents,
rich stuff my dear, the very best.
Lo ba-ña-mos...

5. All that public to and fro-ing,
she watches as it comes and goes,
with him tucked, dear, in a manger
pulled from under the donkey's nose.
Lo ba-ña-mos...

6. Winter solstice 'twas my dear,
shivery damp and animal stink,
Worship, palaver, gifts and all -
what was going on do you think?
Lo ba-ña-mos...

*English chorus: Wash him clean, wipe him dry,
Hush you, shush you, rock-a-bye, rock-a-bye.*

Fig. 6.3 "The Midwife's Carol," Hymn by Ian Sowton and Becca Whitla

Among the active members of the congregation is the author of "The Midwife's Carol," Ian Sowton. Ian can often be found cheerfully assisting with the washing of the dishes after soup on Sunday mornings, or sorting books for the book sale to raise money for the parish's refugees.[42] When Ian asked me to write music for his text, saying he wanted something folky, I set to work on the tune. My roommate at the time, community member Ian Digby (and future husband of The Christmas Story director), helped make it come alive, by suggesting an additional beat in the chorus and by singing it with me over and over until it flowed and the harmony part emerged. For many years, the two of us sang it together at the Christmas Eve service.

In the carol, Sowton reimagines the Biblical nativity narrative from the perspective of a midwife. In the subversive tradition of Biblical midwives Shifra and Puah who deceive the Egyptian Pharaoh in order to save Hebrew children (Exodus 1:15–22), Sowton's midwife tells the tale of Jesus' birth. The messiness of childbirth is not sanitized away: verse three begins "He's breathing well, the cord's tied off, her afterbirth's come free, my dear." The midwife describes the chaos at the scene with shepherds bursting in to pay their respects, and "three fine scholar blokes" squeezing in. The midwife defends the new mother by telling the scholars to "buzz off, you lot and let her rest." Sowton's text represents the kind of expansive language and imagination which Duck advocates as a way to lift up the eschatological ministry of Jesus "who proclaimed God's love for all and by his actions lifted up women, the poor, children, and others society rejects or devalues" and lives out a "new reality and provide(s) a foretaste of God's reign in the world."[43]

---

[42] Sowton joined together his theology, literary training, and passion for poetry in producing inclusive language versions of the Hebrew Scripture lessons and the Psalms (published in a Psalter by the parish in 2007). He was born in Beijing China in 1929 into a Salvation Army family, and lived in a Japanese Internment camp from 1942 to 1945, coming to Canada in 1947. A retired English professor and poet, he was an advocate for the study of women and Canadian writers throughout his teaching career, and notable for his steadfast support of the establishment of a doctoral women's studies program at York University in Toronto. He also adapted well-loved eighteenth- and nineteenth-century hymns into gender inclusive language and wrote several original hymns, a couple of which were published in the Canadian Anglican hymnal *Common Praise*, all of which were also published in the congregation's 2007 hymnbook.

[43] Ruth C. Duck, "Expansive Language in the Baptized Community," in *Primary Sources of Liturgical Theology*, ed. Dwight W. Vogel (Collegeville, MN: The Liturgical Press, 2000), 289–90.

Read decolonially, "The Midwife's Carol" offers another way of telling the story of Jesus' birth by (re)inserting women's embodied knowledges into the narrative. The story is transformed into an intentional site where the agency of women is named, affirmed, and dignified, a place where women's knowledge is welcomed and nurtured. Faced with the dangerous challenges of navigating real borders as they are forced to return to their home to be taxed, Mary and Joseph are met in the political border space of a borrowed stable by the midwife. The messy non-rational and visceral reality of birthing counters the sanitized and romanticized version of the story of the birth of Jesus, especially Luke's version and inherited interpretations of it, expressed in the culture at large and in traditional carols, including those sung before and after The Christmas Story.

Border thinking draws its strength from precisely the kind of border knowledges that are affirmed in women's embodied knowledge about birthing. Walter Mignolo distinguishes between "modern" knowledge/epistemology and border knowledge by developing the concept of border gnosis, which he describes as "knowledge from a subaltern perspective ... conceived from the exterior borders of the modern-colonial world-system."[44] He does not assume that only people who come from "such and such a place could do X." Yet, he also insists that border thinking can only come from a subaltern perspective, cautioning against territorial perspectives which risk instead an appropriation of "colonial differe/a/nces [where they become] an object of study rather than as an epistemic potential."[45] This seeming contradiction, this incommensurability—to which we will return in Chap. 7—between the possibility of any person engaging in border thinking, on the one hand, and the insistence that it must *be from, come from*, and *be at* a subaltern locus of enunciation, on the other, exposes the tension of trying to engage in acts of solidarity with the marginalized.[46]

Certainly, women's knowledge about birthing falls outside the purview of traditional modern scientific, rationalist framing. The text of "The Midwife's Carol" provokes a reclaiming and celebration of this other way of knowing. The song helps the story to be retold from this perspective,

---

[44] Mignolo, *Local Histories*, 11.

[45] Mignolo, *Local Histories*, 45.

[46] Mignolo's emphasis on the "links between the place of theorizing ([from Paul Gilroy] *being from, coming from*, and, *being at*) and the locus of enunciation," foregrounds for me the importance of questions of leadership as well as the relationship between theory and action. Ibid., 115.

reconfiguring it, and invites those who sing it to enter into the story from a different vantage point. For Sowton, writing "The Midwife's Carol" was primarily an attempt to "desentimentalize" the story of Jesus' birth. He wanted to provide an alternative to the kind of sentimental middle-class version of the story that is pervasive. In fact, Sowton falls into the camp that does not support The Christmas Story production for this reason. He has not once attended a performance. Instead, he imagined the story "from the perspective of a working-class midwife, an ordinary person whose job it was to assist at the birth."[47] As such, Sowton's poem celebrates his own working-class Salvation Army roots. A detailed textual analysis, beyond the scope of this study, would reveal Sowton's literary accent—"fine strong mum," "hush you, shush you, rock-a-bye," "my dear," "three fine scholar blokes," "buzz off, you lot,"—something he describes as "not English, not Canadian, but reflecting his own mongrel inheritance." Hinting at his own complex autobiographical narrative, Sowton explains that his "father was born in Sweden and went to school in India and my mother was from New Zealand."[48] The varieties of speech and cultural influences were enriched by Sowton's childhood in China. Above all though, Sowton also insists that his move to desentimentalize the story is rooted in an incarnational theology which does not shy away from the "blood, sweat, and tears of an actual birth."[49]

But the colonial element is still at play in the authorship of the song. However powerful and provocative the words may be; however much they may evoke a decolonial reclaiming of another way of knowing; however much the singers, especially women, may experience liberation through the affirmation of women's perspectives and the implied critical interrogation of power structures; the fact remains that the text was written by a "white," middle-class, heterosexual man. Even my own participation in the creation of the song as the tune-writer is fraught with the coloniality of my being a "white," educated, middle-class person, though it could also be argued that my involvement mitigates somewhat against Sowton's male subjectivity.[50]

---

[47] Ian Sowton, personal conversation with the author (3 October 2017).

[48] Ibid.

[49] Ibid.

[50] When I composed the tune, I had not yet experienced birthing. I was accompanied by midwives in the births of my two children, so as I continued to sing it I gained a new appreciation for the song.

Sowton's appropriation of the voice of a woman adds a certain incom-mensurability to the dynamics. He *is* celebrated among the women in the congregation, many of whom are committed feminists, for his work using emancipatory language and as an ally to women. But there could be said to be a residual heteronormative androcentric colonizing force at play here. Questions about representation persist. What if the text had been written by a woman? By a midwife? Did Sowton's privilege—and mine—afford us more recognition for the song we had created? Though "white" women also draw on women's collective, embodied knowledge in prac-tices of birthing, how could we/I have been more aware of racialization in the conception of the song—and of economic disparity, for that matter? And yet, the song has been embraced by the community and (re)signified as subversive and liberative, with a subalternity (at least of women) poured onto it—even in the midst of, or despite, its inherent coloniality of author-ship. The authors have been accepted as allies in the process, claimed as part of the struggle to resist oppressive power structures and reclaim other ways of knowing.

The fact that "The Midwife's Carol" became its own beloved "tradi-tion" at Holy Trinity illuminates this potential for allyship. Sowton is well aware of these issues and in his own writing, teaching, and academic work, insists that there is no such thing as objectivity. He believes that it is essen-tial to be "clear where you're coming from" which in his case is as a "white, middle-class, male, well aware of his privilege."[51] Yet, when he wrote the hymn out of a desire to emphasize the fleshy reality of God's incarnational act by daring to imagine a "working-class" woman and midwife telling the story, he was also claiming, or owning, what he calls the universality of the story as part of his own Christian faith.[52] For him it was a way to tell the story from a different perspective, from below, an act of solidarity in which he was promoting another way of knowing the story of Jesus' birth. His work in writing this carol, and in inviting me to collaborate with him, could be described as contributing to an articulation of another way of understanding the event by re-telling the story from a woman's perspective.

This impulse to tell the story otherwise is also affirmed in the fact that the song is meant to belong to and be sung in community. The singing of the song, in all its complexity of authorship, identity (of the creators and

[51] Ibid.
[52] Ibid.

the singers), relationship, context, and community, can be articulated along the lines of what Alberto Moreiras proposes as relational or perspectival subalternism and "counterhegemonic" praxis which we examined in Chap. 3.[53] Rooted in relationship, the community of singers articulates a counter-narrative that opposes hegemonic canons, transforms the way the biblical nativity narrative is understood, and liberates the community to imagine another way of being. Ultimately, the benefits of this kind of approach affirm the fact that liberation does not only benefit subjugated people but perpetuates social and epistemic "self-liberation of those who live and act within the structure of belief of modernity and colonialism."[54]

My experience of leading "The Midwife's Carol" was deepened in the intercultural work of planning the bilingual service with the San Esteban community. By singing the chorus in Spanish, the two communities literally navigated the borders between languages in this one song (just as they had also done in other hymns that alternated between the languages, including in the singing of the songs that accompanied the *Posadas* ritual). What could be described as their "border singing" corresponds with what I have articulated as syncopation, the navigating between languages, cultures, communities, and between people—a mode of being to which I was committed in my work to encourage the two communities to sing together.

BORDER(ED) LIVES, BORDER LITURGY

My experience of syncopation in working with these communities reflects the joys and challenges of working interculturally toward liberating congregational singing. The incorporation of the *Posadas* as another way of knowing, telling, and enacting the Christmas story lifted up the lived experience of the San Esteban community. Their leadership, and the sharing of their struggles of daily life, deepened and concretized the two communities' enactment of the ritual. It became a portrayal of their own lived reality, witnessed to and accompanied by the Anglo-speaking congregation. Then when both communities sang about the birth of Jesus from the

---

[53] Alberto Moreiras, "Hybridity and Double Consciousness," *Cultural Studies* 13 (3) (1999): 373.

[54] Mignolo, *Local Histories*, 125. Though Mignolo is referring to "postcolonial theories" here, he is drawing on the pioneering work of liberation philosophers Paulo Freire and Enrique Dussel, among others. Freire and others develop the idea of liberation for both the oppressor and oppressed. See, for example, Paulo Freire, *Pedagogy of the Oppressed*, trans. Myra Bergman Ramos (New York: Herder and Herder, 1971).

embodied perspective of the midwife, they also embraced another way of knowing, lifting up the knowledges of women.

At the same time, neither the *Posadas* nor "The Midwife's Carol" are uncomplicated in their use of marginalized voices. The risk of mis-appropriation and of silencing or distorting those voices looms large. In the case of the *Posadas,* the risk of appropriating the ritual as an exotic "other" was mitigated by the authenticity and integrity of the ritual because of the participation of the San Esteban community. The *Posadas* were transformed into a rebuke of present systems of oppression and exclusion. The appropriation of a woman's voice in "The Midwife's Carol" was potentially problematic, but the embracing of the song by the two communities and especially by women, allowed the subversive vision of God's incarnation, in the messy, painful, risky birth of a human child, to be foregrounded. Both ritual expressions included Spanish and English as the planners attempted to integrate and celebrate interculturality in the worship of the two communities.

Together, these rituals expressed an in-between-ness which could be characterized as border liturgy. The real borders experienced in the lives of the people played out in the liminal spaces between languages and cultures as people worshiped together. The risky, even dangerous reality of some congregation members interfaced with the privileged reality of others because, as Gloria Anzaldúa notes, "borderlands are physically present wherever two or more cultures edge each other, where people of different races occupy the same territory, where under, lower, middle and upper classes touch, where the space between two individuals shrinks with intimacy."[55] These moments of border liturgy provoke the reclaiming of other ways of knowing drawn from the particular experiences of the mar-ginalized, including elements from outside of the Anglo-North Atlantic coloniality of power. They also promote a critical interrogation of present power structures, including what is traditionally done in worship, as well as how it is done.

This worship in a decolonial key through these concrete, communal, and relational rituals affirmed other ways of being and liberated partici-pants to engage in transformative action in the world. For members of San Esteban, the rituals were an affirmation of their daily struggle to survive and thrive. For members of Holy Trinity, they were acts of solidarity and

[55] Gloria Anzaldúa, *Borderlands/La Frontera: The New Mestiza* (San Francisco: Aunt Lute Books, 2007), 19.

engagements in counterhegemonic praxes which challenged the (liturgical) status quo.[56] This rich engagement is not without significant challenges, of course. It takes a serious and steadfast commitment, which requires energy, vision, and patience. It is hard work. Some Holy Trinity community members, for instance, resisted these liturgical innovations by expressing their discomfort with so much Spanish, longing for things to be done the "way we used to do it." In the end, a lack of committed leadership and determination from the two communities meant that the *Posadas* was ultimately discontinued in the Christmas Eve service.

Still, the *Posadas* and "The Midwife's Carol" did contribute—if only for a time—to the transformation of how people from the two communities understood themselves and each other. They also affirmed the transforming potential of similar initiatives for The Christmas Story, outlined at the beginning of the chapter. Through these other ways of knowing, we were able to move from "tradition" to innovation and renewal, (re)claiming a ritual from the underside (the *Posadas)* and (re)inventing a new practice ("The Midwife's Carol").

And yet, even these "decolonial turns" can potentially limit the type of re-orientation I am proposing if those involved are not open to a fundamental transformation of the status quo. Liberating congregational singing (and liturgy) is more than simply reclaiming other ways of knowing. A robust re-orientation places the weight of an epistemological force on those other ways of knowing for re-interpreting reality and re-evaluating Euro North Atlantic traditions. Liberating singing actually demands an openness to conversion, to *metanoia*. It invites a critical stance of recognition which has cultural, social, and political implications that in turn affects our relationships, our communities, and our institutions/churches. It provokes liberating actions which entail epistemological reconfigurations, including an interrogation of inherited epistemes; an openness to alternative traditions and new initiatives; and a recognition, acknowledgement, and celebration of the fragile spaces that have already been opened up by those who find themselves on the underside. With all of this in mind, we turn now to the singing of a Toronto trade union choir to glean some incipient principles for a liberating liturgical theology. As we shall see, their

---

[56] As already noted, I am generalizing about members of each community. I am particularly aware of the fact that there are Holy Trinity members who struggle with discrimination based on a number of factors. Similarly, there are members at San Esteban who might not characterize their lives as a "daily struggle to survive and thrive."

singing exhibits a mode of doing theology and embodying sacramental praxes, all animated by the liberating action of the Holy Spirit.

BIBLIOGRAPHY

Anzaldúa, Gloria. 2007. *Borderlands/La Frontera: The New Mestiza.* San Francisco: Aunt Lute Books.

Bennet, J.C. 2017. How Formal Anglican Pew-Renting Worked in Practice, 1800–1950. *The Journal of Ecclesiastical History* 68 (4): 766–783. Cambridge: Cambridge University Press.

Bhabha, Homi K. 1994. *The Location of Culture.* New York: Routledge.

Church of the Holy Trinity. Church Website. http://www.holytrinitytoronto.org/wp/. Accessed 21 June 2017.

———. A Very Brief History. http://www.holytrinitytoronto.org/wp/about/a-very-brief-history/. Accessed 21 June 2017.

Du Bois, William Edward Burdhardt. 1904. *The Souls of Black Folks; Essays and Sketches.* Chicago: A.C. McClurg & Co.

Duck, Ruth C. 2000. Expansive Language in the Baptized Community. In *Primary Sources of Liturgical Theology*, ed. Dwight W. Vogel, 286–294. Collegeville: The Liturgical Press.

———. 2013. *Worship for the Whole People of God: Vital Worship for the 21st Century.* Louisville: Westminster John Knox.

Elizondo, Virgilio. 2007. Living Faith: Resistance and Survival. In *Galilean Journey: The Mexican-American Promise*, 32–46. Maryknoll: Orbis Books.

Franciscan Media. Las Posadas: A Mexican Christmas Tradition. https://www.franciscanmedia.org/las-posadas-a-mexican-christmas-tradition/. Accessed 11 June 2017.

Freire, Paulo. 1971. *Pedagogy of the Oppressed.* Trans. Myra Bergman Ramos. New York: Herder and Herder.

Go Forth into the World. https://johnian.wordpress.com/2012/02/05/go-forth-into-the-world/. Accessed 9 May 2018.

Kelly, Deirdre. 2013. Angels in the Dark: The Church of the Holy Trinity's A Christmas Story. *Critics at Large*, December 20. http://www.criticsatlarge.ca/2013/12/angels-in-dark-church-of-holy-trinitys.html. Accessed 8 June 2017.

Kervin, William S. 2017. Joyful Is the Dark: Expansive and Emancipatory Language. In *Gathered for Worship: A Sourcebook for Worship Committees, Leaders, and Teams*, 36–39. Toronto: United Church Publishing House.

King's College Cambridge. A Festival of Nine Lessons and Carols: Service Booklets from Previous Years. http://www.kings.cam.ac.uk/files/services/festival-nine-lessons-2015.pdf. Accessed 6 June 2017.

Matovina, Timothy M. 1998. Liturgy, Popular Rites, and Popular Spirituality. In *Mestizo Worship: A Pastoral Approach to Liturgical Ministry*, ed. Virgilio P. Elizondo and Timothy M. Matovina, 81–91. Collegeville: The Liturgical Press.

Medina, Néstor. 2019. Latinaos, Culture and the Bible. In *Reading In-Between: Biblical Interpretation in Canada*, ed. Néstor Medina, Alison Hari-Singh, and HeyRan Kim-Cragg. Eugene: Pickwick.

Mignolo, Walter D. 2000. *Local Histories/Global Designs: Coloniality, Subaltern Knowledges, and Border Thinking*. Princeton: Princeton University Press.

———. 2009. Epistemic Disobedience, Independent Thought and Decolonial Freedom. *Theory, Culture & Society* 26 (7–8): 151–181. http://waltermignolo.com/wp-content/uploads/2013/03/epistemicdisobedience-2.pdf. Accessed 25 July 2018.

Monbiot, George. 2016. Neoliberalism – The Ideology at the Root of All Our Problems. *The Guardian*, April 15. https://www.theguardian.com/books/2016/apr/15/neoliberalism-ideology-problem-george-monbiot. Accessed 16 June 2020.

Moreiras, Alberto. 1999. Hybridity and Double Consciousness. *Cultural Studies* 13 (3): 373–407.

Olaiz, Hugo. How to Celebrate a Mexican Posada: A Packet for Lay Leaders, Musicians, and Clergy. *Chartered Committee on Hispanic Ministry, Episcopal Diocese of North Carolina*. http://www.tens.org/download_file/view/221/. Accessed 11 June 2017.

Quijano, Aníbal. 2000. Coloniality of Power, Eurocentrism, and Latin America. *Nepantla: Views from the South* 1 (3): 533–580. http://www.unc.edu/~aescobar/wan/wanquijano.pdf. Accessed 25 July 2018.

The Christmas Story. 75th Anniversary Programme. https://www.thechristmasstory.ca/commemorative-program. Accessed 6 June 2017.

———. History of the Pageant. https://www.thechristmasstory.ca/history-of-the-pageant. Accessed 6 June 2017.

———. Music. https://www.thechristmasstory.ca/music. Accessed 6 June 2017.

Vincent, Donovan. 2015. Three Torontonians Taking Their Turn in the Spotlight This Christmas. *The Toronto Star*, December 20. https://www.thestar.com/news/insight/2015/12/20/three-torontonians-taking-their-turn-in-the-spotlight-this-christmas.html. Accessed 9 June 2017.

Wikipedia. Pew. https://en.wikipedia.org/wiki/Pew. Accessed 21 June 2017.

———. Las Posadas. https://en.wikipedia.org/wiki/Las_Posadas. Accessed 13 June 2017.

CHAPTER 7

Liberating the Song Bird

INTRODUCTION

We begin with an assertion—liberating congregational singing is animated by none other than the Holy Spirit. Preferentially present in the borders of our lives, she provokes us to interrogate empire at the heart of our singing, invites us to celebrate other ways of singing which come from the margins, and coaxes us to liberate our singing and liberate with our singing. Thus understood as a germinating force that permeates our singing, and our lives, the Holy Spirit also vivifies the incipient principles for a liberating liturgical theology proposed in this chapter.

My experience with the Hotel Employees and Restaurant Employees (H.E.R.E.) Local 75 Choir from Toronto is the praxical lens through which these themes are explored. The choice to examine a setting outside the church is a deliberately provocative move on my part because the Holy Spirit is not confined to a church building and is not limited to certain rites and certain hymns. Indeed, one could say that the Holy Spirit defies the limits of coloniality, beckoning us toward the risky business of border singing, whether on a picket line, at a protest, or in a church service. A process of liberating congregational singing frees us to be open to these dynamic in-between, life-giving, spirit-infused, intercultural, and multilingual spaces wherever and whenever we encounter the Divine.

© The Author(s) 2020
B. Whitla, *Liberation, (De)Coloniality, and Liturgical Practices*,
New Approaches to Religion and Power,
https://doi.org/10.1007/978-3-030-52636-8_7

Ain't You Got a Right to the Tree of Life!

Ain't you got a right to the tree of life!
So rocky was the road—so dangerous is the journey!
I know you had a hard time, I know you're tired.
Our life will be sweeter, our life will be sweeter...
You can tell all my brothers, you can tell all my sisters...
Ain't you got a right to the tree of life![1]

We are gathered as usual on Wednesday evening in the spring of 1999. This is my last rehearsal before I head off with my husband for a musical tour in Europe with our newborn daughter, Emma. A few weeks back, I taught the choir a new song: "Ain't You Got a Right to the Tree of Life." Linette, a member of the choir, throws her head back, closes her eyes, and beats the slow rhythm of the lament with her hands. Another member lets her voice float up to intone the haunting major seventh of the chord. We hush our voices as we sing and imagine how "our life will be sweeter." We raise our voices to proclaim the good news to our brothers and sisters. After the reprise of the first verse, the choir stills.

Sensing the mood, one member suggests we sing "Amazing Grace." At the end of the song, there is a discernible shift in the feeling in the room. The members decide that they need to pray over me to protect me before I leave. One woman starts pacing around the room uttering "Jesussss" under her breath. I am not sure what to do. I am the leader of this trade union choir, but the members of the choir have taken control and the rehearsal has become a prayer meeting of which I am the focus. I allow myself to give up control and give in to what is happening. Members offer prayers for my safety and the safety of my family. After several minutes, things wind up. Something has happened. I feel moved, blessed, and deeply honored to be present.

---

[1] The song is based on a version collected by Guy and Candie Carawan, *Ain't You Got a Right to the Tree of Life? The People of Johns Island, South Carolina—Their Faces, Their Words, and Their Songs* (Athens, GA and London, U.K.: Brown Thrasher Books, The University of Georgia Press, 1966). For a recorded version of the H.E.R.E. Choir, see H.E.R.E. Local 75 Choir, "Ain't You Got a Right," in *I Still Have Joy,* Compact Disk Recording, (Toronto: Deep Down Productions, 2004, CD).

Historical Context

Between 1998 and 2005, every Wednesday, the Hotel Employees and Restaurant Employees Union Local 75 Choir (H.E.R.E. Choir) gathered at Holy Trinity Anglican Church in downtown Toronto. Even though we were a trade union choir, we sang spirituals and church songs as well as union songs. We joined our voices together in a profoundly concrete engagement. Acknowledging the hard reality and struggles of daily life for choir members, we sang about the "rocky road," the "dangerous journey," the suffering through hard times, and the bone-tired exhaustion that haunted the members of the choir. I was the middle-class white choir leader of this group of Caribbean-Canadian women who cleaned the rooms at Toronto's fanciest hotels. Their singing was an expression of their daily challenges and struggles and an extension of their inner cry to God in song.[2]

Members of the H.E.R.E. Local 75 Choir mostly came to Canada through Canada's immigration policy called the "West Indian Domestic Scheme," which operated officially from 1955–1967 and made it possible for young Caribbean women to immigrate to Canada as domestic workers.[3] These women were part of the first wave of an important surge in post-war immigration in the second half of the twentieth century, especially in Toronto, where the cultural fabric of the city was deeply enriched by immigrants from the Caribbean, especially Jamaica.[4] By the 1990s, these women had become elder immigrant women working to support their families living in both Canada and in the Caribbean. Some of them worked as unionized workers in downtown hotels.

The West Indian Domestic Scheme allowed Caribbean women to work as nannies and housekeepers for wealthy families. Awarded

---

[2] At one longer session when the women were sharing their stories, it came to light that, with one exception, every member of the choir had left young children behind in the Caribbean, often for many years, in order to immigrate to Canada. The one exception was a woman whose two children had died as infants.

[3] Erica Lawson, "The Gendered Working Lives of Seven Jamaican Women in Canada: A Story About 'Here' and 'There' in a Transnational Economy," *Feminist Formations* 25, no.1 (Spring 2013):138–56; Frances Henry, "The West Indian Domestic Scheme of Canada," *Social and Economic Studies* 17, no.1 (March 1968):83–91.

[4] The "National Act of 1948" also attracted labourers from Jamaica. This program and others were shown to be racist Canadian immigrant policies designed to discriminate against "non-whites. See Wikipedia, "Jamaican Canadians," accessed July 6, 2017, https://en.wikipedia.org/wiki/Jamaican_Canadians

landed-immigrant status upon entry, they were subject to a one year probationary period in which they were especially vulnerable to sexual exploitation, racist attitudes, and poor working conditions.[5] Even after they had official status, life was not easy. Choir members shared with me that their children were often mistreated back in Jamaica because family members who were caring for them resented the extra work despite the fact that their mothers sent money home. When their children were finally sent for, they sometimes barely recognized their own mothers. Literacy was also a challenge for members. It took me several months to realize that a couple of women who were constantly staring at me were actually looking at me so they could get the words of the songs. Still, these women persevered against all odds and wove their lives together to form a vibrant strand in the polycultural fabric of Toronto and Canada.[6]

Beyond "Border Thinking"

As already noted, many people in Canadian communities (and elsewhere) live a "borderland" existence in a very real sense. Some members in the community of San Esteban, for instance, face struggles to be able to legally stay in Canada. Others encounter enormous daily barriers as they seek to establish a life for themselves as new immigrants. Many still confront overwhelming obstacles even after being in the country for a long time. Discrimination based on identity, whether through racialization, language, gender, class, sexual orientation, ability, age, and so on, functions to create borders between people and to create spaces into which some are welcomed and others are not. People are constantly navigating these borders of our lives—a process I have described for myself as syncopation—as they

[5] See Erica Lawson's article for an analysis of the intersecting and complex strands of gender, race, and class, especially in the context of globalizing movements of people. Lawson writes about the legal case of seven Jamaican women who were initially granted landed immigrant status as domestic workers and subsequently issued with deportation orders. Lawson, "Gendered Working Lives." Also of note, Frances Henry assesses the program from her perspective in 1968. Incidents of racism and unwelcome are striking. Frances Henry, "The West Indian Domestic Scheme of Canada," *Social and Economic Studies* 17, no. 1 (March 1968).

[6] Jamaican Canadians, or Canadian citizens of Jamaican descent and Jamaican-born permanent residents of Canada, number 256,915 and Jamaican Canadians comprise about 30% of the entire Black Canadian population, according to the census of 2010. Statistics Canada, "The Jamaican Canadian Community," accessed July 5, 2017, http://www.statcan.gc.ca/pub/89-621-x/89-621-x2007012-eng.htm. See also: Wikipedia, "Jamaican Canadians."

move between clearly defined spaces while inhabiting the in-between zones, the liminal borderlands, where people with different identity markers and from different ethno-cultural backgrounds meet, interact, and engage in intercultural activities. These issues are made all the more conspicuous—and tragic—by the xenophobic direction of the Trump administration in its inhumane treatment of migrants at the border between the USA and Mexico.[7]

The women in the H.E.R.E. Local 75 Choir in Toronto were not strangers to the harrowing reality of borderland existence. Their daily struggles with borders and boundaries, sometimes tedious, sometimes agonizing, which they shared at rehearsals, illuminate the at times overwhelming experience of immigrants more generally. By leaving "home," these women became travellers/sojourners/migrants and battled discrimination and a sense of dislocation and loneliness. They coped with new ways of doing things and strove to establish a new sense of home, belonging, and personhood. At the level of basic governmental bureaucracy, symbols of personhood were sometimes dehumanizing, determined as they are by a number of "plastic artifacts—your health card, your SIN card, your bank card, your driver's licence and so on—[without which] you do not exist because you cannot officially be seen."[8] As already pointed out, they also wrestled with the heart-wrenching fact that their children had been left behind. If and when they were reunited, they began the arduous work of trying to overcome their children's sense of abandonment and the legacy of mistreatment by those who had looked after them.[9] All of these and other struggles were fought amid expectations that they would have the means to support family, friends, and even the floundering economy at "home."[10]

---

[7] Jonathan Blitzer, "A New Report on Family Separations Shows the Depths of Trump's Negligence," in *The New Yorker,* December 6, 2019, accessed, March 10, 2020, https://www.newyorker.com/news/news-desk/a-new-report-on-family-separations-shows-the-depths-of-trumps-negligence

[8] Olive Senior, "Crossing Borders and Negotiating Boundaries," in *Jamaica in the Canadian Experience: A Multiculturalizing Presence,* ed. Carl E. James and Andrea David (Halifax and Winnipeg: Fernwood Publishing, 2012), 15. A SIN card is a social insurance number, equivalent to the SSN-social security number in the USA.

[9] Ibid., 21.

[10] Beverly Mullings, Kay-Ann Williams, and Alexander Lovell, "Myths and Realities: The Challenge of Social Transformation Through Canada/Jamaica Diasporic Exchange," in *Jamaica in the Canadian Experience: A Multiculturalizing Presence,* ed. Carl E. James and Andrea Davis (Halifax & Winnipeg: Fernwood Publishing, 2012), 294.

The experience of the women in the choir—like the members of the San Esteban community—elucidate the stark reality of border(ed) existences. Borders can certainly be geographic and/or physical, for instance, when the undocumented are threatened with deportation; an airport or border check point becomes threatening and dangerous and a church sanctuary can become a literal refuge. At the same time, all those marked as "other," unwanted, or "inferior" because of race, ethnicity, gender, class, sexual orientation, ability, and so on, experience the suffering of stigma and exclusion to some extent.[11] Other borders are more fluid and harder to pinpoint when institutional, educational, cultural, interpersonal, or psychological barriers prevent some people from crossing certain borders and make it easy for others. In the present climate of increased xenophobia and the rise of the political right globally, the stakes are high as the reality of violence is palpably evident.

Let us return to Walter Mignolo's proposal of border thinking. He insists that it is not "thinking *about* borders" but "requires dwelling in the border," which would ostensibly involve reckoning with the kind of messy complex reality just described.[12] Indeed, the principles involved in border thinking, as he articulates them, provoke a fundamental challenge to Eurocentric modes of thinking, being, and doing. More specifically, he argues that border thinking involves delinking from Europe's "hegemonic epistemology" which perpetuates the "myth of universal history" and the subalternization of "other" knowledges.[13] To repeat in Mignolo's words, "border thinking becomes, then, the necessary epistemology to delink and decolonize knowledge and, in the process, to build decolonial local histories, restoring the dignity that the Western idea of universal history took away from millions of people."[14] It challenges us to imagine "other" (decolonial) ways of thinking, being, doing, (and feeling).[15]

---

[11] Robert Pitter writes about the challenges of growing up as the son of Jamaican immigrants. In order to succeed in Canadian society where the white Anglo dominant culture was the measure of success, he always had "to be twice as good." Robert Pitter, "Always Have to Be Twice as Good: Reflections of an Athlete, Coach and Academic," in *Jamaica in the Canadian Experience*, 155–60.

[12] Walter D. Mignolo, *Local Histories/Global Designs: Coloniality, Subaltern Knowledges, and Border Thinking* (Princeton: Princeton University Press, 2000), xvi, xv.

[13] Ibid., xvii, x, 13.

[14] Ibid., 10.

[15] As already noted, the idea of other ways of feeling have recently been articulated in Latin American decolonial circles. See, for example Arturo Escobar, *Sentipensar con la Tierra:*

Mignolo makes it clear that he is looking to articulate a mode of thinking from the subaltern perspective of Latin America.[16] We can imagine that such a mode of thinking could also be articulated from the perspective of members of the H.E.R.E. Local 75 Choir. The elemental challenge such a shift engenders—of delinking from Europe and embodying other ways of being—is monumental. What is less clear in Mignolo's proposal is what "subaltern" means and how such a perspective might actually be enacted. For instance, he advocates using "Amerindian categories of thought and Afro-Caribbean experiences without converting them into exotic objects of study,"[17] but he does not disentangle how his own social location as a "white" man of Italian descent teaching at a USA academic institution problematizes his engagement of these issues. Key questions emerge: Does Mignolo himself dwell at the border, a condition he claims is necessary for border thinking? How does his social location relate to the subalternity he is advocating? How does he justify using thinking, categories, and experiences from Indigenous and Afro-descendant contexts without citation?[18] What are some specific examples of how border thinking can engage in "conscientious epistemic, ethical, and *aesthetical* political projects" or more simply, "thinking and doing decolonially?"[19] By not concretely dealing with these questions, his proposal remains theoretical and abstract, however much he himself may believe that "emancipation *as* liberation means not only the recognition of the subalterns but the erasure of the power structure that maintains hegemony and subalternity."[20]

Nuevas Lecturas Sobre Desarrollo, Territorio y Diferencia (Medellin, Colombia: Ediciones UNAULA, 2014).

[16] See especially Mignolo, "Chapter 3: Human Understanding and Local Interests: Occidentalism and the (Latin) American Argument," in *Local Histories*, 127–171.

[17] Ibid., 144.

[18] Mignolo has been criticized for his poaching of Indigenous thinking. See Sylvia Rivera Cusicanqui, "Chhixinakax Utxiwa. una Reflexión Sobre Prácticas y Discursos Descolonizadores," in *Modernidad y Pensamiento Descolonizador*, comp. Mario Yupi (La Paz: U-PIEB – IFEA, 2006),3–16. Along similar lines, Ramon Grosfoguel writes about the connections between economic, epistemic, and ontological extractivism. He documents Mignolo's mis-appropriation of the ideas of Cusicanqui and Leanne Betasamosake Simpson (from Canada). Ramon Grosfoguel, "Del 'Extractivismo Economico' al 'Extractivismo Epistemco' y al 'Extractivismo Ontologico': Una Forma Desctructiva de Conocer, Ser y Estar en el Mundo." *Tabula Rasa Bogota-Colombia* 24 (enero-junio 2016) (in English: "From 'Economic Extractivism' to 'Epistemical Extractivism' and 'Ontological Extractivism:' A Destructive Way to Know, Be and Behave in the World.").

[19] Mignolo, *Local Histories*, xvi, xvii.

[20] Ibid., 125.

The other fundamental problem with the way Mignolo articulates border thinking is that he remains caught in Eurocentric binarist modes however much his proposal seeks to delink from Europe. He does confront the problem of the subject-object binary in Eurocentric thinking and distinguishes between "ordering the world in dichotomies" and "thinking from dichotomous concepts," which he argues is a "key configuration of border thinking." Still he insists that border thinking is a "dichotomous locus of enunciation."[21] Certainly an oppositional stance is productive in border thinking as part of thinking, being, doing, (and feeling) decolonially "emerging *from* and responding *to* colonial legacies at the intersection of Euro/American modern history."[22] However, Mignolo could go further. By rejecting Eurocentric dichotomous modes of thinking, the subaltern/dominant binary in particular is more effectively liberated to encompass the real multiplicity and intersectionality of border(ed) living. Border thinking could then be reimagined to include the multiple and diverse intercultural interactions in which people shift between identity spaces within themselves, in relation to other people, and in response to the multiple contexts which they inhabit. In short, Mignolo's articulation of border thinking is too abstract and too dualist, delimiting the real dynamism of the contexts and peoples he is seeking to describe and celebrate.

As we saw earlier, Gloria Anzaldúa moves beyond binary configurations and articulates identity multiply in her *mestiza* consciousness. She also concretizes her proposal by rooting her idea of the borderlands at the real border, rising out of her own painful experience, thus helpfully articulating challenges in the bluntest possible terms. She lays bare the grim realities—as well as the complexity and intermixture—of the life in-between, at the "borderlands," where inhabitants are identified as the "squint-eyed, the perverse, the queer, the troublesome, the mongrel, the mulato, the half-breed, the half dead; in short, those who cross over, pass over, or go through the confines of the 'normal.'"[23] She starkly articulates the perils of a borderland existence:

> do not enter, trespassers will be raped, maimed, strangled, gassed, shot. The only 'legitimate' inhabitants are those in power, the whites and those who

[21] Ibid., 85.

[22] Ibid., 95.

[23] Gloria Anzaldúa, *Borderlands/La Frontera: The New Mestiza* (San Francisco: Aunt Lute Books, 2007), 25. Anzaldúa intentionally mixes Spanish and English—for example, here, she spells *mulato* in the Spanish way.

align themselves with whites. Tension grips the inhabitants of the border-lands like a virus. Ambivalence and unrest reside there and death is no stranger.[24]

Such a reality was very familiar to the Afro-descendant Caribbean members of the choir.

Anzaldúa's proposal, which describes the violent reality of the border-lands and includes naming the dynamics of power based on white suprem-acy, destabilizes the subaltern/dominant binary of Mignolo's border thinking, allowing the real and far more complex dynamics of identifica-tion processes to be understood interculturally as people—dominant-identified; subalternized, to use Mignolo's language; and those in-between, the intermixed—interact in border(ed) spaces. Néstor Medina celebrates this strength of Anzaldúa's work by noting that "Anzaldúa appropriates difference and the fluidity of identities as the alternative to the dominant discourse of homogeneous, hermetically sealed identities. Her proposal unsettles, disturbs, breaks from contemporary dominant frames for inter-preting reality, cultures, and describing identity, resisting airtight defini-tions, categories, and iron-cast frames."[25] He argues that "her discussion on *borderlands* … [invites] us to create new language and possibilities for conceiving multiple intersecting identities in people."[26]

Let me be clear that I am not proposing abandoning the idea of border thinking as Mignolo articulates it.[27] I am however suggesting that it needs to be expanded to encompass the complex concrete realities beyond Eurocentric dichotomies. It could then better include what Medina names as the "multiple intersection identities in people." This opening up would also account for the kind of syncopated movements that many people make between spaces and cultures as they confront borders, cross borders, disrupt borders, are prevented from crossing borders, cross in one direc-tion and not the other, look over borders, and even reimagine and recon-figure borders. These multiple identities and experiences are drawn together in the in-between space of our collective singing—border sing-ing—where they contribute to a variegated web of interaction from which people draw multiple meanings and in which they experience the irruption of the Holy Spirit.

[24] Ibid., 26.
[25] Néstor Medina, *Mestizaje: (Re)Mapping Race, Culture and Faith in Latina/o Catholicism* (Maryknoll, NY: Orbis Books, 2009), 124.
[26] Ibid., 137.
[27] I am also not abandoning my responsibility to confront my own privilege as "white."

Border Singing

Border singing as it is proposed here, and to draw a parallel with Mignolo's border thinking, confronts Eurocentric modes of singing; lifts up other ways of knowing/singing particularly from oppressed groups, and welcomes epistemic disobedience. But the border singing of the women in the H.E.R.E. Local 75 Choir is more than this. It is not simply an abstract, idealized, or romantic singing imagined from the safe spaces of the ivory tower, but the real singing of people who wrestle every day with their own extreme vulnerability, marginalization, and dislocation as Anzaldúa and Medina have articulated them. Border singing affirms their concrete lived reality as a source of knowledge and makes space for the women to voice their experience of life, work, and the Divine in song. It thus affirms their singing as a *locus theologicus,* as a point and time of encounter with the Divine. It is also potentially transformational, when all of these factors come together, as a liberating force.

A theological lens on border singing—or border thinking or border living—invites us to look beyond a "liberated *from*" to a "liberated *for.*" Certainly the deconstructive modes of postcolonial scholarship and the more constructive and praxical modes of decolonial thinking help us to imagine liberating congregational singing *from* coloniality, or from musi-coloniality. We can interrogate the coloniality in congregational singing through Bhabha's notions of mimicry and Third Space and embrace modes of resistance expressed in other ways of knowing, epistemic disobedience, and border thinking along the lines of decolonial thinking. But the question remains liberating *for* what purpose?

Other ways of knowing, being, doing, and feeling certainly do suggest an-other possible vision for the world, which may be imagined in Christian language, as an eschatological proleptic orientation. Such "other" visions have always already been present in the flipping of hymns from the hymnic canon by oppressed communities. They have also been embodied as other ways of knowing/singing in local songs and rituals. These instances point to occasions when singers are actively engaged in sounding this other vision in and through their singing.

Similarly, when the women gathered for H.E.R.E. Local 75 Choir rehearsals, our lived concrete realities were enfolded into our experience of singing. Empowered from their marginal location in society, singing from the experience of their border(ed) living, choir members sang out, embodying defiance against the "patriarchal and racist social and ecclesial structures" of their daily lives.[28] The palpable hope that we experienced and the transformative power of our collective voices were understood by members of the choir to be infused by a dynamic energy that brought us closer together in the struggle, what they would certainly have called the Holy Spirit, even though it was a "secular" trade union choir. This pneumatological lens invited us to understand our work as liberating *for* the building of a better world, as we voiced a vision of the kin-dom of God's justice, peace, and radical love both in rehearsals and out *in* the world. Every Wednesday our bodies vibrated with the shared task of intertwining identity, theology, and ideology in a dynamic that welcomed our encounters with the Divine as experienced momentary irruptions of the Holy Spirit.

TURNING TOWARD THE SPIRIT, THE SUBVERSIVE HOLY BREATH OF LIFE

As we have seen, an enriched definition of border singing includes complex processes in which the voices of minoritized and marginalized peoples interplay with the dominant voices of those with more power. Given the messy, painful, potentially conflictual nature of this mingling, how is it possible to imagine such an interaction as a liberating liturgical force? In fact, it is precisely the messy, painful, and potentially conflictive nature of engagements across difference that prepares us for the kind of profoundly transformative potential which is required in liberating processes.

This dynamic and fluid mutual engagement between human beings who strive to enact the liberating message of the Gospel through border singing is enabled by the liberating action of none other than the Holy Spirit. In this space in-between, the Spirit's subversive dancing and singing invites us to seek her. We find her in the silenced utterances of "others" beyond the edges of prevailing Eurocentric paradigms of the Enlightenment. She is also present the spaces of our border singing where she irrupts, disrupts, and is disclosed in the concrete reality of people's daily lives, especially those of the marginalized, like the women of the H.E.R.E. Local 75 Choir.

---

[28] Loida I. Martell-Otero, "Introduction: Abuelita Theologies," in Zaida Maldonado Pérez, Loida I Martell-Otero, Elizabeth Conde-Frazier, *Latina Evangélicas: A Theological Survey from the Margins* (Eugene, OR: Cascade Books, 2013), 9.

A pneumatological optic is also articulated by many liturgical theologians who see the Holy Spirit as the essential liturgical enlivener.[29] However, this emphasis on the Holy Spirit tends to be derivative, overly abstract, and somewhat under-developed, too frequently coming across as something of an afterthought. Whatever the focus has been—whether a theological orientation toward God or Jesus; a liturgical articulation of ecclesiology, soteriology, or eschatology; a focus on the sacraments; or an exploration of the word (and words), music, or the community—liturgical theologians have not made a pneumatological approach in liturgy a priority, however much some may argue that the Holy Spirit is an essential animating principle.

If, as these liturgical theologians have argued, the Holy Spirit is the necessary enlivener, the active and activating divine force in liturgy, then let us consider how a liturgical theology which focuses on liberation as the primary and prophetic (liturgical) action of the Church and her people might be understood to be animated by the Holy Spirit as a *liberating* liturgical force. Above all, the pneumatological force which galvanizes the liberating action of the Church and her people is not an abstract notion, as it is so often in liturgical and theological circles. Rather, the Holy Spirit is understood as imminent rather than transcendent, and material rather than metaphysical. She is active in the daily lives of the marginalized, among whom are members of the H.E.R.E. choir, accompanying them as a subversive, disrupting, disturbing, liberating, and indomitable force, who challenges the status quo, especially for the ways in which it is oppressive.

---

[29] A survey of Dwight Vogel's *Primary Sources in Liturgical Theology* demonstrates this optic. In "Mystery and Liturgy," Odo Casel notes that because "*Pneuma* is the breath of God, from which supernatural life flows," liturgy therefore is "born of the fullness of the Spirit, and love, [and] becomes a work of beauty and wisdom," (31). Gordon Lathrop, whose liturgical approach is primarily Christological, similarly asserts in "A Rebirth of Images: On the Use of the Bible in Liturgy," that the force which animates the word is the "life-giving Spirit flowing from the side of the crucified Jesus Christ" (233). Likewise, Jean Jacques von Allmen undergirds his soteriological approach with an insistence on the efficacious and eschatological necessity of the Holy Spirit in the anamnesis in "The Cult as Recapitulation of the History of Salvation" (136). Finally, Robert Taft's widely respected approach to Orthodox liturgics insists that the Holy Spirit is the "enabler of Christian worship," the "life of Christ in us, both lived and celebrated," as well as "the presence before faith." See his essay "What Does Liturgy Do? Toward a Soteriology of Liturgical celebration: Some Thesis" (141, 144). All examples from Dwight W. Vogel, ed., *Primary Sources of Liturgical Theology* (Collegeville, MN: The Liturgical Press, 2000).

Liberationist evangélica theologians Zaida Maldonado Pérez, Loida I. Martell-Otero, and Elizabeth Conde-Frazier affirm these qualities of the Holy Spirit. For them, she is "the wild child of the Trinity, the Holy Subversive One, (who) calls us to stir things up, to become 'devoted tongues' of fire that will dare to proclaim truth to power so that we can get from the question, 'what does this mean?' to the question, 'what shall we do?,' which will change our churches, our communities, and the world."[30] They insist that the Spirit—incarnated, embodied, and contextual—is experienced in the concrete daily struggles of the most marginalized and oppressed, especially women. They understand the Spirit as "an imminent, personal Presencia," as the "One who draws near to speak, comfort, reveal, touch, strengthen, anoint, encourage, heal and bring to new life."[31] It is these embodied materializations of the Spirit in the most unlikely places—the expressions of a singing, dancing life force—which make her an affront to epistemologies of the Enlightenment with their empirical rational evidence and argumentation.

Speaking from her own Indigenous context in South Ontario, *Kanienkeha* United Church of Canada minister Susan Beaver remarks that she understands the Holy Spirit not as "wild" energy, but as warm, loving, gentle, uniting, and comforting.[32] A positive use of "wild child" is problematic in her context because "wild child" is a reminder of racial epithets she—along with other Indigenous children—experienced when she was a child. As part of the dynamic of the Trinity, she understands the Spirit to radiate love, particularly in community contexts where peoples' lives are shattered by the ongoing legacies of colonialism and the ever-present reality of coloniality. As such, the Spirit changes to meet the needs of the contexts in which she is moving. She is a shape-shifting trickster, as Beaver describes her, who can heal Indigenous peoples and communities or disturb and disrupt where there is a need for confrontation and challenge against oppressive forces.[33] Whichever form the Holy Spirit takes, she can be imagined as an essential and arousing liturgical life-force and a perichoretic dance partner to the other persons of the Trinity. As an expression of the Divine, which is all-enveloping, womb-like, constantly

---

[30] Zaida Maldonado Pérez, Loida I Martell-Otero, and Elizabeth Conde-Frazier, "Dancing with the Wild Child: Evangélicas and the Holy Spirit," in *Latina Evangélicas*, 31.

[31] Pérez, Martell-Otero, and Conde-Frazier, "Dancing with the Wild Child," 21, 19.

[32] *Kanienkeha* is the Indigenous word for "Mohawk."

[33] Beaver, personal conversation with the author (8 January, 2018).

creating and recreating, ushering forth new life, and liberating humanity to be co-workers in building God's kin-dom of justice, the Holy Spirit permeates all of life.

Of course, the Divine birthing process is not easy. The painstaking process of birthing life also provokes palpitations internal to the Divine and experiences of birth pangs in the pulsations of life, resulting in pain, suffering, and what we name as evil, causing pain and sadness even to the Divine. Of primary and non-derivative importance (i.e., as a partner in the perichoretic dance and not merely an emanation from God or Christ), the Holy Spirit understood this way is also present in the concrete, collective, religious expression of communities in worship. Broadly speaking, this "worship" also includes the choir of women that gathered every Wednesday at Holy Trinity under the auspices of a secular trade union. Martell-Otero describes this transformational impact of the Spirit in and through worship, especially among the marginalized:

> Through the outpouring of the Spirit, God's fullness is experienced in concrete ways. The congregation sings, and people—especially the women, whether young or old—raise their hands in a joyous dance, speak in tongues, prophesy, weep, and hug. Lives are transformed. ... Each of these experiences counters their experiences of injustice. For those left voiceless can now speak in tongues. Those with no future now prophesy. Those torn from their countries, communities, and families have forged a new family amid the congregation ... the dreams and visions empower them to develop new ministries to fight for justice and transformation for their communities: they see what is and know what should be.[34]

This articulation of the (liberating) Spirit also affirms the multivalent and plurivocal dynamics of border singing. She is an omni-present, uncontainable, and provocatively subversive force, and at the same time tender and preferentially present in the border(ed) spaces of our living. Active throughout creation history, animating the Word of Genesis and John— understood here more along the lines of the Latin *verbum* or the Spanish *verbo*, as the active "verb" rather than the static "word"—she is uncapturable, un-silenceable, and un-restrainable. She embraces the messy and at times dangerous reality of a borderline or borderland existence experienced by many in our communities, accompanying those who suffer

---

[34] Loida I. Martell-Otero, "Neither 'Left Behind' Nor Deciphering Secret Codes: An Evangélica Understanding of Eschatology," in *Latina Evangélicas*, 121.

discrimination and violence. The life-giving and life-birthing divine processes which the Spirit embodies push people together, including members of the choir as they sang with each other, including me, as leader.

The work of the Spirit also makes tangible the Divine siding with the poor and marginalized as an intrinsic element of the Divine outworking. She enters the visceral, painful, messy reality of the people, just as God sent Jesus to be among us, especially those at the margins. She sings at these margins, drawing us beyond prevailing rationalistic Eurocentric paradigms which tend to dominate approaches to worship. She also dances at the centre, de-centering the status quo. Her role as an energizing force for worship—and for all of life—is revealed in the concrete, collective, embodied religious expressions of communities in worship. She is at the heart of the principles for a liberating liturgical theology to which we now turn.

LIBERATING LITURGICAL THEOLOGY

The principles for a liberating liturgical theology proposed in the remainder of this chapter are inspired by Latin American liberation theologian Juan Luis Segundo and LatinaXo theology, particularly from the work of Latino-Canadian Néstor Medina. It is important to note that these theologies rise out of the experience of particular peoples from particular places, peoples often minoritized because of "race" and culture, and marginalized in other ways because of language, class, education, dis/ability, and sexual orientation. My own experience is different, and in engaging them, I do not wish to co-opt them. Yet, they inspire and provoke me, energizing my own commitment to living out a liberating praxis by challenging me to interrogate my privilege and power and helping me to imagine a world other-wise. They offer important insights for this theological work on liturgy, animating theo-liturgical principles which in turn respond to the multiple and diverse realities of today's church contexts. Choosing Latin American liberation and LatinaXo theologies as alternative sources to predominant patriarchal Euro-centric approaches to theology and liturgy is also in itself a decolonial move which affirms other epistemological modes beyond Euro-North-Atlantic centres of power.

Juan Luis Segundo: The Church Reimagined

For Segundo, a theology of liberation begins not with the theoretical, but with social praxis, a commitment to liberation itself.[35] This action-reflection-action orientation prioritizes concrete historical experience as a hermeneutic source and is accompanied by a commitment to a social and ideological praxis of liberation by the church—which for Segundo *is* the people—in the world. The church's efficacy can only be measured by its concrete communal actions in the real world on behalf of the oppressed, including in its sacramental expressions and liturgies. Segundo's thinking continually circles back to the need to situate theology—and liturgy—inside a commitment to liberation which responds to the real-life, historically-situated, concrete reality of the people.

In such a paradigm, the Church is radically re-imagined as an agent working to enact the liberating love which is at the heart of Christianity. The Church as "sign" thus demonstrates its prophetic and immanent function in tangible work on behalf of the poor and oppressed, *in* the world. Segundo advocates against a Church set apart from the world, ministering to the world from afar, "capable of deciding what was authentic liturgical worship without confronting the world," but instead calls the Church to "plunge itself into this love that builds up humanity in history."[36] The women of the H.E.R.E. choir were being church in this way. We were "worshiping" through our singing by confronting systems of oppression at demonstrations, rallies, and on the picket line. Even at weekly rehearsals our singing nourished us to continue to face the daily struggles of our lives and encouraged us to continue to work at building up humanity through the union's work, and our own witness, in the world.

Such broad interpretations of the "Church" and "worship" are consistent with Segundo's approach. For instance, though he appreciates the particularity of Roman Catholic sacramental rites, he also views sacramentality much more broadly as encompassing all liturgical actions and, potentially, all of life. He argues that the sacraments (and liturgical actions) are meant to be signs that not only shape Christians into liberating agents in community, but also simultaneously demonstrate the significance of the sacrament as a liberative sign. In other words, "the sacraments are [the] *means* to form and set in motion an ecclesial community" which will then

---

[35] Juan Luis Segundo, *Liberation of Theology*, trans. John Drury (Oregon: Orbis, 1976), 84.
[36] Juan Luis Segundo, *The Sacraments Today, Volume Four of a Theology for Artisans of a New Humanity*, trans. John Drury (New York: Orbis, 1974), 117, 7.

be actualized as a liberating force; the "signified is also realized."[37] Without these two sacramental functions—the formation of liberating/liberated communities and the signification of Christian principles of liberation through the sacraments—the sacraments run the risk of becoming empty gestures. As an illustration, he notes that the Eucharist loses its meaning when its signification—"the possibility of loving each other and of transforming this love into an impetus and a message for the entire human community"—is disconnected from real community and hence from reality.[38]

For Segundo, a liberating approach is also dependent on its ability to conscientize the people for prophetic liberating work on behalf of the church—using Paulo Freire's parlance—in a dialogic process that is also self-reflective.[39] This consciousness-raising function of the sacraments and liturgies is directly connected to the prophetic function of the Church; "the revolution signified by Christian sacramentality consists in leading the whole community to carry out a prophetic function."[40] Yet, in order to become, to be, and to remain prophetic and authentic—and in parallel with the self-reflective, praxical, and liberationist orientation of this book—Segundo insists that liturgical processes, and indeed theological engagements, require a constant dialogue and self-critical process, a merging of reflection and action. They must become praxis to empower Christian "reflection, activity, and hard work on behalf of the transformation of the world."[41]

---

[37] Ibid., 107, 21.

[38] Ibid., 4, Gustavo Gutiérrez also makes this connection between liberating practice and liberating liturgy explicit: "Without a real commitment against exploitation and alienation and for a society of solidarity and justice, the Eucharistic celebration is an empty action, lacking any genuine endorsement by those who participate in it." Gustavo Gutiérrez, *A Theology of Liberation*, trans. Caridad Inda and John Eagleson (Maryknoll, NY: Orbis, 1973), 265.

[39] See Segundo, "A Community in Dialogue in Sacraments," in *The Sacraments Today*, 90–100; Paulo Freire, *Pedagogy of the Oppressed*, trans. Myra Bergman Ramos (New York: Herder and Herder, 1971).

[40] Segundo, *The Sacraments Today*, 36.

[41] Ibid., 98. In later work, Segundo proposes the four-fold hermeneutic circle as a praxical mode for biblical interpretation which similarly begins with experience as the source of reflection. See Segundo, *Liberation of Theology*, 9. He also writes about "being liberative" rather than simply "talking about" theology, which resonates in a liturgical mode with Aidan Kavanagh's assertion that liturgy is primary theology. See Aidan Kavanagh, "On Liturgical Theology," in *Primary Sources of Liturgical Theology*, ed. Dwight W. Vogel (Collegeville, MN: The Liturgical Press, 2000), 91–100.

Segundo's emphasis on the whole of human reality—in all its contextual particularity and historicity—as a locus for liturgical expression and celebration, is thus affirmed. He connects this approach, with its concrete communal orientation, to a liturgical interpretation of the sacraments as part of life and as the "broad domain of liturgy."[42] In the broadest sense then, the members of the H.E.R.E. choir, as prophetic agents in the world, can be understood to have enacted liberating liturgy through their/our singing. We were engaged in action that signified/articulated an-other world, a world which challenged and transformed the ideological status quo through the liberating action of the union's work, including through our singing.

Principles for a liberating liturgical theology, along the lines of Segundo, challenge traditional Euro-North Atlantic approaches to liturgy in four crucial ways. First, liberating approaches to liturgy must be rooted in an actual concrete commitment to liberation. Second, they draw on highly contextual approaches to biblical, liturgical, and theological interpretations which emphasize particular rather than universal expressions of Christianity.[43] Third, liberating liturgical principles would insist on the fundamental ideological and political nature of human action, which for Christian liturgy means that the Church may not remain apart from the world; liturgy, like theology must emerge from and speak to the lived reality of the people. Finally, the necessary process of historical praxis—which requires people to engage in a combination of critical reflection and action—encourages people to constantly transcend themselves as they work toward an eschatological transformation of the world.

It must be noted that some liberationist echoes can be heard among liturgical theologians, though to my knowledge none of them fully articulates a liberative liturgical theology, per se.[44] For instance, David Newman,

---

[42] Segundo, *The Sacraments Today*, 34.

[43] For liturgical theologian Anscar Chupungco, plurality and contextuality are part of the Church's prophetic and eschatological role through the Holy Spirit: "in gathering together the scattered fruits of the Word sown among the peoples, the Church brings about by the power of the Holy Spirit the eschatological fullness when God will be all in all." Anscar J. Chupungco, "The Theological Principle of Adaptation," in *Primary Sources of Liturgical Theology*, ed. Dwight W. Vogel (Collegeville, MN: The Liturgical Press, 2000), 250.

[44] To be clear, I am also not attempting to articulate a fully developed liturgical theology at this point nor survey the breadth of the discipline. Rather I am simply making the point that the liberationist themes and their broader liturgical implications are evident in some theological and methodological trajectories of liturgical theology. Of note in this regard is Anscar Chupungco who contributed to the Vatican II document on liturgy *Sacrosanctum concilium* from his particular context of the Philippines. *Sacrosanctum concilium* affirmed local expres-

inspired by the legacy of liberation theologies, quotes Segundo when he insists that liturgical theology requires a "praxis-based methodology." It must never, Newman argues, "focus narrowly on liturgy" but needs to be action-oriented because it also encompasses elements of pastoral care, social action, and mission.[45] He further notes that liturgical theology ought to be rooted in the concrete lives of the people, drawing on popular (meaning grass roots) experience and knowledge, rather than only academic theory.

Likewise, liberation-oriented resonances are evident in the work of liturgical theologians Don Saliers and Ruth Duck.[46]Saliers, who acknowledges the influence of feminist and liberation theologies in his work, advocates a liturgical approach that brings our "humanity at full stretch" before God so that our study of liturgy may be "everywhere and always the study of what real men and women do and suffer in their lives."[47] In a similar vein, Ruth Duck insists that her work to expand—one could say liberate—liturgical language must be communal, dialogical, and contextual. For her, this work to be inclusive lifts up once again the eschatological ministry of Jesus—as we noted in our discussion of "The Midwife's Carol"—the ministry of one "who proclaimed God's love for all and by his actions lifted up women, the poor, children, and others society rejects or devalues" and lives out a "new reality and provide(s) a foretaste of God's reign in the world."[48]

sions of Christianity and advocated for the "fully conscious and active" participation of the laity. Pope Paul VI, "Constitution on the Sacred Liturgy Sacrosanctum Concilium," II: 14, accessed October 27, 2017, http://www.vatican.va/archive/hist_councils/ii_vatican_council/documents/vat-ii_const_19631204_sacrosanctum-concilium_en.html

[45] David R. Newman, "Observations on Method in Liturgical Theology," *Worship* 57, no.4 (1983):381.

[46] I remind the reader that "liberating" as it is used throughout this book is based on the multiple intersecting markers of social identification which undergird coloniality: race, gender, class, education, dis/ability, sexual orientation, and so on. Such an approach reflects the current rich display of diverse approaches in liberationist theologies (black, mujerista, feminist, evangélica, etc.). It goes beyond the class analysis approach of early liberation theologians to affirm the reality of the complex web of factors that supports the colonial matrix of power. For an excellent summary of current streams in liberation theologies, see Elsa Tamez, "Teología de la Liberación," in *Quedan Dios y los Pobres: Textos Sobre la Teología de la Liberación*, ed. Alejandro Dausá (La Habana: Centro Memorial Dr. Martin Luther King, Jr, 2008).

[47] Don E. Saliers, "Human Pathos and Divine Ethos," in *Primary Sources of Liturgical Theology*, ed. Dwight W. Vogel (Collegeville, MN: The Liturgical Press, 2000), 278, 277.

[48] Ruth C. Duck, "Expansive Language in the Baptized Community," in *Primary Sources of Liturgical Theology*, ed. Dwight W. Vogel (Collegeville, MN: The Liturgical Press, 2000), 290, 289.

LIBERATING LITURGY: THE HOLY SPIRIT ENLIVENS
AND LIBERATES THE WORK OF THE PEOPLE

My turn to the Spirit echoes and draws upon LatinaXo approaches, particularly from the work of Néstor Medina, which affirm an imminent, embodied understanding of the Holy Spirit as an active and animating presence in people's lives and in the life and work of the church.[49] Like their Latin American liberation theologian colleagues, LatinaXo theologians emphasize the importance of understanding theology in relation to specific concrete historical locations and they privilege the life and work of the people as sources of theology. Yet, LatinaXo theologians more explicitly focus on the presence and work of the Spirit as the animating force in the places, lives, and work of the people.[50]

Still, and echoing my earlier concerns regarding the lack of attention to the Spirit in liturgical theology, LatinaXo approaches to pneumatology tend to be derivative, often articulating "the activity of the Spirit as incomprehensible outside of the work of Christ."[51]Medina argues that a

---

[49] Each of these approaches involves different experiences, trajectories, and theological paths. I do not intend to lump them together as monolithic, but the diverse range of these articulations is beyond the scope of this chapter. The articulations of a Latino-Canadian theologian (Medina), for example, are different from those of a Mexican-American (Anzaldúa, DeAnda), Puerto-Rican (Martell-Otero, Villafañe), Cuban-USA (Goizueta, Espín, González), or a Honduran-USA (García-Johnson), to name a few. For a recent survey of different approaches in LatinaXo theology, see Orlando O. Espin, ed. *The Wiley Blackwell Companion to Latino/a Theology* (New Jersey: John Wiley & Songs, Ltd., 2015).

[50] For example, Orlando Espín's work echoes antecedents in Latin American liberation theologies which emphasize action-orientation and the concrete and historically rooted experience of the people as a source for theology. But he further argues that pneumatology must also be rooted in service to others. See Orlando O. Espín, *Grace and Humanness: Theological Reflections Because of Culture* (Maryknoll, NY: Orbis Books, 2007), 8. Oscar García-Johnson similarly sees God's work *through* the Spirit revealed in the everyday *(lo cotidiano)*. He further asserts the profoundly subversive character of the Spirit who guides "our people to learning the most *subversive language ever,* spirituality." Oscar García-Johnson, *The Mestizo/a Community of the Spirit: A Postmodern Latino/a Ecclesiology* (Eugene, OR: Pickwick Publications, 2009), 25.

[51] Néstor Medina, "Theological Musings Towards a Latina/o Pneumatology," in *The Wiley Blackwell Companion to Latino/a Theology,* ed. Orlando O. Espín (New Jersey: John Wiley & Sons, Ltd., 2015), 177.

"Latina/o pneumatology needs to go beyond regurgitating traditional understandings of the Spirit as subordinate to Christ or the Father."[52] Into this gap he proposes germinative principles for a LatinaXo pneumatology which help to amplify and deepen Segundo's nascent liberative liturgical principles as I have developed them.

Segundo's principles can be summarized and expanded using three broad categories. First, they are concrete, engaged with and in the world in the historically and geographically located and culturally conditioned lives of the people. In this way, the Church's role is prophetic and immanent, exhibited in tangible work on behalf of the excluded, *in* the world, including through its "sacramental" expressions and liturgies. Medina's work suggests that the Holy Spirit can be understood to animate the concrete so that it becomes embodied and particularized especially by highlighting the experience of women, particularly Latinas.

Second, they rise out of community: the Church, understood as the whole community, is responsible, above all—to quote again Segundo's evocative call—to "plunge itself into [the] love that builds up humanity in history."[53]Medina helps us see how the communitarian is made richer through LatinaXo concepts like *convivencia* (living with), *familia,* and *fiesta.* Finally, these liberative liturgical principles are transformational: liberating liturgy is an active embodiment of the ideological and theological principles of liberation. By liberating liturgy and engaging in liturgy that is liberating, the people are actually engaged in a communal praxis of liberation as agents working to enact the liberating love which is at the heart of Christianity. With Medina's pneumatological optic, this transformational impetus is given life through a theology of *acompañamiento* (accompaniment). Let's consider each of these in more detail.

The Concrete

First, and resonating with the evangélica theology of Martell-Otero, Maldonado-Pérez,   and   Conde-Frazier,   Medina   insists   that   a

---

[52] Ibid.
[53] Segundo, *The Sacraments Today,* 7.

LatinaXopneumatology will include Latinas' embodied experiences. Such an inclusion will enable us "to speak about the divine Spirit as present/ active/enfleshed in the material world and not detached or disembodied as often appears among traditional pneumatologies."[54] He describes the Spirit as "impregnated with life, creating and sustaining," and oozing "with life-giving energy like a womb within which life irrupts and erupts."[55] An embodied approach to the Spirit thus enhances notions of immanence and emphasizes LatinaXo and liberation insistences on historical, concrete, everyday life (*lo cotidiano*), as well as on experience as a source of and location for theology and the irruption of the Divine.

Ada María Isasi-Díaz writes that *lo cotidiano* is "at the heart of *mujerista* theology and … is important to all liberation theologies and struggles" and Oscar García-Johnson succinctly describes *lo cotidiano* as a combination of "action, *sentimiento* (feeling, which in the Latino/a sense is a form of aesthetic reasoning), and ideals."[56] Affirming the porous boundary between worship and the rest of life, García-Johnson also notes that everyday life is experienced "holistically and aesthetically within practices of the community, music, humor, and religious celebrations."[57] Neomi De Anda, with Medina affirms that *lo cotidiano* is also the space where "people face the complex and messy reality of suffering, shame, brokenness, and struggle toward transformation of their world and reality," where, resonating with Segundo, people make "their faith concrete and historical."[58]

Liturgically speaking, this emphasis on concrete lived experience as a theological source challenges us to understand the Holy Spirit's role in enlivening our worship. She is present in the whole-life experiences of the people which in turn become sources and locations for liturgical theology and for liturgy itself, especially through the experiences of the most marginalized and particularly the experiences of marginalized women, so

---

[54] Medina, "Theological Musings," 181.

[55] Ibid.

[56] Ada María Isasi-Díaz, "Lo Cotidiano: A Key Element of Mujerista Theology," in *Journal of Hispanic/Latino Theology*, 5–17. Vol 10, No 1 (2002), 6 and García-Johnson, *The Mestizo/a Community*, 19.

[57] Ibid.

[58] Neomi DeAnda and Néstor Medina, "Convivencias: What Have We Learned? Toward a Latino/a Ecumenical Theology," in *Building Bridges, Doing Justice: Constructing a Latino/a Ecumenical Theology*, ed. Orlando Espin (New York: Orbis, 2009), 188.

neglected in religious practices.[59] As we have seen, the experience of daily life is also permeated with a variety of border experiences as people navigate the borders between cultures, languages, class and status, and geographic locations, among other things. When expressed as worship, the particular concrete experiences of the marginalized give voice to the experiences of those who are without voice in society and who are forced to navigate these multiple borders.

The singing of the women in the H.E.R.E. choir is a clear example of how empowered voices, animated by the Holy Spirit in collective expressions, can be understood as this kind of worship. The Holy Spirit, as liturgical enlivener, affirms religious expressions that come from "the very matrix of life as it is lived by the marginalized and oppressed."[60] Such worship, particularly when the concrete experience of the marginalized is a theological and liturgical source, echoes Don Saliers' affirmation of humanity at full stretch—the range of human experience and expression from anguished lament to ecstatic joy. Saliers writes that expressions of concrete lived reality embody the "ongoing mutuality of God and the pathos of our human life," where the "cry of pain may co-mingle with our praise and our thanks" in solidarity with and as a collective expression of the whole Church.[61]

---

[59] LatinaXo theologians, especially but not only in Roman Catholic contexts, argue that popular religiosity is also affirmed as such a source. Roberto Goizueta calls it "the communal and aesthetic character of praxis." The very things that characterize popular religious expressions—they often tend to be woman-centered, syncretistic, and un-contained—make them at once subversive of more ordered liturgical traditions and also a potentially rich, enlivening source for those traditions. Roberto Goizueta, "Rediscovering Praxis: The Significance of U.S. Hispanic Experience for Theological Method," in *We Are a People! Initiatives in Hispanic American Theology*, ed. Roberto Goizueta (Minneapolis, MN: Fortress Press, 1992), 63.

[60] Martell-Otero, "Abuelita Theologies," 6.

[61] Saliers, "Human Pathos and Divine Ethos," 280. David Power likewise affirms the importance of ordinary, everyday life in the embodied liturgical expressions for which he advocates. For instance, he notes, that the "bodily things that Christian liturgy incorporates are more ordinary, more daily, more domestic. They are the life of every day." David N. Power, "Ritual and Verbal Language," in *Primary Sources of Liturgical Theology*, ed. Dwight W. Vogel (Collegeville, MN: The Liturgical Press, 2000), 188.

Community

Second, Medina's pneumatology enriches our notion of community with *convivencia* (literally "living with"), which he describes as a complex concept which encompasses a rich web of characteristics that define a particularly Latina/o understanding of the dynamic nature of community. Deeply relational, *convivencia* "points to the *act* of living and sharing life with someone(s) within the context of the larger community."[62] Set in the context of daily life (*lo cotidiano*) and encompassing all of life, he further argues that *convivencia* entails a relational ethos or theology that "comes from the community (*en conjunto)* and belongs to the community (*de conjunto).*"[63] For Medina, the Spirit is an indispensable element of this relational collective dynamic and is found "in the midst of these struggles ... injecting new energy to continue in the struggle for life."[64] His expansive characterization of *convivencia* also includes an acknowledgement of three other important LatinaXo community dynamics: (1) the reality of basic survival in LatinaXo communities (or *sobre-vivencia*); (2) the prevalence of celebration (or *fiesta*) even in contexts of violence and exclusion; and (3) the importance of family (or *familia*).[65]

Medina notes that the relationality encompassed in *convivencia* (particularly through its emphasis on family and community) is expressed "in people's religious celebrations, rites and customs, which [in turn] identify the human interconnection with the divine."[66] For Justo González, worship as *fiesta* similarly draws on the LatinaXo notion of *familia*—not the kind of nuclear (exclusive) family exemplified in the dominant culture, but an "extended family that includes all sorts of relatives, and whose limits are never clearly defined."[67] *Familia* engenders notions of "a vast assemblage of people who are related in a multiplicity of ways, so that they have a sense of belonging, but not necessarily of excluding others."[68] These community oriented/familial/festal qualities of *convivencia*, energized by the Spirit, can expand ways of understanding community and worship to

[62] Medina, "Theological Musings," 181.
[63] DeAnda and Medina, "Convivencias," 185.
[64] Medina, "Theological Musings," 182.
[65] Ibid.
[66] Ibid.
[67] Justo L. González, "Worship as Fiesta," in *Primary Sources of Liturgical Theology*, ed. Dwight W. Vogel (Collegeville, MN: The Liturgical Press, 2000), 256.
[68] Ibid.

include the diversity of people, identities, and liturgical traditions present in our churches.[69]

They also broaden our understanding of the spaces and times that can embody worship to include the rehearsal of a trade union choir, our singing at a demonstration, or the raising up of a song on a picket line. For our purposes, *convivencia* helpfully opens up the community oriented aspect of our liberating liturgical theology, by reclaiming the primacy of the role of the Holy Spirit in the very act of sharing life and liturgy, even in the direst of circumstances, amidst the pain and suffering of life and amongst those who are focused on survival. It underscores the importance of rooting liturgy—and singing—in the life of particular communities, with special attention to the voices of the marginalized and excluded.

Transformative Liberating Accompaniment

Finally, Medina's pneumatological expansion of Roberto Goizueta's theology of accompaniment (*acompañamiento*) can deepen our understanding of the transforming impetus of a liberating liturgical theology. For Goizueta, accompaniment is more than simply an "ethical-political activity moving in a particular historical direction (e.g., toward a more just society)." It is the "already" of a concrete LatinaXo praxis of theological behaviour in which Latinas/os walk with each other in a communal action that is concrete, physical, and historical.[70] It is "the ethical-political interaction between and among those persons walking together" in which the people walk with Jesus, knowing that Jesus walks with them, the whole process affirming personhood and a vision of the kin-dom of God.[71] Medina takes Goizueta's christologically based theology of *acompañamiento* with its focus on Jesus as the "source of our community, our solidarity, and therefore, our liberation" and infuses it with a pneumatological

---

[69] As Medina notes, "it is the Spirit that energizes Latinas/os toward celebración-convivencia." He also emphasizes the importance of community-based ritual expressions, like the posadas we examined in the last chapter, when he notes that "we see this determination in the multiple religious cultural celebrations of quinceañera, posadas, pilgrimages, birthdays, and so on, all of which make explicit the aspirations of the people and their obstinate refusal to give up." Medina, "Theological Musings," 182.

[70] Goizueta, *Caminemos con Jesús*, 207.

[71] Ibid.

emphasis by arguing that "acompañamiento takes place precisely because of the agency work of the Spirit."[72]

For those from the dominant culture, *acompañamiento* can be understood as the "not yet" of the kin-dom of God and a clarion call to side and enter into solidarity with the poor, self-consciously and intentionally "being with" and "walking with" the poor who God loves preferentially *because* God loves us all.[73] This "not yet," to which we return shortly, is not an eschatology of escapism, however. Rather, it has a proleptic orientation of anticipation that emphasizes the possibility of change and the crucial role of the agency of the people, especially the marginalized, in bringing it about, all in collaboration with the Divine. It affirms that the pain and suffering of this world cannot be the last word. Yet at the same time, glimpses of the Divine take place amidst, in, and in-between experiences of pain, death, and suffering. Indeed, this authentic relational justice, when built on a foundation of genuine intersubjectivity "between particular, unique others" presupposes a solidarity in the midst of suffering together *with* the poor and marginalized (and not for them) before genuine pluralism can be achieved.[74]

Medina draws together his pneumatological proposal by noting that *acompañamiento* acknowledges the "inspiring, energizing, and empowering activity of the Spirit as Latinas/os find the strength to acompañar each other in the midst of incredible difficulties and learn to convivir."[75] Rooted in the concrete historically-situated lives and struggles for survival by real people, "convivencia is [thus] a prerequisite of acompañamiento."[76] It also reorients our thinking about pneumatological activity from "creation to resurrection, to the birth of the church and sustaining of creation" with a methodological inversion which prioritizes the Spirit's activity as equal in the perichoretic activity of the Trinity and not as derivative from God or Christ.[77]

Our initial theo-liturgical principles for liberating liturgy drawn from Segundo—concrete, communitarian and transformational—are thus widened through this pneumatological optic. In, through, and with the presence and power of the Holy Spirit, we draw on our concrete experiences

---

[72] Ibid., 209; Medina, "Theological Musings," 184.
[73] Goizueta, *Caminemos con Jesús*, 177, 178.
[74] Ibid., 13.
[75] Medina, "Theological Musings," 184.
[76] Ibid.
[77] Ibid.

of daily life (*lo cotidiano*), especially from the margins, expressing the full range of human affections from deepest suffering to ecstatic joy. We worship together as an extension of living with each other and sharing our lives (*convivencia*). Finally, this Sprit-filled, dynamic, relational, embodied process depends on a commitment to accompany each other (*acompañar*), to live into liberating our lives and transforming our communities, preferentially opting for the most marginalized.

In this way liberating singing becomes an extension of living a liberating praxis. It also suggests ecclesiological transformation, to which we return shortly. Our work liberating liturgies can then spill out beyond the walls of our church buildings into our lives as a prophetic witness in and to the world, blurring the boundaries and borders between our sacraments—understood here to encompass all liturgical actions—and all life.[78] This "sacramental nature of action" allows us to interpret the transforming love at the heart of Christianity, action made possible by the Holy Spirit, as revelatory and deeply embodied: "divine action [which] occurs 'in,' 'with,' and 'under' human action."[79] Our liturgical actions can be understood to prophetically reach out and encompass our whole lives, liberating us to live together and truly accompany each other, as we celebrate life as an intercultural holy fiesta which can begin to actualize the beloved community of God's kin-dom.

RISKS AND CHALLENGES

Affirming liberation and LatinaXo theo-ethical approaches, Eldín Villafañe reminds us that "true"—and I would say liberating—worship must include social justice and solidarity with the oppressed: "from Amos to Isaiah God's people are challenged to place their worship praxis—offerings, fasting, music, liturgy—within the context of *just action (dikaioma)* to the poor and the oppressed."[80] Noting that it is the power of the Spirit which

---

[78] Orthodox theologian Alexander Schmemann echoes this approach to liturgy in which the world (creation) is understood broadly as God's primary sacrament. Alexander Schmemann, "The Task and Method of Liturgical Theology," in *Primary Sources of Liturgical Theology*, ed. Dwight W. Vogel (Collegeville, MN: The Liturgical Press, 2000), 54–62.

[79] Paul Waitman Hoon, "Liturgical Action in Light of the Word," in *Primary Sources of Liturgical Theology*, ed. Dwight W. Vogol (Collegeville, MN: The Liturgical Press, 2000), 241.

[80] Eldín Villafañe, *The Liberating Spirit: Toward an Hispanic American Pentecostal Social Ethic* (New York: University Press of America, 1992), 187.

enables the community of the Spirit (the church) to "reflect and witness to the values of the Reign of God," he connects such Spirit-animated and biblically mandated practices of worship to the eschatological purpose of just action for the poor and oppressed.[81] But a word of caution is needed here.

As attractive and enlivening as Latin American and LatinaXo approaches are, a hermeneutics of deep respect and self-critical awareness is needed in order to engage with them outside of their original contexts and especially from a White Anglo dominant culture perspective. Emerging out of communities where the *fiesta* happens in contexts of what Medina names as "violence and exclusion," where basic survival is the order of the day, such theo-liturgical approaches offer a calling to account for liturgical practitioners and theologians, like myself, who are from dominant "white" Anglo North Atlantic cultural contexts. Put another way, we who benefit from the ongoing legacy of colonialism must be scrupulous in our attempts to engage with people whose painful experience is that of being outside, of "not quite belonging," something of which I was keenly aware as the middle-class "white" leader of the H.E.R.E. Local 75 choir.[82]

As already argued, for those from the dominant culture, *acompañamiento* can be understood as the "not yet" of the kin-dom of God, a proleptic orientation and eschatological commitment we must make to be continually building God's kin-dom. But, what does that mean tangibly? Goizueta notes that this kind of accompaniment "implies the transgression of discriminatory barriers."[83] It also requires a syncopated disruptive movement between spaces which compels us to inhabit border spaces and invites us to engage relationally in cross-border thinking—and, I would add, cross-border being, cross-border feeling, and of course, cross-border singing and worshipping. It is essential for people from the dominant

---

[81] Ibid.

[82] Justo L. González, "Hispanic Worship: An Introduction," in ¡Alabadle! Hispanic Christian Worship, ed. Justo L. González (Nashville: Abingdon Press, 1996), 19. Roberto Goizueta spells out the power dynamics: "No authentic dialogue is possible between teachers and students, masters and slaves, men and women, rich and poor, Anglo and Hispanic—unless and until the asymmetrical power relationships are corrected. Otherwise, the most visible, influential, and powerful voice in the dialogue will continue to be that of the wealthy, white, male Anglo—de facto. This is true however noble the intentions of the individual wealthy, white, male Anglo. What makes true dialogue impossible is not his personal intentions, but his particular socio-historical situation, that is, the role he plays within an unequal social structure." See Goizueta, Caminemos con Jesús, 181.

[83] Ibid., 206.

culture to avoid the liberal peril of merely paying lip service to this monumental task. A real move into border spaces is a dislocating and risky business. It requires a *kenotic* relinquishing of power (as we noted in Chap. 2).[84] Authentically "being" in a border space is a relational move which requires nothing short of a conversion to an-other as a radical act of love to give up power, following Jesus of Nazareth.

When I conducted the H.E.R.E. Local 75 Choir, I was challenged to reconfigure myself as a choir leader. On one hand, I learned to teach orally, to play by ear without a score, to be ready to abandon the Eurocentric modes of my musical training. On the other, when choir members wanted proper choir robes in union colours, and later traditional Jamaican outfits, we made it happen. As the White Anglo dominant culture leader of the choir, I constantly interrogated my methods and commitment, returning week after week even when my own life's circumstances made it a real challenge. Over time, I worked to cultivate leadership within the membership of the choir and partnered with a Jamaican-Canadian co-leader who became a close friend. The women of the choir also showed up week after week despite the monumental challenges of their lives. Together we made the commitment to enter a border space in a syncopated movement, engaging each other and accompanying each other across our differences, and in so doing co-articulating a vision of the community of God through our singing.

Goizueta sums up the connections between this kind of *acompaña-miento* and the liberating love at the heart of the gospel message when he writes that "only in and through the concrete *act* of accompaniment do we love others as 'others,' as equals, and are we, in turn, loved by them."[85] In a striking similarity to the way decolonial scholars talk about other ways of being, thinking, doing, and feeling, he writes that accompaniment "as action, or praxis … includes not only 'being' with another or feeling with another, but also 'doing' with another."[86] Indeed, when these praxes occur in the border(ed) spaces of our lives, they have the potential to re-form us as we reflect on our actions and their implications. Indeed, a commitment to liberating action through liturgical expression, in this case singing, can result in a profound and dislocating *metanoia*, a change of

---

[84] I remind the reader that Medina calls this move pneumatological cultural kenosis, "Cultural Theology of the Spirit."

[85] Goizueta, *Caminemos con Jesús*, 206.

[86] Ibid.

heart and life, for the marginalized and for those who are from the dominant culture and yearn to accompany those on the margins.[87]

When it comes to border singing and beginning to actualize principles of a liberating liturgical theology, the multiple complex processes described throughout this book are crucial. From the self-critical processes involved in autobiographical narratives and committing to a liberating praxis of life; to examining coloniality in what and how we sing; to welcoming sung expressions of resistance; to affirming other ways of knowing embodied in songs and in their singing—we must give up Eurocentric modes and embrace the painstaking process of conversion which requires us to become something other than what we are. In recognizing our complicity with systems of coloniality, we seek to change ourselves, convert others, and live in solidarity with those on the underside of modernity.[88] We give up the comfort of what we know in the ways we think, live, act, and feel in the world.

We can affirm that members of the H.E.R.E. Local 75 Choir understood our shared work along these lines. Our singing expressed our concrete daily struggles into which we welcomed the subversive Holy Spirit; she animated our lively—and sometimes argumentative—discussions, joined in our raw and boisterous singing together, and nudged us forward when our actions as a choir—and as a trade union—creatively danced along the edges of what was permitted. The Holy Spirit joined us, in all our fragile human-ness to affirm the beauty of our beloved community and to help us embody, however fleetingly, a weekly Wednesday glimpse of God's beloved community. The lamentation "Ain't You Got a Right" voiced an anticipatory vision of a sweeter future life where everyone does

---

[87] When people sing engaged in a social praxis of liberation, their very act of singing can enable the transformative purposes of liberation to emerge and be actualized, understood, of course, to be animated by the liberating action of the Holy Spirit. As a performative action, singing thus actually becomes liberating. Through the singing of the H.E.R.E: Local 75 Choir, for instance, choir members witnessed to their concrete lived reality and formed and enfolded themselves into a vocal community prepared—or conscientized—for the work of liberation. Along similar lines, Don Saliers remarks that living liturgy is performative. He suggests that liturgy is more than a performance which simply repeats a ritual, but is actually a transformative process whereby the liturgical action is actualized through its performance. Saliers, "Human Pathos and Divine Ethos," 276.

[88] To be clear, giving up Eurocentric modes is not the same as giving up European modes. As we saw in Chap. 4, the entrenching of coloniality also meant some European traditions and peoples were consigned to the underside. Reclaiming these traditions and voices is also part of the complex task of liberating congregational singing.

have the right to the tree of life and is invited to join together as co-workers empowered to help build God's kin-dom in the here and now. Prophetically witnessing and calling to the wider family or *familia*—"all my brothers and sisters," the choir would "raise up" this song in a performative gesture that became liberating in rehearsal and out in the world.

Our singing, what could be understood in the broadest sense as liturgical action, was sacramental praxis; we began by simply showing up and singing together, little by little reflecting upon and making sense of our lives in political and theological terms through our singing. Whenever and wherever we sang, we accompanied each other, and we accompanied fellow trade unionists, protesters, the homeless, or the undocumented victims and survivors of the collapse of the Twin Towers on September 11, 2001 (the undocumented victims who perished were members of the H.E.R.E. union). We sang on picket lines, at demonstrations, at trade union conferences, and at multi-faith services. We sang in Windsor, Ontario, at the very real border between Canada and the USA to protest against a G8 meeting across the river in Detroit. The crowd was pepper-sprayed while we were singing.

These radical risky acts of love and protest through singing are what true liberating encompasses. This kind of risk is articulated in the liberating message of Jesus of Nazareth and embodied in his life and death. When singing together in community gives concrete expression to our shared commitment to liberation, it challenges us to be liberated *for* God's vision for humanity and it can become a liberating praxis of community singing! The women of the H.E.R.E. choir modelled such a praxis when we taught each other and learned from each other, conscientizing ourselves for our singing as holy liberating work. But a wholesale adoption of this celebration of what humanity is liberated *for*, especially in its expressions from the underside and from border spaces, must be also accompanied by the work of liberating *from*, an endeavour in which we have been engaged throughout these pages. The work and grace of the Holy Spirit in and through our singing guides us through the risks of dismantling coloniality and interrogating the theological and ecclesial centres/truths of our traditions, even as we work together to build God's beloved community.

BIBLIOGRAPHY

Anzaldúa, Gloria. 2007. *Borderlands/La Frontera: The New Mestiza*. San Francisco: Aunt Lute Books.

Blitzer, Jonathan. 2019. A New Report on Family Separations Shows the Depths of Trump's Negligence. *The New Yorker*, December 6. https://www.newyorker.com/news/news-desk/a-new-report-on-family-separations-shows-the-depths-of-trumps-negligence. Accessed 10 Mar 2020.

Carawan, Guy, and Candie. 1966. *Ain't You Got a Right to the Tree of Life? The People of John's Island, South Carolina—Their Faces, Their Words, and Their Songs*. Athens/London: Brown Thrasher Books, The University of Georgia Press.

Chupungco, Anscar J. 2000. The Theological Principle of Adaptation. In *Primary Sources of Liturgical Theology*, ed. Dwight W. Vogel, 247–252. Collegeville: The Liturgical Press.

DeAnda, Neomi, and Néstor Medina. 2009. Convivencias: What Have We Learned? Toward a Latino/a Ecumenical Theology. In *Building Bridges, Doing Justice: Constructing a Latino/a Ecumenical Theology*, ed. Orland Espín, 185–196. New York: Orbis.

Duck, Ruth C. 2000. Expansive Language in the Baptized Community. In *Primary Sources of Liturgical Theology*, ed. Dwight W. Vogel, 286–294. Collegeville: The Liturgical Press.

Escobar, Arturo. 2014. *Sentipensar con la Tierra: Nuevas Lecturas Sobre Desarrollo, Territorio y Diferencia*. Medellín: Ediciones UNAULA.

Espín, Orlando, ed. 2007. *Grace and Humanness: Theological Reflections Because of Culture*. Maryknoll: Orbis Books.

———, ed. 2015. *The Wiley Blackwell Companion to Latino/a Theology*. Malden: John Wiley & Songs, Ltd.

Freire, Paulo. 1971. *Pedagogy of the Oppressed*. Trans. Myra Bergman Ramos. New York: Herder and Herder.

García-Johnson, Oscar. 2009. *The Mestizo/a Community of the Spirit: A Postmodern Latino/a Ecclesiology*. Eugene: Pickwick Publications.

Goizueta, Roberto. 1992. Rediscovering Praxis: The Significance of U.S. Hispanic Experience for Theological Method. In *We Are a People! Initiatives in Hispanic American Theology*, ed. Roberto Goizueta, 51–78. Minneapolis: Fortress Press.

———. 1995. *Caminemos con Jesús: Toward a Hispanic/Latino Theology of Accompaniment*. New York: Orbis Books.

González, Justo L. 1996. Hispanic Worship: An Introduction. In *¡Alabadle! Hispanic Christian Worship*, ed. Justo L. González, 9–28. Nashville: Abingdon Press.

———. 2000. Worship as Fiesta. In *Primary Sources of Liturgical Theology*, ed. Dwight W. Vogel, 255–260. Collegeville: The Liturgical Press.

Grosfoguel, Ramón. 2016. Del 'Extractivismo Económico' al 'Extractivismo Epistémico' y al 'Extractivismo Ontológico:' Una Forma Destructiva de Conocer, Ser y Estar en el Mundo. *Tabula Rasa. Bogotá – Colombia* 24 (enero–junio): 123–143.

Gutiérrez, Gustavo. 1973. *A Theology of Liberation.* Trans. Caridad Inda and John Eagleson. Maryknoll: Orbis.

H.E.R.E. Local 75 Choir. 2004. Ain't You Got a Right. In *I Still Have Joy.* Compact Disk Recording. Toronto: Deep Down Productions, CD.

Henry, Frances. 1968. The West Indian Domestic Scheme of Canada. *Social and Economic Studies* 17 (1): 83–91.

Hoon, Paul Waitman. 2000. Liturgical Action in Light of the Word. In *Primary Sources of Liturgical Theology*, ed. Dwight W. Vogel, 239–242. Collegeville: The Liturgical Press.

Isasi-Díaz, Ada María. 2002. Lo Cotidiano: A Key Element of Mujerista Theology. *Journal of Hispanic/Latino Theology* 10 (1): 5–17.

Jagessar, Michael N. 2015. Holy Crumbs, Table Habits, and (Dis)Placing Conversations—Beyond 'Only One is Holy'. In *Liturgy in Postcolonial Perspectives: Only One Is Holy*, ed. Cláudio Carvalhaes, 223–240. New York: Palgrave Macmillan.

Kavanagh, Aidan. 2000. On Liturgical Theology. In *Primary Sources of Liturgical Theology*, ed. Dwight W. Vogel, 91–100. Collegeville: The Liturgical Press.

Lawson, Erica. 2013. The Gendered Working Lives of Seven Jamaican Women in Canada: A Story About 'Here' and 'There' in a Transnational Economy. *Feminist Formations* 25 (1, Spring): 138–156.

Martell-Otero, Loida I. 2013a. Introduction: Abuelita Theologies. In *Latina Evangélicas: A Theological Survey from the Margins*, ed. Zaida Maldonado Pérez, Loida I. Martell-Otero, and Elizabeth Conde-Frazier, 1–13. Eugene: Cascade Books.

———. 2013b. Neither 'Left Behind' Nor Deciphering Secret Codes: An Evangélica Understanding of Eschatology. In *Latina Evangélicas: A Theological Survey from the Margins*, ed. Zaida Maldonado Pérez, Loida I. Martell-Otero, and Elizabeth Conde-Frazier, 108–126. Eugene: Cascade Books.

Medina, Néstor. 2009. *Mestizaje: (Re)Mapping Race, Culture and Faith in Latina/o Catholicism.* Maryknoll: Orbis Books.

———. 2015. Theological Musings Towards a Latina/o Pneumatology. In *The Wiley Blackwell Companion to Latino/a Theology*, ed. Orlando O. Espín, 173–189. Malden: John Wiley & Sons, Ltd.

Mignolo, Walter D. 2000. *Local Histories/Global Designs: Coloniality, Subaltern Knowledges, and Border Thinking.* Princeton: Princeton University Press.

Mullings, Beverly, Kay-Ann Williams, and Alexander Lovell. 2012. Myths and Realities: The Challenge of Social Transformation Through Canada/Jamaica Diasporic Exchange. In *Jamaica in the Canadian Experience: A Multiculturalizing Presence*, ed. Carl E. James and Andrea Davis, 294–309. Halifax/Winnipeg: Fernwood Publishing.

Newman, David R. 1983. Observations on Method in Liturgical Theology. *Worship* 57 (4): 377–384.

Pérez, Zaida Maldonado, Loida I. Martell-Otero, and Elizabeth Conde-Frazier. 2013. Dancing with the Wild Child: Evangélicas and the Holy Spirit. In *Latina Evangélicas: A Theological Survey from the Margins*, ed. Zaida Maldonado Pérez, Loida I. Martell-Otero, and Elizabeth Conde-Frazier, 14–32. Eugene: Cascade Books.

Pitter, Robert. 2012. Always Have to Be Twice as Good: Reflections of an Athlete, Coach and Academic. In *Jamaica in the Canadian Experience: A Multiculturalizing Presence*, ed. Carl E. James and Andrea David, 155–160. Halifax/Winnipeg: Fernwood Publishing.

Pope Paul VI. Constitution on the Sacred Liturgy. *Sacrosanctum Concilium*. http://www.vatican.va/archive/hist_councils/ii_vatican_council/documents/vat-ii_const_19631204_sacrosanctum-concilium_en.html. Accessed 27 Oct 2017.

Power, David N. 2000. Ritual and Verbal Language. In *Primary Sources of Liturgical Theology*, ed. Dwight W. Vogel, 180–190. Collegeville: The Liturgical Press.

Rivera Cusicanqui, Sylvia. 2006. Chhixinakax Utxiwa. Una Reflexión Sobre Prácticas y Discursos Descolonizadores. In *Modernidad y Pensamiento Descolonizador*, compiled by Mario Yupi, 3–16. La Paz: U-PIEB – IFEA.

Saliers, Don E. 2000. Human Pathos and Divine Ethos. In *Primary Sources of Liturgical Theology*, ed. Dwight W. Vogel, 276–283. Collegeville: The Liturgical Press.

Schmemann, Alexander. 2000. The Task and Method of Liturgical Theology. In *Primary Sources of Liturgical Theology*, ed. Dwight W. Vogel, 54–62. Collegeville: The Liturgical Press.

Segundo, Juan Luis. 1974. *The Sacraments Today, Volume Four of a Theology for Artisans of a New Humanity*. Trans. John Drury. New York: Orbis.

———. 1976. *Liberation of Theology*. Trans. John Drury. Oregon: Orbis.

Senior, Olive. 2012. Crossing Borders and Negotiating Boundaries. In *Jamaica in the Canadian Experience: A Multiculturalizing Presence*, ed. Carl E. James and Andrea David, 14–22. Halifax/Winnipeg: Fernwood Publishing.

Statistics Canada. The Jamaican Canadian Community. http://www.statcan.gc.ca/pub/89-621-x/89-621-x2007012-eng.htm. Accessed 5 July 2017.

Tamez, Elsa. 2008. Teología de la Liberación. In *Quedan Dios y los Pobres: Textos Sobre la Teología de la Liberación*, ed. Alejandro Dausá. La Habana: Centro Memorial Dr. Martin Luther King, Jr.

Villafañe, Eldín. 1992. *The Liberating Spirit: Toward an Hispanic American Pentecostal Social Ethic*. New York: University Press of America.

Vogel, Dwight W., ed. 2000. *Primary Sources of Liturgical Theology*. Collegeville: The Liturgical Press.

Wikipedia. Jamaican Canadians. https://en.wikipedia.org/wiki/Jamaican_ Canadians. Accessed 6 July 2017.

CHAPTER 8

A Call to Conversion

By paying attention to other ways of singing—which are already present among us, resisting colonial structures and pointing beyond coloniality—we can construct and embody congregational singing practices as part of a liberating theo-liturgical praxis. The singing of a hotel workers choir, the singing of a dynamic, embodied Latin American song of praise (*El Espíritu de Dios*), the bilingual, bicultural Christmas celebrations of English and Spanish speaking congregations, and the various moments when communities flip traditional hymnody—all embody a sacramental praxis of liberating singing. In spite of the experience of exclusion due to oppressive social structures, marginalized communities don't passively accept songs but actively reconfigure them, (re)create them, and turn them into spaces that prophetically announce hope.

Communities draw strength and a theological mandate from their concrete daily lived reality. Their ways of feeling, being, knowing, and living out their faith affirm and celebrate the diversity of humanity as multiple diverse expressions of the *imago dei*. Indeed, they offer a pathway for the churches to follow. Animated by the Holy Spirit, people, especially those who are excluded, can thus exemplify and model ways of liberating liturgy. What then are some of the implications for being and doing church that we can draw from such contexts? What does this experience say to the churches?

Above all, the act of singing can be a space of liberation. When people incorporate their wisdom and forms of knowledge in the act of singing,

© The Author(s) 2020   229
B. Whitla, *Liberation, (De)Coloniality, and Liturgical Practices,*
New Approaches to Religion and Power,
https://doi.org/10.1007/978-3-030-52636-8_8

singing can become a sacramental space where glimpses of the realm of God are experienced. Through the Holy Spirit, we are liberated *for* this work.

Yet singing is not an innocent or neutral activity. Coloniality affects singing—and song leading—and intensifies it as a terrain fraught with social markers like racialization, gender, class, dis/ability, and so on. It is essential to uncover and recognize the resulting power dynamics in order to move in a liberating direction. And congregational song leaders are never neutral in relation to singing spaces. Singing can be a contested space in which both colonization and decolonization are operative. When it comes to singing in a decolonial key, it is crucial that song leaders engage in self-reflective processes that include self-examination in terms of privilege and power. They must also create the conditions for those who sing to develop a self-critical understanding in order to prepare the foundation for liberating congregational singing. Furthermore, song leaders and communities need to make space for the flourishing of expressions from excluded and marginalized ethno/cultural groups in order for liturgy to become liberating.

This kind of liberating liturgical theology requires a rigorous and critical self-reflective stance institutionally as well as personally, in the kind of processes outlined in these pages. At their peril, churches, in their eagerness to embrace a vision of what humanity is liberated *for*, often neglect this work, the work of liberating *from*. Being transformational/liberating needs both a commitment to build God's beloved community and to confront forces that work against this divine intent. My study signals at least three integrated and broad categories of ongoing work the churches should consider.

First, a process of ecclesial/institutional autobiographical narrative is crucial. In it, we can draw on techniques like those outlined in Chap. 3, especially unforgetting. But an ecclesial autobiographical narrative which tells our stories cannot remain theoretical. For example, in Canada, the churches are challenged by processes like the Truth and Reconciliation Commission to root this storytelling in reconciliatory and transformative action. For Euro-Canadian settlers, immigrants, and Indigenous peoples in Canada, reconciliation invites liberating action, a building up of God's community. But being liberated for reconciliation through truth-telling requires ongoing liberation from our collective coloniality of being. Some church communities and institutions have already begun this work and I pray that the momentum will be strong long into the future.

The second category of work flows out of the first and will entail unmasking and confronting coloniality in our liturgies, including in our songs and singing, as part of facing the many ways coloniality continues to be operative in our churches and our lives. This confrontation involves confessing our complicity with coloniality, historically as well as in current practices. However, confessing is but a first superficial and incomplete step. It must be followed and complemented by public acknowledgement and a dynamic and active unmasking and dismantling of coloniality, particularly in inherited canons of hymnody.

The third category of this work would contribute to the dismantling of coloniality by creating spaces for the voices of the marginalized and excluded to sing and be heard. It will mean celebrating and reclaiming the diverse, myriad forms of singing incarnated from every community in every corner of the world and affirming other ways of knowing. Indeed, when we engage in critical autobiographical narrative, begin to unmask and dismantle the structures of colonization, and confront coloniality in liturgy, then our work of liberating *from* oppressive systems and structures synchronizes with the liberating work of the Holy Spirit. When we engage in this complex process of liberation, we glimpse the divine intent in what we are liberated *for.* Liturgy becomes leitourgia (λειτουργία), the work of the people, at once liberated and liberating. Liturgically speaking, this critically reflective communal praxical process can foster collaborative liberating practices as human and Divine, through the Holy Spirit, accompany each other in becoming coworkers, building and embodying the kin-dom of God.

Concretizing how such a praxis might be lived out in particular communities needs to be worked out in those communities. Each place and time, each person, each community, encompasses multiple factors in terms of identity, history, and concrete lived experiences. The tools developed throughout this book could be adapted and expanded in different contexts, in Canada and beyond, to discern what liberating congregational singing might look and sound like locally. In addition, the techniques and critical analyses could also be adapted and applied to other settings in church communities, church institutions, seminaries, and beyond.

Liberating liturgical projects can also impact, enrich, and change the way we do theology, understand divine activity and the work of Christ, and offer practical strategies for what it means to be and do church. Such expressions, articulations, and practices would need to draw on multiple voices, especially the marginalized, as well as different disciplines within the realm of liturgics and beyond. Our task would not be to articulate a single neatly packaged or systematic theology—"a" theology—but to provide inroads for multivocal and interdisciplinary avenues toward sustained ongoing conversations in the realm of liberating liturgical theologies.

To that end, this book is a concrete expression of how the disciplines of practical/liturgical theology and theology can be better woven together. My insistence that when the people sing, they are actually doing theology emphasizes this point. It is the people—church communities, congregations—who are breaking down the division between disciplines *on the ground*. They are helping us to learn and discern how our theologies and practices can continue to be decolonized, liberated, and reclaimed. And because disciplinary silos are yet another example of Eurocentric epistemic structures, an intermixing of disciplines is also a decolonial move. Accordingly, the critical engagement with post and decolonial theories in these pages can also spark conversations in wider theoretical circles about the limits and possibilities of these discourses in a variety of settings. At the same time, recent theological forays into decolonial thinking, including those in this volume, suggest ways in which liberationists can enrich their approaches through careful considerations of the impact of coloniality and its hegemonic reach into all realms of theology.

To be sure, liberating congregational singing entails nothing short of a profound epistemological and theological reorientation for song leaders and communities who are committed to it, as well as for church leaders and institutions. The accompanying changes will require leaders to work compassionately in and from their communities to be effective. It is a painstaking process whereby we account for the violence inflicted by coloniality (and Christianity). It entails a deep engagement and risk-taking which dislocates or "*dis*places" inherited theological and ecclesial centres/ truths to such an extent that many aspects of our theologies and practices may become unrecognizable.[1] It is even possible that churches could risk decolonizing themselves out of existence. True ecclesial transformation

---

[1] Michael, N. Jagessar, "Holy Crumbs, Table Habits, and (Dis)Placing Conversations— Beyond 'Only One is Holy'," in *Liturgy in Postcolonial Perspectives: Only One is Holy*, edited by Cláudio Carvalhaes, (New York: Palgrave Macmillan, 2015), 224. Jagessar recognizes this inherent challenge when he notes that "Christianity has been too preoccupied with a terrifying singularity—one Lord, one faith, one baptism, one God, etc." Noting that "our diverse landscape (faiths, peoples, cultures) is a plural reality," he proposes that we invert the "'logic of oneness'—[which] must be critically engaged with, given its imperializing and totalizing tendencies" Ibid., 226, 227.

entails a risk that is of this magnitude and amounts to conversion for churches to an-other way of thinking, being, doing, and feeling. It is a monumental task with a kenotic imperative and urgency at its heart. It demands that those with power create spaces for other voices to be heard. It also demands that those who have power relinquish it, following Jesus of Nazareth, by entering into solidarity with the marginalized and excluded, and helping to create the structures of the long-awaited kin-dom.

APPENDIX: VERSIONS OF "O STORE GUD"

© The Author(s) 2020

235

B. Whitla, *Liberation, (De)Coloniality, and Liturgical Practices*,
New Approaches to Religion and Power,
https://doi.org/10.1007/978-3-030-52636-8

O store Gud – original	English
Text: Carl Boberg 1885 Music: Svensk folkmelodi, tryckt 1889 For the original nine verses, see: "O Store Gud," accessed July 28, 2018, http://runeberg.org/smfsang/0010.html,	Thomas Girmalm – Personal conversation, July, 2016
1. O store Gud, när jag den värld beskådar som du har skapat med ditt allmaktsord, hur där din visdom väver livets trådar och alla väsen mättas vid ditt bord //: då brister själen ut i lovsångsljud: o store Gud, o store Gud ://	O great God, when I see the world as you have created with your word of omnipotence how there your wisdom weaves the threads of life and all creatures are fed at your table //Then the soul bursts out in sound of praising O great God, O great God
2. När jag hör åskans röst och stormar brusa och blixtens klingor springa fram ur skyn, när regnets kalla, friska skurar susa och löftets båge glänser för min syn	When I hear the voice of thunder and the roar of storms And flashes of lightning run out from the sky When the rains cold, fresh showers whisper And the (rain)bow of promise is shining for my sight
3. När sommarvinden susar över fälten, när blommor dofta invid källans strand, när trastar drilla i de gröna tälten vid furuskogens tysta, dunkla rand	When the summer wind is whispering over the fields When flowers smell (like blossom but for smell) beside the spring When birds (specific) are singing in the green tents At the edge of the quiet dark pine forests
4. När jag i Bibeln skådar alla under som Herren gjort sen förste Adams tid, hur nådefull han varit alla stunder och hjälpt sitt folk ur livets synd och strid,	When I watch all the wonders of the Bible As the Lord has done, since the time of the first Adam How graceful He has been during all these times And helped His people out of their sin and battle/struggle of life
5. När tryckt av synd och skuld jag faller neder vid Herrens fot och ber om nåd och frid, och han min själ på rätta vägen leder och frälsar mig från all min synd och strid,	When pressed down by sin and guilt, I fall down At the feet of the Lord and beg grace and peace And He, my soul, on the right way leads And saves me from all my sin and struggles (battles)
6. När en gång alla tidens höljen falla och jag får skåda det jag nu får tro, och evighetens klara klockor kalla min frälsta ande till dess sabbatsro //: då brister själen ut i lovsångsljud: Tack, gode Gud, tack, gode Gud! ://	When one time all the shrouds of time shall fall And I will behold that I now receive faith, And the clear bells of eternity call My saved spirit to its Sabbath rest //Then the soul bursts out in sound of praising Thanks good God, thanks good God

Fig. A.1 Swedish-English translation of *"O Store Gud"*

How Great Thou Art, words by Stuart Hine, 1949

© 1949, 1953 The Stuart Hine Trust CIO. All rights in the USA its territories and possessions, except print rights, administered by Capitol CMG Publishing. USA, North and Central American print rights and all Canadian and South American rights administered by Hope Publishing Company. All other North and Central American rights administered by The Stuart Hine Trust CIO. Rest of the world rights administered by Integrity Music Europe. All rights reserved. Used by permission.

1. O Lord my God! When I in awesome wonder
Consider all the *works Thy hand hath made.
I see the stars, I hear the *rolling thunder,
Thy power throughout the universe displayed.
> *Refrain:* Then sings my soul, my Saviour God, to Thee;
> How great Thou art, how great Thou art!

2. When through the woods and forest glades I wander
And hear the birds sing sweetly in the trees;
When I look down from lofty mountain grandeur
And hear the brook and feel the gentle breeze:

3. And when I think that God, His Son not sparing,
Sent Him to die, I scarce can take it in;
That on the cross, my burden gladly bearing,
He bled and died to take away my sin:

4. When Christ shall come with shout of acclamation
And take me home, what joy shall fill my heart!
Then *I shall bow in humble adoration,
And there proclaim, my God, how great Thou art!

Author's original words are "works," "mighty" and "shall I bow" (Word changes approved for use in North America.)

Other verses by Hine, not generally used. See Wikipedia, "How Great Thou Art," accessed, July 28, 2018, https://en.wikipedia.org/wiki/How_Great_Thou_Art.

O when I see ungrateful man defiling
This bounteous earth, God's gifts so good and great;
In foolish pride, God's holy Name reviling,
And yet, in grace, His wrath and judgment wait.

When burdens press, and seem beyond endurance,
Bowed down with grief, to Him I lift my face;
And then in love He brings me sweet assurance:
'My child! for thee sufficient is my grace.'

Fig. A.2   "How Great Thou Art," words by Stuart Hine, 1949

The Covenant Hymnal #19
"O Mighty God, When I Behold the Wonder"
Translation by E. Gustav Johnson (1893-1974),
©1973 Covenant Publications, reprinted with
permission, all rights reserved.

1.O mighty God, when I behold the wonder
Of nature's beauty, wrought by words of thine,
And how thou leadest all from realms up yonder,
Sustaining earthly life with love benign,

Refrain:
With rapture filled, my soul thy name would laud,
O mighty God! O mighty God! (repeat)

2.When I behold the heavens in their vastness,
Where golden ships in azure issue forth,
Where sun and moon keep watch upon the fastness
Of changing seasons and of time on earth.

3. When crushed by guilt of sin before thee kneeling,
I plead for mercy and for grace and peace,
I feel thy balm and, all my bruises healing,
My soul is filled, my heart is set at ease.

4. And when at last the mists of time have vanished
And I in truth my faith confirmed shall see,
Upon the shores where earthly ills are banished
I'll enter Lord, to dwell in peace with thee.

The hymn appeared in *The Covenant Hymnal* in 1931
with 5 verses (#12), in 1973 (as above) and in 1996,
(alongside Hines' text, #9).

The New Century Hymnal #35
"O Mighty God, When I Survey in Wonder,"
Translation and harmonization © 1994. The Pilgrim
Press. Used with permission, all rights reserved.

1.O mighty God, when I survey in wonder
The world that formed when once the word you said,
The strands of life all woven close together,
The whole creation at your table fed,

Refrain:
My soul cries out in songs of praise to you,
O mighty God! O mighty God! (repeat)

2.When your voice speaks in rolls of thunder pealing,
Your lightning power bursts in bright surprise;
When cooling rain, your gentle love revealing,
Reflects your promise, arcing through the skies.

3. The Bible tells the story of your blessing
So freely shed upon all human life;
Your constant mercy, every care addressing,
relieving burdened souls from sin and strife.

4. And when at last, the clouds of doubt dispersing,
You will reveal what we but dimly see;
With trumpet call, our great rebirth announcing,
we shall rejoin you for eternity.

Refrain: (verse 4)
Then we will sing your praise forever more,
O mighty God! O mighty God! (repeat)

See also: Glen Wiberg, "Sightings in Christian Music," in *Pietistan* 17, No 1 (Summer 2002), accessed
July 28, 2018, http://www.pietisten.org/summer02/sightings.html, Accessed April 10, 2020.

Fig. A.3 Other English Translations of *"O Store Gud"*

"Cuán Grande Es Él" by Arturo W. Hotton, 1958.

Accessed June 28, 2018, https://es.wikipedia.org/wiki/Cu%C3%A1n_grande_es_%C3%89l.

Cuán Grande Es Él, 1958	English Translation, mine
1.Señor, mi Dios, al contemplar los cielos, El firmamento y las estrellas mil. Al oír tu voz en los potentes truenos Y ver brillar al sol en su cenit. *Coro:* Mi corazón entona la canción. ¡Cuán grande es Él! ¡Cuán grande es Él!	Lord, my God, when I contemplate the heavens, the firmament and the thousand stars. Hearing your voice in powerful thunder, Seeing the sun shining in its zenith *Refrain:* My heart sings this song: How great He is! How great He is!
2.Al recorrer los montes y los valles Y ver las bellas flores al pasar. Al escuchar el canto de las aves Y el murmurar del claro manantial. *Coro*	When I walk through the mountains and valleys, And seeing the beautiful flowers in passing. Listening to the birds singing And the murmur of the clear spring. *Refrain*
3.Cuando recuerdo el amor divino, Que desde el cielo al Salvador envió. Aquel Jesús que por salvarme vino, Y en una cruz sufrió y por mi murió. *Coro*	When I recall the divine love which from heaven sent the Saviour, That Jesus came to save me and in a cross suffered and died. *Refrain*
4.Cuando el Señor me llame a su presencia, Al dulce hogar, al cielo de esplendor. Le adoraré, cantando la grandeza De su poder y su infinito amor. *Coro*	When the Lord calls me to his presence, To his sweet home, the splendorous heavens. I will adore Him, singing the greatness Of his power and infinite love.

"Cuán Grande Tu" by René Castellanos Morente.

From the bulletin of his funeral, personal collection of the author.

Cuán Grande Tu	EnglishTranslation, mine
1.Señor, mi Dios, cuando de asombro lleno Contemplo al cielo que tu mano creó. Y me estremezco ante el horrento trueno Y el mundo en luz que tu poder formó *Coro:* Entonces canta mi alma, oh Dios, a Ti: ¡Cuán grande Tú! ¡ Cuán grande Tú!	1.Lord, my God, when I am full of wonder I contemplate the sky that your hand created. And I shudder at the tremendous thunder And the light of the world that your power formed. *Refrain:* Then sing my soul, oh God, to You: How great You! How great You!
2.Cuando en los árboles del bosque espeso Escucho tierno al pájaro cantar; Y allá en el monde siento al fresco beso Del viento y oigo el río murmurar. *Coro*	When in the trees of the thick forest I listen tenderly to the singing of the bird; And there on the grass I feel the fresh kiss From the wind and I hear the river murmuring. *Refrain*
3.Y cuando pienso en Dios que ofrece a Cristo De tanto amor no alcanzo comprensión Por mí en la cruz muriendo estuvo listo A dar su sangre y darme salvación. *Coro*	And when I think of God who offers Christ Out of so much love I cannot understand He was ready to die on the cross for me To give his blood and give me salvation. *Refrain*
4.Cuando al Señor en gloria vuela un día, Y me conduzca al celestial hogar; Le adoraré, y en rapto de alegría ¡Cuán grande tú!, mi Dios, he de cantar. *Coro*	When to the Lord in glory I will fly one day, And he will lead me to the heavenly home; I will adore him, and in rapture of joy How great you, my God, I will sing.

Fig. A.4 Spanish Versions of *"O Store Gud"*

BIBLIOGRAPHY

Airhart, Phyllis. 2014. *A Church with the Soul of a Nation: Making and Remaking the United Church of Canada*. Montréal: McGill-Queens.

Anglican Church of Canada. 1998. *Common Praise: The Hymnal of the Anglican Church of Canada*. Toronto: Anglican Church of Canada.

———. Apology to Native People. https://www.anglican.ca/wp-content/uploads/2011/06/Apology-English.pdf. Accessed 22 Apr 2020.

———. 'High' and 'Low' Church. *Frequently Asked Questions*. http://www.anglican.ca/ask/faq/high-low-church/. Accessed 21 Jan 2017.

Anzaldúa, Gloria. 2007. *Borderlands/La Frontera: The New Mestiza*. San Francisco: Aunt Lute Books.

Applebaum, Barbara. 2015. Flipping the Script… and Still a Problem: Staying in the Anxiety of Being a Problem. In *White Criticality Before Anti-Racism: How Does It Feel to Be a White Problem?* ed. George Yancy, 1–19. London: Lexington Books.

Arnold, Richard, ed. 2004. *English Hymns of the Nineteenth Century: An Anthology*. New York: Peter Lang.

Augustine. 1997. *The Confessions*. Trans. Maria Boulding. New York: New City Press.

Badke, David. Nightingale. In *The Medieval Bestiary: Animals in the Middle Ages*. http://bestiary.ca/beasts/besat546.htm. Accessed 25 July 2018.

Bannerji, Himani. 2000. *The Dark Side of the Nation: Essays on Multiculturalism, Nationalism and Gender*. Toronto: Canadian Scholars' Press Inc.

———. 2004. Geography Lessons: On Being an Insider/Outsider to the Canadian Nation. In *Unhomely States: Theorizing English-Canadian Postcolonialism*, ed. Cynthia Sugars, 289–297. Perterborough: Broadview Press Ltd.

© The Author(s) 2020
B. Whitla, *Liberation, (De)Coloniality, and Liturgical Practices*,
New Approaches to Religion and Power,
https://doi.org/10.1007/978-3-030-52636-8

Baring-Gould, Sabine. Onward Christian Soldiers. http://www.hymnary.org/text/onward_christian_soldiers_marching_as. Accessed 25 July 2018.

Battiste, Marie. 2013. *Decolonizing Education: Nourishing the Learning Spirit.* Saskatoon: Purish Publishing Limited.

Bell, John L. 2000. *The Singing Thing: A Case for Congregational Song.* Chicago: GIA Publications, Inc.

———. 2007. *The Singing Thing Too: Enabling Congregations to Sing.* Chicago: GIA Publications Inc.

Bennet, J.C. 2017. How Formal Anglican Pew-Renting Worked in Practice, 1800–1950. *The Journal of Ecclesiastical History* 68 (4): 766–783. Cambridge: Cambridge University Press.

Bhabha, Homi K. 1994. *The Location of Culture.* New York: Routledge.

———. 1996. Culture's In-Between. In *Questions of Cultural Identity*, ed. Stuart Hall and Paul Du Gay, 53–60. London: Sage Publications Ltd.

Blake, William. And Did Those Feet in Ancient Time. https://hymnary.org/text/and_did_those_feet_in_ancient_time. Accessed 4 Jan 2018.

Blitzer, Jonathan. 2019. A New Report on Family Separations Shows the Depths of Trump's Negligence. *The New Yorker*, December 6. https://www.newyorker.com/news/news-desk/a-new-report-on-family-separations-shows-the-depths-of-trumps-negligence. Accessed 10 Mar 2020.

Boberg, Carl. O store Gud, när jag den värld beskådar. http://runeberg.org/smfsang/0010.html. Accessed 28 July 2018.

Bohlman, Philip V. 1997. World Musics and World Religions: Whose World? In *Enchanting Powers: Music in the World's Religions*, ed. Lawrence E. Sullivan, 61–90. Cambridge, MA: Distributed by Harvard University Press for the Harvard University Center for the Study of World Religions.

Bonner, Carey, ed. 1905. *The Sunday School Hymnary: A Twentieth Century Hymnal for Young People.* London: Novello and Company. https://archive.org/details/sundayschoolhym00nsgoog. Accessed 5 May 2018.

Bradley, Ian. 1997. *Abide with Me: The World of Victorian Hymns.* London: SCM Press.

Bramadat, Paul, and David Seljak. 2008. Charting the New Terrain: Christianity and Ethnicity in Canada. In *Christianity and Ethnicity in Canada*, ed. Paul Bramadat and David Seljak, 3–48. Toronto: University of Toronto Press.

British Home Children in Canada. Sherbrooke, Quebec, Church of England Waifs and Strays. http://canadianbritishhomechildren.weebly.com/church-of-england-waifs%2D%2Dstrays-4468.html. Accessed 25 July 2018.

Brydon, Dianne. 2004. Reading Postcoloniality, Reading Canada. In *Unhomely States: Theorizing English-Canadian Postcolonialism*, ed. Cynthia Sugars, 165–182. Peterborough: Broadview Press Ltd.

Butler, Melvin L. 2014. Singing Like David Sang: Queerness and Masculinity in Black Gospel Performance. In *Readings in African American Church Music and Worship: Volume 2*, compiled and edited by James Abbington, 715–725. Chicago: GIA Publications Inc..

Calvin, John. 1996. Epistle to the Reader. In *Cinquante Pseaumes en Français par Clem. Marot* (1543). Reprinted in Music, David, editor and compiler. *Hymnology: A Collection of Source Readings*. Lanham: Scarecrow Press, Inc.

Calvin Institute of Christian Worship. Nairobi Statement on Worship and Culture. https://worship.calvin.edu/resources/resource-library/nairobi-statement-on-worship-and-culture-full-text. Accessed 16 Apr 2018.

Canadian Museum of Immigration at Pier 21. 1971. Canadian Multiculturalism Policy. https://pier21.ca/research/immigration-history/canadian-multiculturalism-policy-1971. Accessed 3 Feb 2020.

Carawan, Guy, and Candie Carawan. 1966. *Ain't You Got a Right to the Tree of Life? The People of John's Island, South Carolina—Their Faces, Their Words, and Their Songs*. Athens/London: Brown Thrasher Books, The University of Georgia Press.

Carey, Hilary M. 2011. Colonial Missionary Societies: Nonconformists. In *God's Empire: Religion and Colonialism in the British World, c.1801–1908*, 177–205. Oxford: Oxford University Press.

Carvalhaes, Cláudio. 2015. Liturgy and Postcolonialism: An Introduction. In *Liturgy in Postcolonial Perspectives: Only One Is Holy*, ed. Cláudio Carvalhaes, 1–20. New York: Palgrave Macmillan.

Cass, Barbara, and Helen Freeman, eds. 1941. *Awake and Sing! Songs for Singing Democracy*. Toronto: Fellowship for a Christian Social Order.

Chopp, Rebecca S. 1986. Toward Praxis: A Method for Liberation Theology. In *The Praxis of Suffering: An Interpretation of Liberation and Political Theologies*, 134–148. Maryknoll: Orbis.

Christian Congregational Music. Homepage. https://congregationalmusic.org/. Accessed 8 Mar 2020.

Chupungco, Anscar J. 2000. The Theological Principle of Adaptation. In *Primary Sources of Liturgical Theology*, ed. Dwight W. Vogel, 247–252. Collegeville: The Liturgical Press.

Church of the Holy Trinity. Church Website. http://www.holytrinitytoronto.org/wp/. Accessed 21 June 2017.

———. A Very Brief History. http://www.holytrinitytoronto.org/wp/about/a-very-brief-history/. Accessed 21 June 2017.

Collins, Ace. 2003. Onward Christian Soldiers. In *Stories Behind the Hymns That Inspire America: Songs That Unite Our Nation*, 147–154, ed. Ace Collins. Grand Rapids: Zondervan.

Cooper, Thomas. 2010. Blog Post 1: Translatio Studii et Imperii. In *Thomas Cooper Individual Blog*, February 3. http://cantst1.blogspot.ca/2010/02/blog-post-1-translatio-studii-et.html. Accessed 25 Feb 2016.

Coutlhard, Glen Sean. 2014. *Red Skin, White Masks: Rejecting the Colonial Politics of Recognition.* Minneapolis: University of Minnesota Press.

DeAnda, Neomi. 2015. Jesus the Christ. In *The Wiley Blackwell Companion to Latino/a Theology,* ed. Orlando O. Espín, 155–171. Hoboken: John Wiley & Sons, Ltd.

DeAnda, Neomi, and Néstor Medina. 2009. Convivencias: What Have We Learned? Toward a Latino/a Ecumenical Theology. In *Building Bridges, Doing Justice: Constructing a Latino/a Ecumenical Theology,* ed. Orland Espín, 185–196. New York: Orbis.

DeNora, Tia. 1995. *Beethoven and the Construction of Genius: Musical Politics in Vienna, 1792–180.* Oakland: University of California Press.

Diocese of Gauleguaychú. El Espíritu de Dios. http://www.obispadogchu.org.ar/cancionero/09pentecostes/220ElEspiritudeDios.htm. Accessed 25 July 2018.

Diocese of Toronto, Anglican Church of Canada. Diversity Resources. http://www.toronto.anglican.ca/parish-life/diversity-resources. Accessed 4 Feb 2017.

Dowley, Tim. 2011. How Great Thou Art. In *Christian Music: A Global History,* 218. Minneapolis: Fortress Press.

Du Bois, William Edward Burdhardt. 1904. *The Souls of Black Folks; Essays and Sketches.* Chicago: A.C. McClurg & Co.

Duck, Ruth C. 2000. Expansive Language in the Baptized Community. In *Primary Sources of Liturgical Theology,* ed. Dwight W. Vogel, 286–294. Collegeville: The Liturgical Press.

———. 2013. *Worship for the Whole People of God: Vital Worship for the 21st Century.* Louisville: Westminster John Knox.

Dussel, Enrique. 1995. *The Invention of the Americas: Eclipse of "the Other" and the Myth of Modernity.* New York: The Continuum Publishing Company.

Elizondo, Virgilio. 2007. Living Faith: Resistance and Survival. In *Galilean Journey: The Mexican-American Promise,* 32–46. Maryknoll: Orbis Books.

Escobar, Arturo. 2014. *Sentipensar con la Tierra: Nuevas Lecturas Sobre Desarrollo, Territorio y Diferencia.* Medellín: Ediciones UNAULA.

———. 2016. Desde Abajo, por la Izquierda, y con la Tierra: La Diferencia de Abya Yala/Afro/Latino-América. *Intervenciones en Estudios Culturales* 3: 117–136.

Espín, Orlando. 2007. *Grace and Humanness: Theological Reflections Because of Culture.* Maryknoll: Orbis Books.

———, ed. 2015. *The Wiley Blackwell Companion to Latino/a Theology.* Hoboken: John Wiley & Songs, Ltd.

Fennema, Sharon R. 2015. Postcolonial Whiteness: Being-with in Worship. In *Liturgy in Postcolonial Perspectives: Only One is Holy,* ed. Cláudio Carvalhaes, 277–287. New York: Palgrave Macmillan.

Fine, Sean. 2016. Chief Justice Says Canada Attempted 'Cultural Genocide' on Aboriginals. *The Globe and Mail*. http://www.theglobeandmail.com/news/national/chief-justice-says-canada-attempted-cultural-genocide-on-aboriginals/article24688854/. Accessed 25 July 2018.

Fletcher, Wendy. 2008. Canadian Anglicanism and Ethnicity. In *Christianity and Ethnicity in Canada*, ed. Paul Bramadat and David Seljak, 138–167. Toronto: University of Toronto Press.

Franciscan Media. Las Posadas: A Mexican Christmas Tradition. https://www.franciscanmedia.org/las-posadas-a-mexican-christmas-tradition/. Accessed 11 June 2017.

Freire, Paulo. 1971. *Pedagogy of the Oppressed*. Trans. Myra Bergman Ramos. New York: Herder and Herder.

García-Johnson, Oscar. 2009. *The Mestizo/a Community of the Spirit: A Postmodern Latino/a Ecclesiology*. Eugene: Pickwick Publications.

Gibson, Colin. Lift High the Cross (New Zealand Version). In *Canterbury Dictionary of Hymnology*. https://hymnology-hymnsam-co-uk.myaccess.library.utoronto.ca/l/lift-high-the-cross,-the-love-of-christ-proclaim?q=Lift%20high%20the%20cross,%20the%20love%20of%20Christ%20proclaim. Accessed 25 July 2018.

———. Shirley Erena Murray. In *Canterbury Dictionary of Hymnology*. https://hymnology-hymnsam-co-uk.myaccess.library.utoronto.ca/s/shirley-erena-murray?q=erena%20murray. Accessed 25 July 2018.

Gilroy, Paul. 1993. *The Black Atlantic: Modernity and Double Consciousness*. London: Verso.

Global Ministries. Global Praise. https://www.umcmission.org/Find-Resources/Global-Praise. Accessed 27 Oct 2015.

Go Forth into the World. https://johnian.wordpress.com/2012/02/05/go-forth-into-the-world/. Accessed 9 May 2018.

Goizueta, Roberto. 1992. Rediscovering Praxis: The Significance of U.S. Hispanic Experience for Theological Method. In *We Are a People! Initiatives in Hispanic American Theology*, ed. Roberto Goizueta, 51–78. Minneapolis: Fortress Press.

———. 1995. *Caminemos con Jesús: Toward a Hispanic/Latino Theology of Accompaniment*. New York: Orbis Books.

González, Justo L. 1996. Hispanic Worship: An Introduction'. In *¡Alabadle! Hispanic Christian Worship*, ed. Justo L. González, 9–28. Nashville: Abingdon Press.

———. 2000. Worship as Fiesta. In *Primary Sources of Liturgical Theology*, ed. Dwight W. Vogel, 255–260. Collegeville: The Liturgical Press.

Government of Canada. Multiculturalism. https://www.canada.ca/en/services/culture/canadian-identity-society/multiculturalism.html. Accessed 3 Feb 2020.

Grosfoguel, Ramón. 2016. Del 'Extractivismo Económico' al 'Extractivismo Epistémico' y al 'Extractivismo Ontológico:' Una Forma Destructiva de

Conocer, Ser y Estar en el Mundo. *Tabula Rasa. Bogotá – Colombia* 24 (enero–junio): 123–143.

Gunew, Sneja. 2004. *Haunted Nations: The Colonial Dimensions of Multiculturalisms.* New York: Routledge.

Gutiérrez, Gustavo. 1973. *A Theology of Liberation.* Trans. Caridad Inda and John Eagleson. Maryknoll: Orbis.

H.E.R.E. Local 75 Choir. 2004. Ain't You Got a Right. In *I Still Have Joy.* Compact Disk Recording. Toronto: Deep Down Productions, CD.

Haig-Brown, Celia. 2009. Decolonizing Diaspora: Whose Traditional Land Are We On? *Cultural and Pedagogical Inquiry* 1 (1): 4–21.

Hall, Stuart. 1992. The West and the Rest: Discourse and Power. In *Formations of Modernity,* ed. Stuart Hall and Bram Gieben, 185–227. Cambridge: Polity Press in association with the Open University.

———. 1996. Introduction: Who Needs Identity? In *Questions of Cultural Identity,* ed. Stuart Hall and Paul Du Gay, 1–17. London: Sage Publications Ltd.

Hammond, Fred. The Spirit of the Lord. In *The Spirit of David.* http://www.all-music.com/album/the-spirit-of-david-mw0000073417. Accessed 25 July 2018.

Havergal, Frances. Take My Life and Let It Be. https://hymnary.org/text/take_my_life_and_let_it_be. Accessed 4 Jan 2018.

Hawn, C. Michael. 2003a. *Gather Into One: Praying and Singing Globally.* Grand Rapids: Eerdmans Publishing.

———. 2003b. *One Bread, One Body: Exploring Cultural Diversity in Worship.* Wisconsin: Alban Institute.

———, comp. and ed. 2013. *New Songs of Celebration Render: Congregational Song in the Twenty-First Century.* Chicago: GIA Publications.

———. Jesus Shall Reign. http://www.umcdiscipleship.org/resources/history-of-hymns-jesus-shall-reign. Accessed 25 July 2018.

———. How Great Thou Art. https://www.umcdiscipleship.org/resources/his-tory-of-hymns-how-great-thou-art. Accessed 28 July 2018.

———. Lift High the Cross. In *History of Hymns.* http://www.umcdiscipleship.org/resources/history-of-hymns-lift-high-the-cross. Accessed 25 July 2018.

Henry, Frances. 1968. The West Indian Domestic Scheme of Canada. *Social and Economic Studies* 17 (1): 83–91.

Hildegard of Bingen. 1990. *Scivias.* Trans. Columba Hart and Jane Bishop. New York: Paulist Press.

Hoon, Paul Waitman. 2000. Liturgical Action in Light of the Word. In *Primary Sources of Liturgical Theology,* ed. Dwight W. Vogel, 239–242. Collegeville: The Liturgical Press.

Hope Publishing Company. How Great Thou Art. *hopepublishing.com.* https://www.hopepublishing.com/find-hymns-hw/hw4894.aspx. Accessed 19 June 2020.

Hughes, Derrick. 1986. *Bishop Sahib: A Life of Reginald Heber*. West Sussex: Churchman Publishing Ltd.

Hutchinson, Roger. 1975. *The Fellowship for a Christian Social Order: A Social Ethical Analysis of a Christian Socialist Movement*. PhD dissertation, Toronto School of Theology, University of Toronto.

———. 1989. The Fellowship for a Christian Social Order: 1934–1945. In *A Long and Faithful March: "Towards the Christian Revolution" 1930s/1980s*, ed. Harold Wells and Roger Hutchinson, 17–29. Toronto: United Church Publishing House.

Ingalls, Monique, Carolyn Landau, and Tom Wagner. 2013. *Christian Congregational Music: Performance, Identity, and Experience*. Farnham: Ashgate Publishing.

Isasi-Díaz, Ada María. 2010. Kin-Dom of God: A Mujerista Proposal. In *In Our Own Voices: Latino/a Renditions of Theology*, ed. Beahamín Valentín, 171–189. Maryknoll: Orbis.

———. 2002. Lo Cotidiano: A Key Element of Mujerista Theology. *Journal of Hispanic/Latino Theology* 10 (1): 5–17.

Isasi-Díaz, Ada María, and Eduardo Mendieta, eds. 2012. *Decolonizing Epistemologies: Latina/o Theology and Philosophy*. New York: Fordham University Press.

Jagessar, Michael N. 2015. Holy Crumbs, Table Habits, and (Dis)Placing Conversations—Beyond 'Only One Is Holy'. In *Liturgy in Postcolonial Perspectives: Only One Is Holy*, ed. Cláudio Carvalhaes, 223–240. New York: Palgrave Macmillan.

Jagessar, Michael N., and Stephen Burns. 2011. *Christian Worship: Postcolonial Perspectives*. Sheffield: Equinox.

Johnson, E. Gustav. 1973. O Mighty God, When I Behold the Wonder #19. In *Covenant Hymnal*. Chicago: Covenant Publications.

Johnson, Sarah Kathleen. 2018. On Our Knees: Christian Ritual in Residential Schools and the Truth and Reconciliation Commission of Canada. *Studies in Religion* 47 (1): 3–24.

Joy Bringer Ministries. How Great Thou Art. http://www.joy-bringer-ministries.org/hymns/hgta.pdf. Accessed 28 July 2018.

Kairos. Blanket Exercise. http://kairosblanketexercise.org/. Accessed 25 July 2018.

Kalssen, Helen, ed. 1990. *International Songbook*. Carol Stream: Mennonite World Conference.

Kavanagh, Aidan. 2000. On Liturgical Theology. In *Primary Sources of Liturgical Theology*, ed. Dwight W. Vogel, 91–100. Collegeville: The Liturgical Press.

Keller, Catherine, Michael Nausner, and Mayra Rivera, eds. 2004. *Post-Colonial Theologies: Divinity and Empire*. Danvers: Chalice Press.

Kelly, Deirdre. 2013. Angels in the Dark: The Church of the Holy Trinity's A Christmas Story. In *Critics at Large*, December 20. http://www.criticsatlarge. ca/2013/12/angels-in-dark-church-of-holy-trinitys.html.   Accessed   8 June 2017.

Kervin, William S., ed. 2011. *Ordered Liberty: Readings in the History of United Church Worship*. Toronto: United Church Publishing House.

———. 2017. Joyful Is the Dark: Expansive and Emancipatory Language. In *Gathered for Worship: A Sourcebook for Worship Committees, Leaders, and Teams*, 36–39. Toronto: United Church Publishing House.

Khodorkovsky, Maria. 2008. Traduttore, Traditore. *Beyond Words—Language Blog*, October 9. http://www.altalang.com/beyond-words/2008/10/09/ traduttore-traditore/. Accessed 25 July 2018.

Kimbrough, S.T. 1995. Charles Wesley and the Poor. In *The Portion of the Poor: Good News to the Poor in the Wesleyan Tradition*, ed. M. Douglas Meeks, 147–190. Nashville: Kingswood Books.

———., ed. 2007. *Music and Mission: Toward a Theology and Practice of Global Song*. New York: GBGMusik.

King, Thomas. 2004. Godzilla Vs. Post-Colonial. In *Unhomely States: Theorizing English-Canadian Postcolonialism*, ed. Cynthia Sugars, 184–190. Toronto: Broadview Press Ltd.

King's College Cambridge. A Festival of Nine Lessons and Carols: Service Booklets from Previous Years. http://www.kings.cam.ac.uk/files/services/festival-nine-lessons-2015.pdf. Accessed 6 June 2017.

Kitchin, George W. Lift High the Cross. http://www.oremus.org/hymnal/l/ l118.html. Accessed 10 Jan 2017.

Kolodziej, Benjamin A. 2004. Isaac Watts, the Wesleys, and the Evolution of 18th-Century English Congregational Song. *Methodist History* 42 (4): 236–248.

Lawson, Erica. 2013. The Gendered Working Lives of Seven Jamaican Women in Canada: A Story About 'Here' and 'There' in a Transnational Economy. *Feminist Formations* 25 (1): 138–156.

Lebans, Crista. 2015. On not Making a Labor of It: Relationality and the Problem of Whiteness. In *White Criticality Before Anti-Racism: How Does It Feel to Be a White Problem?* ed. George Yancy, 69–83. London: Lexington Books.

Lemire, Devon. A Historiographical Survey of Literacy in Britain Between 1780 and 1830. *Constellations*. https://ejournals.library.ualberta.ca/index.php/ constellations/article/viewFile/18862/14652. Accessed 18 Jan 2017.

Lim, Swee Hong. 2008. *Giving Voice to Asian Christians: An Appraisal of the Pioneering Work of I-To Loh in the Area of Congregational Song*. North Charleston: VDM Verlag.

Lim, Swee Hong, and Lester Ruth. 2018. *Lovin' on Jesus: A Concise History of Contemporary Music*. Nashville: Abingdon Press.

Lind, Emily R.M. 2015. I Once Was Lost but Now I'm Found: Exploring the White Feminist Confessional. In *Unveiling Whiteness in the Twenty-First Century: Global Manifestations, Transdisciplinary Interventions*, ed. Veronica Watson, Deirdre Howard-Wagner, and Lisa Spanierman, 229–246. London: Lexington Books.

Luther, Martin. 1965. Preface to Gerog Rhau's Symphoniae Iucundae. In *Luther's Works, American Edition: Volume 53—Liturgy and Hymns*, translated and edited by Ulrich S. Leupold, 321–322. Philadelphia: Fortress Press.

Maduro, Otto. 2012. An(Other) Invitation to Epistemological Humility: Notes Towards a Self-Critical Approach to Counter-Knowledges. In *Decolonizing Epistemologies: Latina/o Theology and Philosophy*, ed. Ada María Isasi-Díaz and Eduardo Mendieta, 87–103. New York: Fordham University Press.

Maldonado-Torres, Nelson. 2007. On the Coloniality of Being. *Cultural Studies* 21 (2–3): 240–270. http://www.decolonialtranslation.com/english/maldonado-on-the-coloniality-of-being.pdf. Accessed 25 July 2018.

Manuel, Arthur, and Grand Chief Ronald M. Derrickson. 2015. *Unsettling Canada: A National Wake-up Call*. Between the Lines: Toronto.

———. 2017. *The Reconciliation Manifesto: Recovering the Land, Rebuilding the Economy*. Toronto: James Lorimer & Company Ltd.

Maracle, Lee. 2004. The 'Post-Colonial' Imagination. In *Unhomely States: Theorizing English-Canadian Postcolonialism*, ed. Cynthia Sugars, 205–208. Toronto: Broadview Press Ltd.

Martell-Otero, Loida I. 2013a. Introduction: Abuelita Theologies. In *Latina Evangélicas: A Theological Survey from the Margins*, ed. Zaida Maldonado Pérez, Loida I. Martell-Otero, and Elizabeth Conde-Frazier, 1–13. Eugene: Cascade Books.

———. 2013b. Neither 'Left Behind' Nor Deciphering Secret Codes: An Evangélica Understanding of Eschatology. In *Latina Evangélicas: A Theological Survey from the Margins*, ed. Zaida Maldonado Pérez, Loida I. Martell-Otero, and Elizabeth Conde-Frazier, 108–126. Eugene: Cascade Books.

Martin, Karen, and Boora Mirraboopa. 2003. Ways of Knowing, Being and Doing: A Theoretical Framework and Methods for Indigenous and Indigenist Research. *Journal of Australian Studies* 27 (76): 203–214. https://doi.org/10.1080/14443050309387838. Accessed 8 May 2018.

Matovina, Timothy M. 1998. Liturgy, Popular Rites, and Popular Spirituality. In *Mestizo Worship: A Pastoral Approach to Liturgical Ministry*, ed. Virgilio P. Elizondo and Timothy M. Matovina, 81–91. Collegeville: The Liturgical Press.

McClary, Susan. 2002. *Feminine Endings: Music, Gender, and Sexuality*. Minneapolis: University of Minnesota Press.

McKay, Stan, and Janet Silman. 1995. *The First Nations: Canadian Experience of the Gospel-Culture Encounter*. Geneva: WCC Publications, World Council of Churches.

McNally, Michael. 2009. *Ojibwe Singers: Hymns, Grief, and a Native Culture in Motion*. St. Paul: Minnesota Historical Society Press.

Medina, Néstor. 2008. Jürgen Moltmann and Pentecostalism(s): Toward a Cultural Theology of the Spirit. In *Love and Freedom: Systematic and Liberation Theology in the Canadian Context*, ed. David John C. Zub and Robert C. Fennell. Toronto: Toronto School of Theology.

———. 2009. *Mestizaje: (Re)Mapping Race, Culture and Faith in Latina/o Catholicism*. Maryknoll: Orbis Books.

———. 2015. Theological Musings Towards a Latina/o Pneumatology. In *The Wiley Blackwell Companion to Latino/a Theology*, ed. Orlando O. Espín, 173–189. Hoboken: John Wiley & Sons, Ltd.

———. 2017. *On the Doctrine of Discovery*. Toronto: Canadian Council of Churches.

———. 2018. *Christianity, Empire and the Spirit: (Re)Configuring Faith and the Cultural*. Leiden: Brill.

———. 2019. Latinaos, Culture and the Bible. In *Reading In-Between: Biblical Interpretation in Canada*, ed. Néstor Medina, Alison Hari-Singh, and HeyRan Kim-Cragg. Eugene: Pickwick.

———. Forthcoming. (De)Cyphering Mestizaje; Encrypting Lived Faith: Simultaneous Promise and Problem. In *The Preferential Option for Culture*, ed. Miguel Diaz. Minneapolis: Fortress Press.

Medina, Néstor, and Becca Whitla. 2019. (An)Other Canada is Possible: Rethinking Canada's Colonial Legacy. *Horizontes Decoloniales/Decolonial Horizons* V.1: 13–42.

Métis Nation. http://www.metisnation.ca. Accessed 3 May 2017.

Mignolo, Walter D. 2000. *Local Histories/Global Designs: Coloniality, Subaltern Knowledges, and Border Thinking*. Princeton: Princeton University Press.

———. 2009. Epistemic Disobedience, Independent Thought and Decolonial Freedom. *Theory, Culture & Society* 26 (7–8): 151–181. http://waltermignolo.com/wp-content/uploads/2013/03/epistemicdisobedience-2.pdf. Accessed 25 July 2018.

Monbiot, George. 2016. Neoliberalism—The Ideology at the Root of All Our Problems. *The Guardian*, April 15. https://www.theguardian.com/books/2016/apr/15/neoliberalism-ideology-problem-george-monbiot. Accessed 16 June 2020.

Monk, W.H., ed. 1861. *Hymns Ancient and Modern for the Use in the Services of the Church with Accompanying Tunes*. London: Novello and Co.

Monk, W.H., and C. Steggall, eds. 1916. *Hymns Ancient and Modern for the Use in the Services of the Church with Accompanying Tunes*. London: William Clowes and Sons, Ltd.

Moreiras, Alberto. 1999. Hybridity and Double Consciousness. *Cultural Studies* 13 (3): 373–407.

Moschella, Mary Clark. 2008. *Ethnography as a Pastoral Practice: An Introduction.* Cleveland: Pilgrim Press.

Mukherjee, Arun. 1998. *Postcolonialism: Living My Life.* Toronto: TSAR Publications.

Mullings, Beverly, Kay-Ann Williams, and Alexander Lovell. 2012. Myths and Realities: The Challenge of Social Transformation Through Canada/Jamaica Diasporic Exchange. In *Jamaica in the Canadian Experience: A Multiculturalizing Presence*, ed. Carl E. James and Andrea Davis, 294–309. Halifax/Winnipeg: Fernwood Publishing.

Music, David, ed. and comp. 1996. *Hymnology: A Collection of Source Readings.* Lanham: Scarecrow Press, Inc.

National Archives. 'Chartists,' Power, Politics & Protest: The Growth of Political Rights in Britain in the 19th Century. http://www.nationalarchives.gov.uk/education/politics/g7/. Accessed 18 Jan 2017.

———. The Struggle for Democracy: Getting the Vote. http://www.nationalarchives.gov.uk/pathways/citizenship/struggle_democracy/getting_vote.htm. Accessed 18 Jan 2017.

Nekola, Anna, and Tom Wagner, eds. 2015. *Congregational Music Making and Community in a Mediated Age.* Farnham, Surrey: Ashgate.

Newman, David R. 1983. Observations on Method in Liturgical Theology. *Worship* 57 (4): 377–384.

Ng, Wenh-In. 2003. Lands of Bamboo and Lands of Maple. In *Realizing the America of Our Hearts*, ed. Fumitaka Matsuoko and Eleazar S. Fernandez, 99–114. Atlanta: Chalice Press.

Ng, Greer Anne Wenh-In. 2008. The United Church of Canada: A Church Fittingly National. In *Christianity and Ethnicity in Canada*, ed. Paul Bramadat and David Seljak, 204–246. Toronto: University of Toronto Press.

Olaiz, Hugo. How to Celebrate a Mexican Posada: A Packet for Lay Leaders, Musicians, and Clergy. *Chartered Committee on Hispanic Ministry, Episcopal Diocese of North Carolina.* http://www.tens.org/download_file/view/221/. Accessed 11 June 2017.

Olwage, Grant. 2005. Discipline and Choralism: The Birth of Musical Colonialism. In *Music, Power, and Politics*, ed. Annie J. Randall, 25–46. New York: Routledge.

Osbeck, Kenneth W. 1982. *101 Hymn Stories: The Inspiring True Stories Behind 101 Favorite Hymns.* Grand Rapids: Kregal Publications.

Parker, Alice. 1991. *Melodious Accord: Good Singing in Church.* Chicago: Liturgy Training Publications.

Peace, Thomas. The Nation-State Is Not What We Think It Is: Teaching Canadian History for a Non-National Perspective. *Active History.* http://activehistory.ca/2014/12/the-nation-state-is-not-what-we-think-it-is-teaching-canadian-history-from-a-non-national-perspective/. Accessed 9 Mar 2020.

Pérez, Zaida Maldonado, Loida I. Martell-Otero, and Elizabeth Conde-Frazier. 2013. Dancing with the Wild Child: Evangélicas and the Holy Spirit. In *Latina Evangélicas: A Theological Survey from the Margins*, ed. Zaida Maldonado Pérez, Loida I. Martell-Otero, and Elizabeth Conde-Frazier, 14–32. Eugene: Cascade Books.

Pitter, Robert. 2012. Always Have to Be Twice as Good: Reflections of an Athlete, Coach and Academic. In *Jamaica in the Canadian Experience: A Multiculturalizing Presence*, ed. Carl E. James and Andrea David, 155–160. Halifax/Winnipeg: Fernwood Publishing.

Plaatjie, Gloria Kehilwe. 2006. Toward a Post-Apartheid Black Feminist Reading of the Bible: A Case of Luke 2.36–38. In *Voices from the Margin: Interpreting the Bible in the Third World*, ed. R.S. Sugirtharajah, 463–483. Maryknoll: Orbis Books.

Poling, James. 2013. Postcolonial Theologies. *Roundtable Response, International Academy of Practical Theology*. Victoria University, University of Toronto, April 13.

Polokwane Choral Society. 2004. *We Keep Singing*. Compact Disc Recording. Toronto: Deep Down Productions.

Pope Paul VI. Constitution on the Sacred Liturgy. *Sacrosanctum Concilium*. http://www.vatican.va/archive/hist_councils/ii_vatican_council/documents/vat-ii_const_19631204_sacrosanctum-concilium_en.html. Accessed 27 Oct 2017.

Porter, Andrew. 1989a. Introduction: Britain and the Empire in the Nineteenth Century. In *The Oxford History of the British Empire, Volume 3, the Nineteenth Century*, ed. Andrew Porter, 1–28. Oxford: Oxford University Press.

———. 1989b. Religion, Missionary Enthusiasm, and Empire. In *The Oxford History of the British Empire, Volume 3, the Nineteenth Century*, ed. Andrew Porter, 222–246. Oxford: Oxford University Press.

Porter, Mark. 2017. *Contemporary Worship Music and Everyday Musical Lives*. Abingdon/New York: Routledge.

Power, David N. 2000. Ritual and Verbal Language. In *Primary Sources of Liturgical Theology*, ed. Dwight W. Vogel, 180–190. Collegeville: The Liturgical Press.

Presbyterian Church of Canada. 1997. *The Book of Praise*. Toronto: Presbyterian Church of Canada.

Quijano, Aníbal. 2000. Coloniality of Power, Eurocentrism, and Latin America. *Nepantla: Views from the South* 1 (3): 533–580. http://www.unc.edu/~aescobar/wan/wanquijano.pdf. Accessed 25 July 2018.

Rainbow, Bernarr. 1970. *The Choral Revival in the Anglican Church (1839–1872)*. London: Barrie & Jenkins.

Regan, Paulette. 2010. *Unsettling the Settler Within: Indian Residential Schools, Truth Telling, and Reconciliation in Canada*. Vancouver: UBC Press.

Richards, Jeffrey. 2002. *Imperialism and Music: Britain, 1876–1953*. Manchester: Manchester University Press.

Rivera Cusicanqui, Sylvia. 2006. Chhixinakax Utxiwa. Una Reflexión Sobre Prácticas y Discursos Descolonizadores. In *Modernidad y Pensamiento Descolonizador*, compiled by Mario Yupi, 3–16. La Paz: U-PIEB—IFEA.

Routley, Eric. 1978. *Church Music and the Christian Faith*. Carol Stream: Agape.

Rudder, Kiara. 2019. Hayden King and Others Question the Effectiveness of Land Acknowledgements. *The Eye Opener*, January 19. https://theeyeopener.com/2019/01/hayden-king-and-others-question-the-effectiveness-of-land-acknowledgemenets/. Accessed 19 May 2019.

Russell, Letty M., J. Shannon Clarkson, and Kate M. Ott, eds. 2009. *Just Hospitality: God's Welcome in a World of Difference*. Louisville: Westminster John Knox Press.

Said, Edward. 2003. *Orientalism*. New York/London: Penguin Classics.

Saliers, Don E. 1998. Liturgical Musical Formation. In *Liturgy and Music: Lifetime Learning*, ed. Robin A. Leaver and Joyce Ann Zimmerman. Collegeville: Liturgical Press.

———. 2000. Human Pathos and Divine Ethos. In *Primary Sources of Liturgical Theology*, ed. Dwight W. Vogel, 276–283. Collegeville: The Liturgical Press.

———. 2007. *Music and Theology*. Nashville: Abington Press.

Scheer, Greg. From Greenland's Icy Mountains. *Hymnary.Org*. http://hymnary.org/text/from_greenlands_icy_mountains. Accessed 4 Feb 2017.

Schmemann, Alexander. 2000. The Task and Method of Liturgical Theology. In *Primary Sources of Liturgical Theology*, ed. Dwight W. Vogel, 54–62. Collegeville: The Liturgical Press.

Schneider, Howard. 1998. Canada: A Mosaic Not a Melting Pot. *The Washington Post*, July 5. https://www.washingtonpost.com/archive/politics/1998/07/05/canada-a-mosaic-not-a-melting-pot/8a4998ed-b04b-491e-b72e-1ef4d8e96d84/. Accessed 3 Feb 2020.

Scott, R.B.Y., and Gregory Vlastos, eds. 1936. *Towards the Christian Revolution*. Chicago: Willet, Clark and Co.

Seeger, Pete. 2009. *Where Have All the Flowers Gone? A Singalong Memoir*. Pennsylvania: Sing Out Corporation.

Segundo, Juan Luis. 1974. *The Sacraments Today, Volume Four of a Theology for Artisans of a New Humanity*. Trans. John Drury. New York: Orbis.

———. 1976. *Liberation of Theology*. Trans. John Drury. Oregon: Orbis.

Senior, Olive. 2012. Crossing Borders and Negotiating Boundaries. In *Jamaica in the Canadian Experience: A Multiculturalizing Presence*, ed. Carl E. James and Andrea David, 14–22. Halifax/Winnipeg: Fernwood Publishing.

Shea, Victor, and William Whitla, eds. 2015. Part One: Contexts. In *Victorian Literature: An Anthology*, 19–179, ed. Victor She and Willian Whitla. Oxford: Wiley Blackwell.

————, eds. Victoria Literature: Supplementary Web Resource. http://high-eredbcs.wiley.com/legacy/college/shea/140518874X/supp/web_contexts.pdf, page 215–215. Accessed 23 Mar 2017.

Shotwell, Alexis. 2015. Unforgetting as a Collective Tactic. In *White Criticality Before Anti-Racism: How Does It Feel to Be a White Problem?* ed. George Yancy, 57–67. London: Lexington Books.

Simpson, Leanne. 2011. *Dancing on Our Turtle's Back: Stories of Nishnaabeg Re-creation, Resurgence, and a New Emergence.* Winnipeg: Arbeiter Ring Publishing.

Six Nations of the Grand River. Community Profile. Accessed 9 Mar 2020. http://www.sixnations.ca/CommunityProfile.htm

Small, Christopher. 1998. *Musicking: The Meanings of Performing and Listening.* Hanover: Wesleyan University Press.

Sosa, Pablo. 2011. Christian Music in Latin America since 1800. In *Christian Music: A Global History,* ed. Tim Dowley, 206–209. Minneapolis: Fortress Press.

Spivak, Gayatri Chakravorty. 1988a. Can the Subaltern Speak? In *Marxism and the Interpretation of Cultures,* ed. Cary Nelson and Lawrence Grossberg, 271–313. Urbana: University of Illinois Press.

————. 1988b. Subaltern Studies: Deconstructing Historiography. In *Selected Subaltern Studies,* ed. Ranajit Guha and Gayatri Spivak. Oxford: Oxford University Press.

Statistics Canada. The Jamaican Canadian Community. http://www.statcan.gc.ca/pub/89-621-x/89-621-x2007012-eng.htm. Accessed 5 July 2017.

Stokes, Martin. 2012. Globalization and the Politics of World Music. In *The Cultural Study of Music: A Critical Introduction,* ed. Martin Clayton, Trevor Herbert, and Richard Middleton, 107–116. New York: Routledge.

Subaltern Knowledges. 2011. Geopolitics of Sensing and Knowing: On (de) Coloniality, Border Thinking, and Epistemic Disobedience. http://eipcp.net/transversal/0112/mignolo/en. Accessed 25 July 2018.

Symonds, John Addington. These Things Shall Be a Loftier Race. http://www.traditionalmusic.co.uk/hymn-lyrics/these_things_shall_be_a_loftier_race.htm. Accessed 25 July 2018.

Tamez, Elsa. 2008. Teología de la Liberación. In *Quedan Dios y los Pobres: Textos Sobre la Teología de la Liberación,* ed. Alejandro Dausá. La Habāna: Centro Memorial Dr. Martin Luther King, Jr.

Taylor, Timothy D. 2007. *Beyond Exoticism: Western Music and the World.* Durham: Duke University Press.

Teillet, Jean. 2019. *The North-West Is Our Mother: The Story of Louis Riel's People, the Métis Nation.* Toronto: HarperCollins.

The Christmas Story. 75th Anniversary Programme. https://www.thechristmass-tory.ca/commemorative-program. Accessed 6 June 2017.

————. History of the Pageant. https://www.thechristmasstory.ca/history-of-the-pageant. Accessed 6 June 2017.

————. Music. https://www.thechristmasstory.ca/music. Accessed 6 June 2017.

The Episcopal Church. Tracts for the Times. http://www.episcopalchurch.org/library/glossary/tracts-times. Accessed 3 Jan 2017.

The Métis. In *Canada's First Peoples*. http://firstpeoplesofcanada.com/fp_metis/fp_metis1.html. Accessed 3 May 2017.

Tracey, James R. 2003. The Weather Underground and the Future of Memory: An Interview with Sam Green. *Contemporary Justice Review* 6 (4): 397–400.

Truth and Reconciliation Commission of Canada. 2015a. Canada's Residential Schools: The History, Part 1, Origins to 1939. In *The Final Report of the Truth and Reconciliation Commission of Canada. Volume 1.* Canada. http://nctr.ca/assets/reports/Final%20Reports/Volume_1_History_Part_1_English_Web.pdf. Accessed 28 July 2018.

————. 2015b. Reports of the Truth and Reconciliation Commission. http://nctr.ca/reports.php. Accessed 3 May 2018.

Tuck, Eve, and Wayne Yang. 2012. Decolonization Is Not a Metaphor. *Decolonization, Indigeneity, Education & Society* 1 (1): 1–40. http://www.decolonization.org/index.php/des/article/view/18630/15554. Accessed 25 July.

United Church of Canada. 1996. *Voices United: The Hymn and Worship Book of the United Church of Canada.* Etobicoke: United Church Publishing House.

United Church of Christ. 1994. O Mighty God, When I Survey in Wonder. In *New Century Hymnal*, #35. Cleveland: The Pilgrim Press.

Villafañe, Eldín. 1992. *The Liberating Spirit: Toward an Hispanic American Pentecostal Social Ethic.* New York: University Press of America.

Vincent, Donovan. 2015. Three Torontonians Taking Their Turn in the Spotlight This Christmas. *The Toronto Star*, December 20. https://www.thestar.com/news/insight/2015/12/20/three-torontonians-taking-their-turn-in-the-spotlight-this-christmas.html. Accessed 9 June 2017.

Vogel, Dwight W., ed. 2000. *Primary Sources of Liturgical Theology.* Collegeville: The Liturgical Press.

Watson, J.R. 1997. *The English Hymn: A Critical and Historical Study.* Oxford: Oxford University Press.

Watts, Isaac. Jesus Shall Reign. http://www.cyberhymnal.org/htm/j/s/jsreign.htm. Accessed 25 July 2018.

Westermeyer, Paul. 1998. *Te Deum: The Church and Music.* Minneapolis: Augsburg Fortress.

Whitla, Becca. 2015. From the Heart of Song to the Heart of Singing. *Touchstone* 33 (1): 53–58.

———. 2017. Singing as *un Saber del Sur*, or Another Way of Knowing. *Toronto Journal of Theology* 33 (2, Fall): 289–294.

———. 2018a. Coloniality in 'Glossary of Key Terms'. In *Decoloniality and Justice: Theological Perspectives*, ed. Jean-François Roussel, 22–24. Saõ Leopoldo: Oikos: World Forum on Theology and Liberation.

———. 2018b. The Colonizing Power of Song. In *Decoloniality and Justice: Theological Perspectives*, ed. Jean-François Roussel, 43–50. Saõ Leopoldo: Oikos: World Forum on Theology and Liberation.

———. 2019. Hymnody in Missionary Lands: A Decolonial Critique. In *Hymns and Hymnody: Historical and Theological Introductions, Volume 2: From Catholic Europe to Protestant Europe*, ed. Benjamin K. Forrest, Mark A. Lamport and Vernon M. Whaley, 285–302. Eugene: Wipf and Stock.

Wiberg, Glen. 2002. Sightings in Christian Music. *Pietistan* 17 (1, Summer). http://www.pietisten.org/summer02/sightings.html. Accessed 28 July 2018.

Wikipedia. Batak Christian Protestant Church. https://en.wikipedia.org/wiki/Batak_Christian_Protestant_Church. Accessed 26 June 2018.

———. Cuan Grande es Él. https://es.wikipedia.org/wiki/Cu%C3%A1n_grande_es_%C3%89l. Accessed 25 July 2018.

———. Grand River (Ontario). https://en.wikipedia.org/wiki/Grand_River_(Ontario). Accessed 3 May 2018.

———. The Historiography of the British Empire. https://en.wikipedia.org/wiki/Historiography_of_the_British_Empire. Accessed 3 Mar 2017.

———. How Great Thou Art. https://en.wikipedia.org/wiki/How_Great_Thou_Art. Accessed 28 July 2018.

———. Jamaican Canadians. https://en.wikipedia.org/wiki/Jamaican_Canadians. Accessed 6 July 2017.

———. Pew. https://en.wikipedia.org/wiki/Pew. Accessed 21 June 2017.

———. Las Posadas. https://en.wikipedia.org/wiki/Las_Posadas. Accessed 13 June 2017.

William & H. James Co. Cast-Iron-Mechanical Banks Sambo Mechanical Bank. https://www.historytoy.com/william-h-james-co-cast-iron-toy-sambo-mechanical-bank. Accessed 18 Mar 2017.

Winsan, Patty. 2017. Are Indigenous Acknowledgements a Step Forward or an Empty Gesture? *The Toronto Star*, December 27. https://www.thestar.com/news/insight/2017/12/27/are-indigenous-acknowledgements-a-step-forward-or-an-empty-gesture.html. Accessed 10 Apr 2018.

World Council of Churches. Member Churches. *World Council of Churches*. https://www.oikoumene.org/en/member-churches/wcc-regions. Accessed 11 Feb 2018.

Yancy, George. 2015. Introduction: Un-Sutured. In *White Criticality Before Anti-Racism: How Does It Feel to Be a White Problem?* ed. George Yancy, xi–xxvii. London: Lexington Books.

Yancy, George C. White Suturing, Black Bodies, and the Myth of a Post-Racial America. *SARTS: Society for the Arts in Religious and Theological Studies.* http://www.societyarts.org/white-suturing-black-bodies-and-the-myth-of-a-post-racial-america.html. Accessed 7 Apr 2018.

Yerichuk, Deanna. 2015. Grappling with Inclusion: Ethnocultural Diversity and Socio-Musical Experiences in Common Thread Community Chorus of Toronto. *International Journal of Community Music* 8 (3): 217–231.

Young, Robert J.C. 1995. *Colonial Desire: Hybridity in Theory, Culture and Race. London.* New York: Routledge.

Index[1]

[1] Note: Page numbers followed by 'n' refer to notes.

© The Author(s) 2020
B. Whitla, *Liberation, (De)Coloniality, and Liturgical Practices*,
New Approaches to Religion and Power,
https://doi.org/10.1007/978-3-030-52636-8

CPSIA information can be obtained
at www.ICGtesting.com
Printed in the USA
LVHW020450101220
673703LV00005B/78

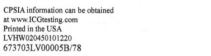

9 783030 526351